The Cruise of the Amaryllis

Other Sailing Classics

The Cruise of the Amaryllis

G. H. P. MUHLHAUSER

With a Memoir by
E. Keble Chatterton

GRANADA
London Toronto Sydney New York

Granada Publishing Limited
8 Grafton Street, London W1X 3LA

First published 1924
Reissued in the Mariners Library by Rupert Hart-Davis Ltd 1950
This edition published by Granada Publishing 1985

British Library Cataloguing in Publication Data

Muhlhauser, G. H. P.
  The cruise of the Amaryllis
  1. Amaryllis *(Yacht)*   2. Voyages around the world
  I. Title
  910.4'1'0924   G440.A/

ISBN 0 246 12761 9

Printed in Great Britain by
Billing & Sons Ltd., Worcester

Thanks are due to the Society of Authors as the literary representative of
the estate of John Masefield for permission to reprint the poems which
appear in this volume.

CONTENTS

MAPS

MEMOIR

THE outstanding feature of George Muhlhauser's character was unquestionably his deep sincerity and devotion to duty. Rugged, honest, straight-to-the-point in his methods, he was one of the finest seamen and navigators, amateur or professional, who ever sailed under the British ensign; and therefore I feel that it is an honour to be asked by his family to add this brief appreciation to the story of his historic round-the-world voyage.

I made his acquaintance first in the summer of 1911, in a Dutch port. I had arrived in Flushing harbour and tied-up; when there sailed out through the lock-gates a well-handled 8-ton cutter and secured astern of *Vivette*. It was his seamanship in working his craft in that narrow waterway which attracted me towards this Englishman, and from that day we became friends.

As far as ever it could be in any man, the salt sea was in Muhlhauser's personality. Born in Surrey during the seventies, and educated at the Merchant Taylor's School, he was always attracted by that fascinating glamour of maritime things and surroundings; and during his school holidays he used to go out roughing it with the fishermen in the North Sea trawlers. It was in fact the North Sea which was not a little responsible for the moulding of his strong, independent, fearless character. On those chilly waters his seamanhood was, so to speak, reared and trained; and when later on he was to be called by business to settle in Essex, he at once set about buying his first craft. This was the little 3-ton sloop-rigged *Camera* in 1901, and in her he sailed with his partner. Four years later he and a couple of friends owned the *Vivid*, and then in 1910 he became owner of the *Wilful* in which I met him that day in Flushing.

It was in her that he sailed to Norway and back in three weeks in July 1914. This, I think, is expressive of George Muhlhauser's character in a manner that no amount of details can convey. For the sheer delight in sailing, from that genuine love of the sea, he spent his brief holiday most of the time out of sight of land, where sound navigation and skilled seamanship were essential. I believe he had with him one sea-sick companion and that the *Wilful* had barely reached Norway when the little craft started back home. Towns and civilization had little attraction for the skipper of the *Wilful*, and then, soon after his return, came that memorable August 4, and we were in for the Great War. So, leaving his own yacht till peace should return, he obtained a commission in the Royal Naval Volunteer Reserve (shortly afterwards being transferred to the Royal Naval Reserve) and set out with his brother yachtsman, the late Stuart Garnett, in command, and a crew consisting largely of Cambridge rowing "blues," in the steam-yacht *Zarefah*.

By a set of circumstances I came across Muhlhauser in this ship off Grimsby during that first autumn of the war, and as navigating officer he performed downright sterling work. This vessel led a charmed life. As flagship of the Admiral of the Minesweepers, she was up and down the North Sea in all weathers, night and day, either in or skirting the very minefields themselves, and escaping total destruction time after time. But presently the *Zarefah* was laid aside and the personnel transferred to the bigger steam-yacht *Sagitta*, and in her he continued in his quiet, unobtrusive manner to do excellent work. I remember a professional mariner (who never met Muhlhauser) once telling me during the war that he had always admired the navigational ability manifested in the *Sagitta*, whose skill seemed exceptional. For in those days, when aids to navigation had been largely removed from the North Sea, it wanted something a good deal more than luck to make sure of your position, especially when you had been out miles from the shore investigating the limits of a newly laid area of mines. And this professional mariner has not yet recovered from the shock when I told him that all three officers of *Sagitta* were amateur yachtsmen.

I saw Muhlhauser several times and dined with him in *Sagitta*, and later on he was to become second-in-command of one of those Q-sailing-ships. Here his ability as an experienced seaman came in most valuable: no better fellow could have been found for the job. I have seen all his diaries for the war, and this period of his service was remarkable; but the finest achievement of all was that affair in February 1918, when as second-in-command he went in the little 557-ton steamer *Tay and Tyne*, hung off that wild Norwegian coast once more, captured the German ore steamship *Düsseldorf* of 1,200 tons, and then he himself with a handful of his men steamed her across to Scotland with no sextant, a compass that was full of deviational error owing to the magnetism in the ore, and with a chart that showed only a bit of the North Sea. Add to this that he got caught in the vilest weather that the North Sea can lash up, that the engines kept breaking down, and there was always a possibility of the Germans in her turning on him, and you will appreciate his anxious time. Furthermore, the nearer he made the north-east of the British Isles, the more likely he was to hit an ill-defined area of recently laid mines. But, without ever sighting anything after leaving the Norwegian coast, he at length picked up the Bell Rock and brought his prize safely up the Firth of Forth.

I remember him coming to see me soon after, and showing me on the chart his course. If Muhlhauser had never done anything else in the war, this exploit thoroughly deserved at least a D.S.C. But he was too genuine a sailorman to push himself into the limelight, and his subsequent work in command of an armed trawler brought him to the end of the war. Thus, practically the whole of his service, whether in armed steam-yachts, Q-sailing-craft or Q-steamship, was carried out in that North Sea which from his boyhood's days he had learned to understand in so many of its moods.

But whilst the war cured many half-hearted men of their sea-fever, in Muhlhauser's case it merely intensified the fire that was burning. At a time when it left most of us unsettled, the coming of peace seemed to open up an entirely new chapter in the life of this keen adventurer. Years ago he had passed the examination for his yacht-master's certificate, and now with his naval service ended he could not reconcile himself to settling down in a business life again until he had navigated his own ship across the oceans of the world. In the summer of 1919 he sold the little *Wilful* and sailed her to Falmouth for her new owner. And then one day in May 1920, he burst in full of enthusiasm.

"I've bought the *Amaryllis*, and you're coming with me round the world."

It was a tempting invitation, but it had to be resisted. How he fared, how he sailed and navigated her, how he took his beloved ship 31,000 miles encircling the globe, how he arrived back in that port of Dartmouth famous for its sailors and explorers, you shall read in the following pages. It is the narrative of a plain, blunt, sincere, deeply honest seafarer who knew every possible thing about his job, but never played to the gallery. As a feat of endurance and of enterprising courage, this one-man show (for on him was all the responsibility) is one of the very finest voyages of the English nation, and if there were a modern Hakluyt alive it would be included in his collection. You will see the proper seamanlike skill with which he carried out his enterprise; the boldness of his projects over so many thousands of miles. There is nothing of the hit-or-miss, splashing-through-risks manner: it is quietly foreseen and ordered, so far as human vision can prepare. And if we have to make any criticism at all it is only in regard to the commissariat department: I suggest that his reliance so much on tinned foods was a mistake.

In assessing Muhlhauser's rank as a sailor it is not too much to place him alongside Voss, Slocum, and even Drake. He had the spirit of these three; the same daring independence, the pioneering zeal to navigate strange waters in a small ship, and the skill to win through. Such an achievement as the voyage of *Amaryllis* means something more than a mere yachting cruise: it shows that in these days of 50,000-ton liners, with swimming-baths and ballrooms, there does exist the real British sea feeling; there are still men in a war-weary world inspired to go round the globe in small ships. This plucky trip will certainly have its beneficial influence on yachting, and, indeed, the effects are already showing themselves.

MEMOIR

It seems as if her skipper had been destined to perform this splendid voyage and then come ashore with that as his final chapter of sea-life. I saw the *Amaryllis* last August in Dartmouth, with her faded blue ensign suggestive of tropical sun and many weathers. And as I rowed down with the ebb there was her owner coming off from the shore; it was the first time we had met since he sailed nearly three years ago. But the sight of him gave me something of a shock. He was looking quite ten years older, and when I offered him congratulations on his magnificent and successful cruise he just laughed. "Thanks—nobody but myself would have been such a perfect fool ever to have done it."

But that was his modesty. He was still anxious—wondering whether he would be able to sell *Amaryllis*, wondering, too, what his future plans would be. I was hoping to see him in the autumn, and then one day I learned that he was ill and had been operated on; the next I knew was that he had passed away. It came as a great shock to all who had followed the voyaging of this fine sailorman. He was buried, as he would have wished it, with, for his pall, the White Ensign under which he had so honourably served, and the Blue Ensign which he had flown from *Amaryllis'* mizzen all over the world. Those two flags exactly symbolized his seafaring life.

And so, within a few weeks of his life's attainment, George Muhlhauser had gone to the great haven for all seafarers. Home was the sailor, home from his travels across the trackless ocean, but his memory will be kept alive in the inspiration which he has left behind.

E. KEBLE CHATTERTON

1924

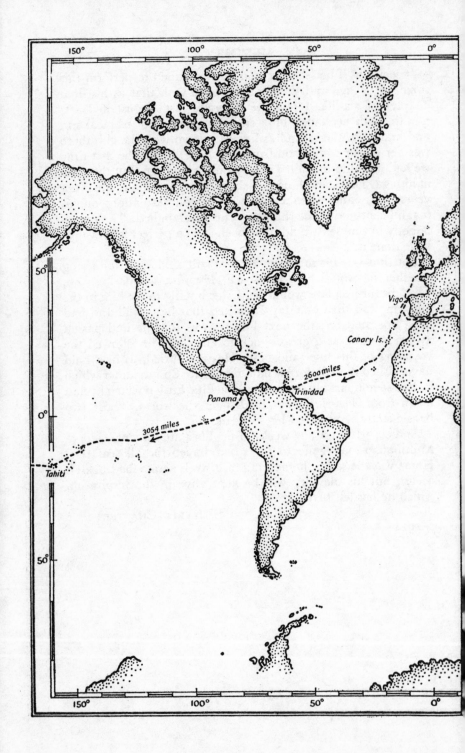

CHAPTER I

OUTWARD BOUND

On a beautiful, still day in early September 1920, the Deputy-Assistant Harbour Master, resplendent in a blue uniform with much gold lace on it, stood on the dock-head at Plymouth, and watched a small yawl-rigged yacht leaving the dock under power. The weather conditions being favourable, i.e. there being no wind and an absolutely smooth sea, she was proceeding at 4 miles per hour, which was the maximum speed at which the "power," a 12/15 h.p. motor, could drive her, even with all things in its favour.

"What ship is that?" the D.A.H.M. asked.

"The *Amaryllis*."

"Where are you bound?"

"Auckland, New Zealand."

As an afterthought he shouted: "Good luck."

Such was our send-off.

At first sight it may seem a remarkable feat to take a small vessel of 28 tons gross, or 36 tons Thames measurement, round the world via New Zealand, and a relatively short time ago it would have been so regarded, but it is now recognized that quite small, well-found vessels are safe even in bad weather. They are not comfortable under such conditions, indeed they are acutely, almost intolerably, uncomfortable, but most of them are safe if properly handled. But it does not do to play tricks, as the sea is without mercy and never forgives. Punishment for a mistake, or error of judgment, is meted out in full on the spot. Though there is, as a matter of actual fact, nothing remarkable about such a voyage, it is unusual since it is not often that the wish to make it, the time, and the necessary knowledge of navigation are combined in the same person. There are many who have the knowledge to do it, but they do not want to, while others want to but have not the time. As a result little ships do not often make really long trips, and, as far as I can learn, the *Amaryllis* is the third smallest to go round the world, and the smallest that has ever sailed round from England, the other two having sailed from America. However that may be, the D.A.H.M., standing on his dock-head, was in no way impressed. On the other hand, the Insurance people were, and on learning where the ship was going raised the premium to an absolutely prohibitive figure, and so *Amaryllis* sailed forth uninsured.

The call of the sea is a peculiar thing. Why anyone who is not obliged to should submit to the confinement, want of society, privations, broken nights, and general unrest and discomfort, to say nothing of the frequently occurring periods of anxiety in a small yacht, with its elementary cooking, on long trips, is difficult to explain to those who are not drawn to the sea. Indeed I do not understand it myself, but at any rate it is a clean sport, and harms no one and nothing, while the fact that one is contending with mighty natural forces, and must depend on one's own efforts to get safely through, gives zest to, and sheds a glow of romance over the undertaking.

Masefield hits off the fascination of the sea extremely well in his *Sea-Fever*:

I must go down to the seas again, to the lonely sea and the sky,
And all I ask is a tall ship and a star to steer her by,
And the wheel's kick and the wind's song and the white sails shaking,
And a grey mist on the sea's face and a grey dawn breaking.

I must go down to the seas again, for the call of the running tide
Is a wild call and a clear call that may not be denied;
And all I ask is a windy day with the white clouds flying,
And the flung spray and the blown spume, and the seagulls crying.

I must go down to the seas again, to the vagrant gypsy life,
To the gull's way and the whale's way where the wind's like a whetted knife,
And all I ask is a merry yarn from a laughing fellow-rover,
And a quiet sleep and a sweet dream when the long trick's over.

It was not until immediately after the Armistice that the idea of making a long cruise suddenly occurred to me. I was then waiting to be appointed to the command of a minesweeper. During the first twenty-six months of the war I had been in the mine-sweeping service, and though I spent the next eighteen months in Q-ships, and wound up in hydrophone trawlers, yet I had not forgotten everything about mine-sweeping and had been promised a ship. One day I was at the Admiralty and was looking idly through a number of Sailing Directions for all parts of the world, and as I read of this harbour and that, and of the history of the discovery of islands and continents the idea took shape in my mind, and speedily grew to a decision, to push out and have a look round as soon as I should be demobilized. This latter event took place in 1919, and with mingled feelings of relief and regret I left the Admiralty a free man and my own master.

I at once began looking round to see what could be had in the way of a suitable craft. Someone told me that a well-known yachtsman was preparing for a trip to the West Indies, and I got into touch with him, and found him in a boat shed on the Dart, brooding over the *Amaryllis*, which he had just bought. She had been hauled out of the water, and all the inside fittings removed, leaving the kelson, timbers, and floors exposed. Everything was in first-rate condition, and I was astounded to learn that she had been built in 1882. There was not a sign of age, or wear, about her. She had been honestly built of well-seasoned timber, and her condition, nearly forty years later, was a credit to her builder, Mr. A. E. Payne, later Summers and Payne, and to those who had looked after her. It will not be necessary to give exact details of her construction, and a brief description will suffice. She is flush-decked, i.e. she has skylights and hatches, but no cabin top, and is 36 tons Thames, 28 tons gross, and 7½ tons net measurement, and is 62 feet over-all, 52 feet on the water-line, 13 feet beam, and draws 10 feet of water. Most of the ballast is iron carried inside, but there are 3¼ tons of lead on the keel. In view of the work before her this arrangement of the ballast was sound, since it is not advisable that a ship which has to knock about the seas in all weathers should carry all the ballast in lead on the keel. Such an arrangement would make her too quick in motion, and would put an undue strain on the masts and gear.

In the fo'c'sle are cots for three men, and a coal stove. Then

17

come the pantry and lavatory, separated by an alleyway leading into the saloon, which is $9\frac{1}{4}$ feet long, with 7 feet floor space between the settees, and 6 feet 1 inch least headroom under the beams. Aft of this is a cabin on the starboard side. The companion ladder to the deck is in the middle, and the small engine is on the port side. Aft of this is my cabin containing two bunks. The sail locker is right aft, and is entered through a hatch on deck.

She struck me as a sound, well-built, and powerful little ship, snugly rigged, and fit to go anywhere. Nevertheless, she is not my ideal cruiser, as she has a counter 10 feet long, is yawl rigged, and steered with a tiller, whereas my preference is for a very short counter, or canoe stern, ketch rig, and wheel steering. Moreover, her draft of 10 feet was rather too much for knocking about amongst coral reefs, though a very good feature from the point of view of keeping the sea.

However, there she was and matters between the owner and myself were soon arranged, and it was agreed that he should have the ship coppered, instal an engine, and that we should then cruise together to the West Indies. Fitting out, however, proved to be a long affair. Everybody seemed to be on strike, and he could not at first get any copper, or castings, and even an engine was unobtainable. The makers of this could not give a promise for delivery, and did not know what it would cost when delivered, and he was finally obliged to put in an American two-cylinder 12/15 paraffin engine, which was very carefully installed, and which proved as satisfactory as marine motors usually are. It started easily, and once running required very little attention, which was lucky, as I am not a mechanic, but it failed me once when I had desperate need of its services. It is, however, hardly fair to lay the blame on the engine for nearly wrecking the ship on that occasion. The engine was prepared to do its part, but the fuel supply went wrong.

Owing to strikes and the difficulty of getting material, nearly a year elapsed before she was ready for sea, and then the owner found that his home affairs prevented him from making the trip at all. As I had waited the best part of a year for him this was distinctly upsetting, to say the least of it, and matters were not improved when I could not find any other suitable ship ready. Ships there were, but fitting them out might have taken another year. In the end I bought the *Amaryllis*, at a price which now seems excessive, and found myself in the proud but rather embarrassing position of being the owner of a ship without a crew. Still it was something to have a good little ship, even if she was forty years old, and I derived much pleasure from planning voyages all over the world. The West Indies attracted me, and then, of course, there was South America, the South Sea Islands, and Australasia, to say nothing of the Mediterranean, India, and the East, or even South Africa. In imagination I visited them all, but in the end came back to the practical things in life, and decided on making a fair wind of it, and going to the West Indies before the North East Trade winds, through the Panama, and across the South Seas before the South East Trades, to Australasia. What I should do then I left time and the Fates to decide, but at the back of my mind was the idea that I should be able to sell the little ship at a nice profit, and return, get another one, and repeat the process. In fact I thought that I had discovered a new industry in which I could pleasantly and profitably spend my declining years. Things did not quite work out according to plan, but of that more anon. The first thing to do, while waiting for the crew to materialize, was to get out a list of the charts required. As I waded through the Admiralty index of charts selecting the ones required, which by the way numbered about 240 at the start and nearly 500 by the time I got home, I could not help wondering what I should have done if I had lived three hundred years ago, and the desire to wander had assailed me. There were then no charts, no accurately made chronometers, no sextants even, no nautical almanacs with information about the Sun, Moon, and stars given in decimals of a minute; no sailing directions, which not only give instructions as to how to get into harbours and what dangers to look out for, but also contain the history and much interesting information about every place dealt with; no Wind and Current Charts; in fact nothing, or very little. Practically all that the undaunted sea-dogs of that period had to speed them on their way were a few

19

crude instruments, an indifferent supply of salted provisions, beer, water, and their own stout hearts.

I spent a month in getting in stores, and going over all the gear to see that it was in good condition, and that everything that was likely to be wanted was there, and at the same time I tried to get a crew together. It became apparent at once that the latter would be a difficult thing to arrange. None of my friends could join. They were mostly struggling, more or less successfully, with their various businesses, and, in addition, the wives of those who were married viewed the suggestion that their husbands should go sailing for a year or two with undisguised contempt and dislike. It became clear to me that these feelings were extended to include me, the originator of the suggestion, and that I was considered a dangerous person for their husbands to know. My friends all proving non-starters I advertised in various papers and journals, and received a meagre crop of replies. Some of my correspondents wanted to get something out of me, others had no qualifications beyond a vague desire to be somewhere else, but David, an Irishman, then in Italy, agreed to join, and a very agreeable, cheerful companion he proved to be all the time he was on board.

As no one else turned up I brought the number on board up to three, the minimum in my opinion for a ship of the size, by signing on a young fisherman for a voyage to New Zealand. At first he was very hard working and diligent, but he soon became slack, and inclined to overstay his shore leave. I pointed out that as I was treating him well he should treat me well, and he agreed that his conduct was wrong, but it failed to improve, and I decided to pay him off. This, however, proved to be impossible. He had signed on for New Zealand, and to New Zealand he had to go, so the Custom House Officer told me when I brought the matter before him. As I could not discharge my man, I bribed him to sign off by giving him a month's wages. Later I found out that his lady-love was at the bottom of the trouble. Whether he was a party to the conspiracy, or whether both he and I were innocent victims of a woman's wiles, I could not discover, but it transpired that the lady did not approve of his signing on for a two-year trip, and persuaded him to overstay his leave regularly, in the hope that I should pay him off in disgust. Things certainly worked out "according to plan," but I am glad that he is the one who is to marry her, and not I. She is a trifle too artful for my taste.

At this point Charles (I will call my companions by their first name), ex-lieutenant R.N.V.R., turned up, and agreed not only to go himself as far as the West Indies, but also to bring his brother. Charles was a first-class seaman, and it was a piece of luck to come across him. His brother John was unused to the sea, but he was a man of many parts, and made himself extremely useful, chiefly in the cooking line.

At last the ship was fitted out, provisioned, and ready for sea in every detail, with the ship's company on board with the exception of David, who was proving very elusive, and difficult to get hold of. Since the day when he agreed to join I had only seen him twice, and had done all the fitting out without his assistance. It was understood that he was putting his affairs in order for a prolonged absence. Apparently it was a complicated and lengthy process, as he put off the date of joining seven times. At last, in desperation, I wired that I was sailing on the next Monday, and that if he wished to take part in the trip he must be on board then. He telegraphed that he would join on the Saturday and that I must not think of sailing without him as the ship would have no luck. I met his train and took him on board with some anxiety. How were things going to work out? He had never seen either Charles or John before, and I had only seen him twice. How were four strange, and totally different temperaments, going to blend? It was a great experiment, and might be a success, or an utter failure from the start. Men who are to be penned up in a small ship for months, living together in close contact, ought to know, and be in sympathy with each other, if friction is to be avoided, but we were all strangers to one another. I felt sure that I could get along very comfortably with David, and also with the other two, but how would they get on with him, and he with them? As it happened, things worked out extremely well, and we were quite a happy family, but it was a great risk to run. Still, there had not been any choice. I had to take a scratch crew, or not start at all, and fortune favoured me. I do not want a better lot of shipmates.

We spent the Sunday in settling in, and left Plymouth on Monday, the 6th September, the Tercentenary of the sailing of the *Mayflower*. In honour of this event the town was gay with bunting, and pageants, but only the D.A.H.M., in solitary glory on the dock-head, marked our departure, and he only in the course of his duty.

On clearing the harbour a course was set to pass well outside Ushant. The plan was to make for Vigo, and then Madeira, and Las Palmas in Gran Canaria, leaving there in the middle of October so as to arrive in the West Indies after the hurricane season.

Having got safely out of the harbour the next thing to do was to arrange the watches. I knew that Charles was a good seaman, and that John was a capable man, though quite ignorant of boats, but how much experience David had I did not know. In the ordinary way in a small ship one man on deck at night to steer and look out is sufficient, but in the circumstances we decided on two watches, four hours on and four hours off duty, with Charles and David in one watch, and John and myself in the other.

David rather upset me at the start by remarking that he hated all work, and especially routine work, and that he proposed to be a passenger to Madeira. This struck me as a most ominous remark, hinting at all kinds of dark possibilities. I consulted Charles, who, as always, had the stub of an extinct cigarette between his lips. He brooded for a time in silence, and then said:

"Is he an Irishman?"

"Yes."

"Oh! that is all right then. It is only a way of speaking. You will probably find him first rate."

And he was correct. David was a cheerful optimist, and always willing and ready to do anything.

He casually remarked on the first day:

"Of course it is madness to take a small ship like this across the Atlantic in the autumn."

"What makes you think that?"

"Oh!" he replied, "a friend of mine, a retired sea captain, told me that it was sheer folly, and that the ship will probably founder."

The fact that I was, according to his information, about to place the ship in a position of great danger did not upset him in the least. He merely referred to the matter in the course of conversation. In vain I quoted to him the Sailing Directions stating that fair winds and fine weather might be expected. He remained unconvinced, but quite undisturbed.

The watches having been fixed the next thing to decide was the question of who was to be cook. The cook is the most important man on board a ship. John saved us all discussion by volunteering for the job, and very well he did it too. He had not had much previous experience, but he soon became expert, and our appreciation of his early efforts encouraged him to attempt loftier flights. He used to study the cookery-book for a time, and would then disappear into the fo'c'sle, whence the sound of Primus stoves going at full blast, and other sounds of activity would issue. At intervals, during the operations, he would appear and feverishly consult the book, and then plunge once more into the fo'c'sle. The final result was always satisfactory, apparently as much to his own surprise as to ours, and meat puddings, jam puddings, hashes, rissoles, curries and stews, scones, cakes, pancakes, and bread graced the table.

The only other special work was navigation, and this fell to my lot, while David ran the engine on the infrequent occasions when it was required. At sea it was very seldom used, but when entering or leaving harbour it was usually running. The mate had no particular job, but he worked hard about the ship, and was always on hand when required.

Things soon settled down on board into sea routine, and by the time the Spanish Coast was sighted everything was working like oiled machinery. The passage took five days. Off Ushant we were becalmed and rolled heavily in an awkward swell, but from the time we got going again we had fair winds and fine weather right across the Bay of Biscay.

On the fifth afternoon the coast should have been in sight, indeed not more than 5 miles off, but a bank of mist lay in that direction, and nothing showed up. A schooner and a steamer were in sight, but no land. I decided to steer in, and told the helmsman, who was at the tiller, or "blooming stick" as he always called it, to pass under the stern of the steamer, which was close and steaming on a parallel course. The wind was well aft and fresh and we were moving through the water faster than the latter, a slow old tramp.

I then went below to look at the chart. On my return a few minutes later I found that instead of passing under her stern the helmsman had, without reflection, decided that it would be more amusing to cross her bow. The natural result of this was that we lost the wind when under her lee, and could then neither cross her stern, nor her bow. We could not even gybe as we found it impossible to get the mainsheet in without coming up to the wind to ease the pressure, and there was not room to do that. It was an undignified position to be in. There was nothing for it but to appeal to the steamer people to give us more room. I waved my arm towards the east, to show that I wanted to go that way, and they very kindly slowed the engines until we had clearance, and could cross their bows. They must have thought us a lubberly lot to put ourselves in such a position.

Shortly afterwards land loomed indistinctly through the mist, and we identified it as Cape Torinana, the point we had been aiming at. That night the wind fell right away to a stark calm, and we drifted about without steerage way, heading now in one direction, and now in another.

The dawn came in thick with rain, which obscured the land, and we started the engine to get close to the coast to try and fix the ship's position, and find out where we had drifted to during the calm night. Islands soon appeared on the starboard hand, which might be either the Islas Ons or the Islas Cies, but which they were I could not determine. As there were no outlying dangers we stood on, but it was not until the islands were abeam that I could be sure that they were the Islas Ons, 5 miles north of the Islas Cies, which guard the entrance to

Vigo Bay. As the wind still continued very light, and the rain very wet, we stood in to the little village of Sangenjo in Pontevedra Bay and anchored. This part of the Spanish coast is cut up into deep bays or fiords, and is very lovely. Mountains of a good height, with villas and houses red roofed and painted white scattered about their bases, look down on the inlets, and in the clear atmosphere make a pleasant picture. As it happened, the atmosphere was very far from clear on the following day; indeed, there was a thick fog and a flat calm, and not being pressed for time, we remained where we were, and entertained various visitors who came off. The first to arrive was the Captain of the Port, rather perturbed by our arrival. I fancy he thought we were smugglers at first, but the large red seal 2 inches in diameter on the Club certificate filled him with subdued rapture. He evidently thought that people with documents bearing such splendid seals must be respectable. Then came two gardes civiles, one of them armed with a rifle. After them a number of schoolboys turned up, and then several parties of residents, and last but not least a fisherman who simply could not be kept off the ship. He wandered around examining all the gear with a critical, professional eye, and we took the smile, which never left his face, to mean approval of what he saw. The next day was still calm, and we ran the few miles to Vigo under power.

Vigo has some fine buildings, but is not otherwise a very attractive town, at least once one is ashore, for it looks well enough from the water; we only stayed there three days.

Drake paid the town a flying visit in 1584, and on his appearance the inhabitants made a bee line for the nearest hill, with the exception of the Governor, who after sending Drake a present of wine and fruit rowed off for a conference which was held in the middle of the harbour.

On the 17th September we weighed and left for Funchal, Madeira, saluting H.M.S. *Téméraire* on the way out. There was very little wind until the next morning when it came fresh from the S.E., with driving rain. At 10 p.m. we had to reef the mainsail, putting in two reefs, and soon afterwards, the wind being then strong and the sea heavy, we hove to on the port tack, heading away from the land. Strictly speaking we should have been hove to on the starboard tack, as it is usual, in that part of the world, for winds which start from the S.E. with thick rainy weather to veer to the N.W., and to avoid being taken aback one should be on the starboard tack, but as I did not know how long the wind would last I did not care to be edging in on the land, and so hove to on the port tack. This was the first time I had tried the little ship in a heavy sea, and I was delighted with the way she behaved. She rode quite easily, with the decks dry, but for spray. At the same time all small vessels are uncomfortable in bad weather, however good they may be as seaboats. The howling of the wind, the pounding of the sea, and the constant and violent motion of the ship itself, all make for unrest and discomfort. Luckily this wind only lasted for one day, and we were then able to proceed. Two days later we were struck by a heavy squall at dark. The afternoon had been calm, no wind at all. Just after noon, heavy black clouds began forming in the northeast, but as they did not seem to get any nearer, and as the barometer was steady, we did not pay a great deal of attention to them, notwithstanding their wicked appearance. At 7 p.m. a dark line showed on the water, and almost immediately the hissing sound of approaching wind could be heard, and in a few seconds it was on us. As the ship had been motionless without way, the first impact of the wind laid her right down, until there was green water up to the skylights, and one of the gratings aft was washed away. She picked herself up at once, she had no more than bowed in acknowledgment of the might of the wind, and went off like a race-horse. It was urgent to get sail off, and after a severe struggle the topsail was dragged down in ribbons. As soon as the halliard was started it thrashed itself to pieces. The mizzen and staysail were then lowered, and the ship was hove to until the squall had screamed itself away. Wet to the skin, for cold rain came with the wind, and chilled, we went below, changed, and had a cup of Bovril, a very cheering drink in the circumstances. One member of the crew, however, who shall be nameless, was not wet. In defiance, or perhaps ignorance, of the rule of the sea which always puts the safety of the ship or her gear before any question of personal comfort, he had gone below when the trouble started, and had calmly donned his oilskins, sea-boots, and sou'wester, and then reappeared properly dressed for the part, when the work was done! He claimed that, owing to the noise of the wind and rain, and general uproar that was going on, he had not heard my pointed remarks as he disappeared below. That squall was the last of what could be described as bad weather until we were the other side of Tahiti, about 8,500 miles away. A period of delightful sailing was about to start, when the wind was nearly always fair, and the weather nearly always fine, except for rain.

After the squall a fresh, fair wind took us in three and a half days to within sight of Porto Santo, an island just east of Madeira, and then dropped, leaving us becalmed. We decided, in the total absence of wind, to start the engine, and David girded up his loins and tackled the job. The engine, however, proved coy and refused to respond, whereupon the mate joined in the struggle, and later John also became involved. The three of them seemed to be quite interested in the case, and happy in taking off various parts, looking inside, and putting them back again. In the circumstances there was no demand for my services or advice, and I sat at the tiller in the glorious sun and smoked a contemplative pipe. I do not claim to be a mechanic, and if anyone else can be induced to look after the engine I am always prepared to stand back and let him smear himself and his clothes with oil and grease, bark his knuckles, get electric shocks, and exhaust himself by turning the fly-wheel. It is only when no one else is willing or available that I appear in the character of engine driver. On this occasion the work continued all day, and just before dark the engine recovered sufficiently from its state of lethargy to give one or two coughs, but only to subside once more into quiescence. And then it suddenly started. No one seemed to have done anything different from what had already been done a dozen times, but motors are like that. They are mysterious things.

At 2 a.m. on the 25th September we brought up in Funchal roadstead, in the midst of several lighters, tugs, and other craft. Seen from the sea, the island is very beautiful. It is mountainous, and the lower slopes are covered with verdure. Houses painted a dazzling white with red roofs appear at intervals, and the town lies at the foot of the hills. The streets are paved with round cobble-stones, and sledges, mostly drawn by oxen, are used instead of wheeled carts. As in Prospero's island "the air breathes upon us here most sweetly," and the climate is delightful. A pleasant spot. One of the things that all visitors are expected to do is to take the funicular train to the top of a hill at the back of the town, have lunch at the Palace Hotel, and then toboggan down the cobbled street in a sledge guided by two men. This we did, as in duty bound. One of our charioteers was sixty-seven years old, and the other was fifty-nine, yet they ran down that hill like two-year-olds. Half-way down we stopped at a small café, and had a bottle of wine, for which we paid an exorbitant price.

An English firm in Funchal repaired the topsail for us, and made a new grating to replace the one washed overboard in the squall, and charged us a staggering price for doing this. When we remonstrated with the manager of the department concerned, he frankly replied that though Madeira was a health resort, neither he nor his firm were there for their health's sake but were out for money, and that as the place lay a long way out in the Atlantic, and there was no competition, anyone arriving with defects to be made good had to pay. Having expressed himself in these terms, he took 2 per cent. off the bill, and we had to be content with that. This same firm was building a harbour launch driven by a Kelvin motor to hold 100 persons and aimed at finishing it in twenty-one days without working overtime. It looked as if they would succeed too. The Portuguese workman seems to be an energetic man, though he is usually supposed to be slothful.

On the 28th September we took in a supply of mangoes, prickly pears, grapes, pine-apples, grenadas, and passion fruit, and weighed at 6 p.m. for Las Palmas in Gran Canaria, shaping our course to pass 20 miles to the eastward of the unlighted and uninhabited Salvage Islands. There is said to be treasure buried there, and at least one party (not ours) has looked for it unsuccessfully. From all accounts there is a lot of treasure hidden in various parts of the world. It seems to have been the way the Middle Ages pirates and privateers banked their loot. They hid it well, and probably more money has been spent in trying to find it than the stuff is worth.

The passage was made under ideal conditions, a warm sun, gentle breeze, and smooth sea, almost purple in colour. Flying fish appeared, the first we had seen. They do not actually fly as a matter of fact, i.e. they do not propel themselves with their wings, but plane along, getting up speed, in some strange way, under the surface. They come out of the water as if shot from a catapult, and cover, perhaps, 100 to 200 yards at a flight. The mate, with hazy recollections of happenings when he was in command of an M.L. during the war, promised us a good supply of flying fish every morning if we put a light on deck at night. We should hear the fish flopping about the deck all night, he assured us. So the light was put out, but the results were very meagre, almost nil in fact. A few were knocked down from time to time by trying to fly through the mast or other obstructions, but the light did not seem to play any part in the matter, as quite as many came on board after it had been discontinued.

In the afternoon of the 1st October the high land of Gran Canaria was sighted ahead. Only the tops of the hills were visible, the lower parts being hidden in cloud. At dark the light on Isleta showed up, and just before 11 p.m. we had anchored in La Laz harbour. It was full of ships, and we toured all round it before we could find a clear spot for anchoring. When we lowered the mainsail the binnacle narrowly escaped being smashed, and my head cracked, through a little mental confusion on the part of the man at the throat halliards, who was under the impression that he had hold of the peak halliards. When the word came "Hold on the peak, lower away the throat," he held on the throat, believing it to be the peak halliards, and urged his opposite number to lower away, with the result that the gaff was lowered right down to the deck, and swept about creating general confusion, while the throat was still half-way up the mast. No harm was actually done, unless the feelings of the culprit were hurt by my remark that persons of average intelligence, working as crew of a sailing-ship, should know, after three weeks on board, which were the peak, and which the throat halliards, and that if they didn't—well, the inference was clear.

Next morning we shifted the ship nearer to the landing-place, and lay with an anchor out ahead, and a stern line on to a small schooner astern. Bumboatmen bothered us all the morning until a ship chandler came off and told us to hoist a flag in the international code—I forget which one it was now—which signified that we had chosen our attendant boat, and all others were to keep off. He said that if any other bumboatmen came on board while that flag was flying we could legally throw them overboard or even shoot them. It seemed a drastic law. Anyway the appearance of the flag at the cross-trees resulted in all the boats moving off.

The harbour of La Laz is about 2 miles from the town of Las Palmas and is a very busy spot, steamers arrive and leave daily, and there is a constant movement in and out of the small local schooners. Some of these brought in cargoes of salted fish, apparently in the last stages of decomposition, judging from the smell. Las Palmas is built along the beach in a valley of palm and other trees, and is an ordinary Spanish town with airy, open-fronted shops. The guide-books, however, give a full description, and I will merely say that we remained in Gran Canaria until the 19th October, waiting for the rainy, hurricane season in the West Indies to finish. The chief items of interest which occurred during our stay were the fact that the mate made tea on one occasion with boiling paraffin instead of boiling water—why there was not an explosion is a mystery—and the appearance on board of a rat, an expectant mother judging from the zeal with which it made nests with scraps of paper. The prospect of being obliged to entertain a mother rat and a number of young ones was very alarming. Traps and poison were tried in vain, and when one night the mate, who was sleeping on deck, leaped up and affirmed that the rat had nibbled his ear we felt that a crisis had arisen. And then John came to the rescue. He had had plenty of opportunities for studying the habits of rats in the trenches, and knew all about them.

"Rats," he said, "do not like the smell of tar. Is there any tar on board?"

There was not, but there was a disinfectant which smelt tarry, and this was poured freely into the bilges, and behind the matchboarding, and that night the rat abandoned ship. Whether it did a tight-rope walk along the stern warp to the schooner, or gallantly leaped into the water, is not known. Anyway it went, and that was the main thing.

Before leaving I got Greenwich Time from H.M.S. *Thistle* which came in. I had previously tried to get it from the Spanish guardship *Infanta Isabella*, but was told on board that their W/T gear was very poor and that they could only hear Santa Cruz, Tenerife, distant about 30 miles as the crow flies, when the conditions were good. It must be a curious installation for a warship.

The Navigating Officer of the *Thistle* also gave me a tracing of "Weir's Azimuth Diagram," which must have taken hours to make. It saved a great deal of calculation. "Big ships must look after little ships," he said, when he handed over the tracing.

On the 19th October we filled up with bananas, oranges, and fresh provisions and prepared to start. Just as we were heaving in the cable, David came on deck and said:

"I do not feel well. There are pains all over my body."

"In that case we had better not start," I replied. "We had better wait and let you see a doctor."

"Oh, no! I shall be all right once we are at sea."

At noon, therefore, we left the harbour for Barbados about 2,700 miles to the westward, but we did not get very far that time as David got worse instead of better, and in the evening he was very uncomfortable and feverish. I consulted the Ship's Medical Guide, without being able to identify his disease, and took his temperature, which was 101°. By that time we had run so far before a fresh N.E. breeze that it was hopeless to think of beating back, and I decided to make Santa Cruz, Tenerife, which was more or less on our way. The breeze held until we were under the lee of the land, and we lay there becalmed all night. At dawn the engine was started to get us clear, and a mile or so further out we found a fresh N.E. breeze, which took us into Santa Cruz harbour, just after dark. Sanchez, the boatman, was alongside even before we had anchored, with a sheaf of American chits of recommendation. He thought we were an American ship. Next morning I called on the British Consul to pay my respects and to get a doctor for David, and in due course one came on board and decided that David had had a chill, but was recovering.

"I would like to come with you, and see your so little ship fighting the waves," the doctor remarked.

I wonder, as a friend of mine used to say when not quite convinced by a statement made.

On the doctor's departure Sanchez came to say that the Harbour Master wanted to see me. Sanchez was our boatman. For a few pesetas a day he had agreed to attend on us with his boat at any hour of the day or night and do the catering and odd jobs for us. It was cheap. Why, the sight of his jolly, round face alone was worth the money, and the presence of his tall, solemn brother during our walks about the town lent a dignity to the party which would otherwise have been wanting.

Sanchez took me to the Capitan del Puerto, a short, stout, pompous, rather over-dressed little man, who was engaged at the moment in choosing socks from a commercial traveller. He kept me waiting while he made a selection of gaudy-coloured hose, and was on the whole rather insolent in his manner. He wanted me to enter, and later clear, my ship, and supply a manifest of the cargo. I explained, through Sanchez, that I had no cargo, and no manifest, and that vessels classed as yachts, and privileged to fly the Blue Ensign, were usually regarded as warships and not as merchantmen and were not required to enter and clear. El Capitan, however, would have none of this. All those islands were strongly pro-German during the war, and he did not propose to make any concessions to an Ingles yacht. I therefore made my way to that unfailing harbour of refuge when in foreign ports, the British Consul, who sent me on to Messrs. Hamilton. These gentlemen very kindly did all the necessary work for a purely nominal sum, and also arranged that Mr. Dyne, one of their managers, should take us to the English Club and make us members.

Meanwhile David was very insistent that we should start at once. He did not like to feel that he was holding us back.

"Three of you can handle the ship," he said, "and I shall soon recover at sea."

But, though I understood how he felt, I could not agree. He might have a relapse, with complications, and get worse instead of better, or he might not recover as quickly as he anticipated, in which case I should have to convey a convalescent right across the Atlantic.

"No," I replied, "there is no hurry, and we will remain here until you are fit, and able to stand your watch. I cannot take the responsibility of starting with a sick man."

In three days, during which we visited Laguna, and were driven out by Mr. Brown to his beautiful house built in the Moorish style, where the chief living-room was the verandah, David had recovered sufficiently to warrant our making a start, and on the 24th October we weighed at 7 a.m. Sanchez came to assist and hove up the stern anchor, which the authorities had insisted on our putting down, and also the second anchor out ahead.

Once outside the harbour a fine, hearty N.E. wind sent us spinning along down the coast and at sunset the Peak of Tenerife was 60 miles distant, showing clearly above the clouds. At last we were fairly off on the 2,600-mile passage across the Atlantic, and a long way it seemed, looking at the blank space on the chart. Moreover, we could not profitably go direct. It was first necessary to run S.W. to ensure finding the true N.E. trade wind, and this made the distance even greater. And soon there was a further reason for keeping south towards the Cape Verde Islands, as John began to complain of pains in his head and limbs. The following day he was worse and obliged to keep to his bunk. We took his temperature, which was slightly up, and his brother went right through the Ship's Medical Guide to try and find a disease corresponding to the symptoms. The only one which seemed to agree was beri-beri, or sleeping sickness. It could hardly be that, and yet, on the other hand, our rice was not of the yellow, unpolished variety. It was white and polished, the sort that causes beri-beri. At this stage of the proceedings, while the mate and I were learning quite a lot about diseases from the Guide, and beginning to think that we ourselves were suffering from several which we had not hitherto suspected, David intervened and decided that John had had a chill. He took up the case with energy, made up the bunk, got John into dry pyjamas, and started nursing him, and feeding him with slops, in a way which would have been a credit to a trained nurse. As a result, two days later John was once more about, and doing his bit, and there was no longer any necessity to think of Cape Verde Islands and Portuguese doctors. After that there was no more sickness, and we all finished the passage in excellent health, in spite of the fact that all the meat came out of tins. The only alternative to tins is to carry a harness cask with the meat in brine, but meat so preserved always seems to me to be unpleasant in smell and flavour, and I much prefer it tinned, as it is then far easier to stow and, stewed up with rice, potatoes or macaroni, onions, and tomatoes, is quite tasty. That is how we prepared it, or else made a dry hash, curry, or rissoles. A lot can be done with tinned meat, but some people consider it dangerous stuff liable to produce ptomaine poisoning. Altogether we did very well as regards feeding. John did most of the cooking, but as we kept up the watches day and night others occasionally had to lend a hand.

Time passed very quickly, and what with two hours at the tiller every six hours, cooking, eating, washing up, sleeping, and handling the sails, there seemed very little leisure. As I had the more interesting job of working out the ship's position daily I did not always assist in washing up. Taking sights and working out the results is rather a fascinating affair, and appeals to one more than washing up greasy dishes, though I did my share of the latter when occasion demanded.

Slowly we crawled across the blank chart, leaving a trail of little circles, enclosing a dot with a date against it, each of which represented the ship's position at noon on that day. The largest-scale chart to be had was still on a very small scale, about 100 miles to the inch, so that the advance from one day to the next seemed to be very slight, though we were actually getting along well, and "making good" an average of 130 miles every twenty-four hours. Though we "made good" only 130 miles daily, we sailed about 150 miles, but, owing to the fact that we could seldom steer the course, we did not approach our port, or make good, the full distance sailed. The wind was always fair, almost too fair, as it was dead astern, which is not the best point of sailing for a fore-and-aft-rigged ship, since one sail blankets or takes the wind from another. To get over this to some extent a spinnaker can be carried on the opposite side to the mainsail, but nothing will make the head sails draw, and the mizzen is almost useless. We carried the spinnaker day and night most of the time, but as the wind shifted frequently and blew anywhere from N.E. to S.E., hardly a day passed when we were not obliged to change the sails over from one side to the other, a process which usually took the best part of an hour. One night the helmsman gybed, involuntarily, all standing. Luckily no great harm was done, but it took a long time, in the dark, to straighten things up and get the ship back on to her course.

The weather was mostly delightful, and all day the white, fleecy, trade-wind clouds would sail quietly along above the horizon, while the nights were lovely, the air soft and warm, and the stars very brilliant. From time to time, however, there was a good deal of rain, blowing about in the form of small local squalls. Sometimes as many as six of these would be in sight at one time in different parts of the horizon, and one night we had a real downpour for five hours, which was so heavy that it gave me a very good idea of what it must be like to sit under a gutter-spout which is going full bore.

The mate had been steering, and he had noticed a heavy bank of cloud to windward. There had been a lot of cloud all the afternoon and evening, with lightning showing all round the horizon, but at midnight this extra black mass appeared, and he called me. It is one of the privileges of the skipper to have a better chance than anyone on board of contemplating the wonders of nature by being called whenever anything unusual is happening, or seems to be about to happen. On this occasion, on being aroused from slumber, I gazed on this black mass with a feeling of strong disfavour, and promptly decided to get the spinnaker off as a start. It was lowered with some difficulty as a

35

fresh puff of wind came with the rain. And then the downpour started, and knocked down the wind and the sea. They had no chance against it, as it appeared to fall, not in drops, but in rods of water. For five hours this went on, and then it gradually ceased, and left me free to go below and take off my soaked clothes.

On the 12th November we were getting near to Barbados, but the sky was quite overcast, as it had been the day before, and I could not get a sight of the sun or stars. This was rather awkward, especially as the rates of two of the chronometers had altered, and they were then nearly 55 seconds adrift, compared with what they should have been on the old rates, but things often happen that way, and it adds a seasoning to life. Further, the difficulty of steering a steady course with the wind frequently working to one side or the other made it advisable to check the position by sights as often as possible. Moreover, the peculiarities of some of the helmsmen were not without effect on the results. One of them, finding the sun rather hot, altered course without mentioning the matter, on one occasion at least, in order to get some shade from the mainsail, and another one appeared one afternoon to take his turn at the tiller with a book under his arm. I gazed at him with concern. Could it be that he proposed to violate all the best traditions of seamen by reading and steering at the same time? That seemed to be his intention as he seated himself with an air of pleasant anticipation.

"That book under your arm, is it to serve as a foot-rest?" I asked.

"Oh, no. No, it is rather interesting, and I thought of glancing at it as I steered."

Thereupon I put on my heavy skipper air, and said:

"Are you aware that the safety of the ship, to say nothing of the crew, depends on the helmsman, and that a touch of the hand, pressure wrongly applied to the tiller, can cause a gybe, and cripple her? If you are really interested in the book I will steer for you while you read."

But, of course, he would not hear of that and put the book away, and the traditions of the sea remained unbroken.

36

In the afternoon the wind fell right away, and then light airs came from all round the compass, with heavy rain, thunder, and lightning. At dark the wind came westerly, and we kept close hauled N.W. until 10 p.m., when we came round to S.W. There is no light on the north end of the island, and I did not care to risk standing on in the dark. At 4 a.m. we came round once more. As it grew light I got the binoculars and started examining the horizon systematically.

John was at the tiller, and he watched me with interest for a few seconds, and then asked: "Are you looking for anything?"

"Yes. I am looking for Barbados, which should be around here somewhere. It is only 18 miles long, and what with no sights for two days, the chronometers a bit out, the current, and one thing and another, I should not be surprised if we missed it altogether."

"Oh, there is land on the starboard bow. Perhaps that is Barbados."

Wily fellow! He had eyes like a hawk, and had seen it at dawn, but he knew I should not see it until I had worked round the horizon with binoculars, and in the meantime he wanted to hear once more about the altered rates of the chronometers, which I had been deploring loudly for several days, as well as declaiming about the extreme inconvenience of not being able to get sights towards the close of a long passage.

CHAPTER II

THE WEST INDIES AND PANAMA CANAL

By noon we were in Carlisle Bay, off Bridgetown, the capital, twenty days out from Tenerife. Launches came bounding out to meet us, bearing representatives of ship-chandling firms, and pulling-boats with more ship-chandlers tried to hook on as we went by; but we evaded them all, and brought up off the careenage. There the Health Officer came alongside, and he was closely followed by the Harbour Master and the Police-

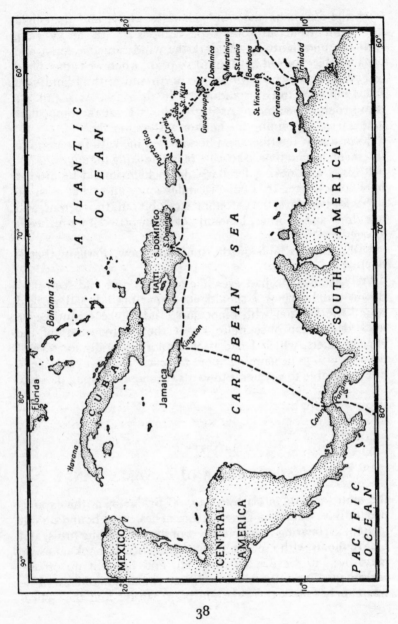

boat. The Harbour Master suggested that we should be quieter anchored near the Police-pier, and the Police-boat, after disappearing for a space, returned to say that we might use their Pier during our stay, by favour of the Commissioner.

The first impression of Bridgetown is distinctly pleasing. Architecturally it is merely a collection of irregular, rather ramshackle buildings, but there is an air of life, good government, prosperity, and quiet purpose about it which produces a good effect. This is as it should be, for did not Barbados, on the occasion of the Boer War, telegraph to the Home Government to urge them to stand up for the rights of the Uitlanders without fear, as Barbados stood behind them?

We landed at the careenage, and met first a negro policeman in a smart uniform, and wearing boots, and then James. The policeman's boots seemed unnecessary, almost wrong, but possibly the fact that James, and the rest of the civilian negro population, went bare-footed invested the boots with an air of distinction. James wore a torn shirt and a ragged pair of trousers, and carried a walking-stick. He greeted us with a most disarming smile, and appointed himself our guide. A guide was not in any way required, but he came in useful once or twice in fetching cabs, and so on, and followed us about as long as occasional small tips were forthcoming. When these ceased he disappeared.

As far as the mate and John were concerned the object of the trip was to find them work in the West Indies, at least that is what I had promised to do in a moment of optimism, as an inducement to them to join, and the first thing was to try and fulfil the promise. Luck favoured us. There was an appointment going for someone to look after the Government craft in the harbour, tugs, water-boats, lighters, and so on, for which the mate was eminently suited, and after some negotiation he was duly appointed, and filled the post to everyone's satisfaction. We also got John work which took him to America, and I have no doubt he is doing well there, as he is a very capable man.

With great regret I watched John pack his gear, and tenderly wrap up his violin, and heard the mate's muttered curses whenever the lid of his clothes' locker fell on his scantily covered head, which it did every few minutes, as he got his things out. We had got on remarkably well together, and it would have been hard to find two more pleasant shipmates. However, they had only agreed to go to the West Indies, and there we were, and they had found what they came to seek. Still it was with great regret that I saw their gear going over the side into the shore boat, and watched them gradually disappear up the careenage.

The next thing was to find someone to replace them. No amateurs were forthcoming, as everyone had his own job to look after, and the only thing was paid assistance. Captain Hancock, in charge of the prison, offered us a noted criminal then serving a long sentence, and we went up to inspect him. His special line seemed to be breaking out of prison, and breaking into houses, both of which he had done several times. For a criminal he was rather prepossessing, and he looked straight at whomever he was speaking to. I asked him if he had been to sea, and could steer and handle sails. He replied that he had been to sea in steamers, but could not steer, and knew little about sails. The temptation to get out of prison by saying he could steer must have been great, but he held to the truth, and remained in prison.

Enquiries from the Harbour Master put us in touch with another James, as black as sin, who claimed to have been twenty years on and off the sea. He was duly signed on as "cook and seaman." And then the Venezuelan schooner *Felicidad* sailed into the bay, and anchored near by. A party of her crew came alongside on their way ashore and appeared to offer to join, but as neither David nor I could speak Spanish we were not quite sure what they said. They were a merry, good-natured, useful-looking lot.

In the evening I sculled over to see the Captain. There were several lads on deck, and one of them, an intelligent youngster, asked if I could speak French. He told me that the Captain was on shore, and enquired whether I would take him as *mousse*, or ship's boy. I told him I must see the Captain before replying. Next morning the Captain came over, and said that we could take the lad if we wanted to, and that he was a "muy bueno muchacho." This sounded well, and we agreed to take him. I gave the Captain some charts of the north coast of South America, which pleased him greatly, and in return he sent over a South American sun hat, a huge affair with a deep, turned-up brim. He also invited me on board his ship, and I went over. There was quite a considerable quantity of live-stock about the decks, chiefly pigs and fowls. The Captain chased a hen and finally caught it under the bowsprit, and offered it to me as a present. However, I did not like to deprive him of it, and, moreover, should not have known what to do with it, though the black "cook and seaman" might have solved that problem. I therefore refused it with many "gratias."

During the morning Stéphane arrived with a small bundle of clothes. He was a bright lad, willing and intelligent, about 90 per cent. white; indeed, but for his woolly hair he would pass for white anywhere, except perhaps in America. I took him round to the Shipping Office to sign him on, and the Harbour Master made the discovery, which seemed to surprise him very much, that Stéphane could write a good hand.

"Why," he said, "what is your religion?"

"Un peu catholique, un peu protestant," replied Stéphane.

"Ah, that accounts for it."

Apparently it is the Protestant part of him which writes.

He could not speak a word of English, and for the first two or three mornings I used to take him round the deck, and tell him the English names for the spars and gear. He was very quick to learn them.

On the evening of the 11th December we regretfully weighed anchor and left for Trinidad. Our stay had lasted nearly a month, and had been very pleasant. Mr. Gill and others had boarded us the day after we arrived, and had made us honorary members of the Clubs, where we met a number of people and were received with the greatest kindness, and where, incidentally, we sampled a bewildering variety of iced swizzles, cocktails, and punches, all very alluring, and most of them potent; the drink I liked best of all, however, was iced lime squash. We had driven out to a sugar plantation in the north end of the island at Mount Prospect, passing strings of brightly clothed negresses walking into the town carrying baskets heaped with fruit and vegetables on their heads. Some of the loads must have weighed about 70 lb., but they carried them with apparent ease. They carry everything on their heads, even a single banana.

We had also been taken over a cotton mill and a modern sugar mill with all the latest machinery, had driven out to see a trial boring for oil, had bathed in the surf at Cranes, and had lunched regularly on Fridays, turtle day, at the Bridgetown Club. At the first lunch there I nearly took the skin off the inside of my mouth by adding half a spoonful of pepper-wine to the turtle soup. Three or four drops are enough. We had also been present at the swearing in of the members of the House of Assembly, and heard the Governor's address. Up to that time I had always thought that a Governor was a figure-head merely, and was quite staggered at the enormous mass of complicated matters and conflicting interests with which he has to deal, as revealed in the address.

Altogether we had had a great time. The Governor, Sir Charles O'Brien, was kindness itself. He invited us to Government House, and came on board with his family to tea, bringing his own cakes, and everyone else was extremely kind and hospitable. Incidentally we had also given one of the Harbour policemen a severe shock. There is always, day and night, a Police-boat rowing about the bay, and a Police-watchman on the Pier. One dark night we came down and walked to the end of the Pier to hail our ship, the signal being a short and a long blast on a loud whistle. I blew, and immediately a black form, up to then invisible, leaped into the air at my elbow. It was the black watchman, who had been asleep, I fear, on duty. The piercing blast of the whistle sounded almost in his ear startled him into life and activity, and his abrupt and unexpected appearance caused me to take a rapid pace to the rear. We both recovered ourselves quickly. I pretended that I had not noticed anything, and he tried to make it apparent to all that he could look out best in a position of repose.

However, we tore ourselves away on the 11th December,

sailing at dusk. Soon after starting I made the discovery that the black cook seaman could not steer. Twice he nearly gybed, and I then sent him away from the tiller.

"I too anxious, sah," he said.

Next day he was also sea-sick. For this he blamed the ship. "Ship jump too much."

It then came out that he was really a chain-maker, and not a sailor, though he had made trips from time to time. I decided to discharge him when we got to Trinidad. When that would be seemed very doubtful. We had heard tales of schooners being weeks trying to get through the Bocas del Draco, at the entrance to the Gulf of Paria in which lies Port of Spain, the capital of Trinidad. The entrance is split up into four by three islands, and there is a strong stream out of the Gulf through the Bocas. If there has been much rain in the Orinoco district the outrush overcomes the inflowing flood, and is very rapid during the ebb. Indeed, Columbus had so much difficulty in getting in that he came to the conclusion that the entrance was guarded by a dragon which kept pushing him out, and he named the entrances the Dragon's Mouth.

On the morning of the second day out from Barbados we were nearing the famous Bocas. In theory, the stream was running in through the entrances, but actually there was a strong outrush, and even with a nice fair breeze we could not advance until David started the engine. We then began to crawl slowly through. The water bubbled and swirled about, and at times the ship did not steer well, but we advanced by degrees, and finally tore ourselves from the embrace of the stream, and emerged into the calm waters of the Gulf, into a fairy scene. Ahead, lost in a rain squall, was Port of Spain, but to port Chacachacare, Huevos, Mono, Gaspar Grande, The Diegos, and Five Islands, crowned with trees, lay beautiful in the sunshine. The rain soon blew up and blotted them out, and when it had passed we were close up to Port of Spain. The water off the town is very shallow, and steamers have to anchor three miles out, but we crept in and brought up in two fathoms half a mile from the piers.

The central part of the island is flat and very fertile, but along the north coast is a range of lofty hills densely wooded, which form a beautiful background to Port of Spain. On the south coast are other hills, not so high, amongst them being the three peaks which gave the island its name when Columbus discovered it in 1498, in his third voyage.

We found Port of Spain an up-to-date place, with electric trams and, as the *West India Pilot* says, "the resources of a civilized town." The streets are filled with a wonderful mixture of races, whites, negroes, coolies from India, Chinese, Spaniards, and blends of all.

While we were there heavy rain fell frequently, to be immediately followed by hot sun, and as a result the place fairly steamed.

We called on the Governor, and delivered our letter of introduction from the Governor of Barbados; were made members of the Clubs; drove out to St. Anne's past the Swannah; but the most important thing we did was to discharge James. We had first to get a Police Permit for him to leave the Colony, then to book his passage, and then to sign him off. He made a fuss at the Shipping Office, and said the Registrar had insulted him, whereupon I told him to sign his name and not be a fool, which really was an insulting remark, but he signed, and said nothing. He then wanted to be rowed out to his steamer, and as this was only fair, I hired a passage for him. He then wanted money for food on the trip, but I gave him biscuits and a tin of bully beef instead, wished him luck, and saw him disappear with a feeling of satisfaction. He still owes me 35*s.* out of what I advanced him when signing him on, after allowing for the fact that we paid his wages until he landed in Barbados again. I fear that James, taking him all round, was a bit of a fraud. No suitable hand could be found at Port of Spain, but we felt sure that we should pick up the right man at one of the islands, and in the meantime could get along with only three on board.

After five days at Port of Spain we left on the 19th December for the pitch lake at La Brea. The wind was fresh, and we got along well under head sails and mizzen, and brought up off Brighton Pier early in the afternoon. Next morning we rowed off to the beach, but could not find anywhere to land, without

jumping into the water, until Mr. R. G. Legge, the engineer
to the company, came down and pointed out a lighter, bumping alongside the pier, on to which we scrambled. There was
nothing dignified about our arrival on the pier. As a matter of
fact, Mr. Legge dragged us up off the lighter by main force.
He then took us up to the office and introduced us to the
Manager, who kindly ordered a car, and sent us round the
premises. We saw the cask factory, where they can make 1,600
casks daily; the engine shop; the cask-filling shed; and finally
the lake itself, which suggested a tidal harbour of about 100
acres with the tide out. Negroes were picking out large lumps of
asphalt and carrying them to trucks running on rails across the
Lake. As the whole surface is in constant slow movement the
rails have to be frequently re-arranged, and the holes resulting
from one day's work are filled up on the morrow by the pitch
welling upwards. Borings have failed to reach the bottom, but
the surface is not as high as it was. Still, there seems to be
plenty of pitch to go on with for the present. Having inspected
the Lake we were driven to some oil wells, one of which
yields oil without pumping, and then, along a pitch road,
bordered with cocoanut-palm-trees, through the old village, a
collection of ramshackle, crazy old huts, past the spick and
span new village to the Company's Hotel, a fine mosquito-
proof building, where the bachelor employés live. There we
were received most cordially, and had lunch, and, later,
dinner, and met Messrs. D'Everteuil, Agostini, Matheson, and
many others. After dinner we visited the bungalow of one of
our hosts and were introduced to various people's wives, one
of the latter "with the gift of the gab very galloppin'" as Mr.
Weller once said. Her words poured out in a continuous stream,
like water from a hose-pipe. I saw her husband watching her
with a certain expression on his face, which may have been
admiration, but I fancy it was some other emotion. From this
lady we gathered that the educated negro—who, by the way,
is never alluded to as a "nigger," as that term is considered
offensive, but as "coloured" or sometimes "African"—is a very
hard-working and ambitious person. Many go home, study,
and take degrees, and come out as successful lawyers and

doctors. I certainly saw in the native quarter at Barbados a roughly painted name, and "Barrister at Law," outside a woefully tumbledown old shack in the last stages of decrepitude, in and round which swarmed a number of little negroes.

Next morning Mr. Matheson sent off a lump of ice, some grape-fruit, and a Spanish-English dictionary to enable David to converse with Stéphane, who spoke French and Spanish but no English, while David spoke English only.

We weighed at 9 a.m., and left for the Bocas on the way to Grenada. The breeze lasted until 1 p.m., and then fell away, whereupon we started the engine as I wanted to get through the Bocas before dark. The tide was ebbing when we got there, and there was a tremendous rush out, so much so that we could hardly steer the ship. The water went out swirling and twisting like a mill race, and we went with it, sometimes broadside on, sometimes heading straight, but getting along with speed. Once clear of the entrance we got into a nasty tide rip for a time, but when out of that found a more regular sea. The wind was fresh, and north of east so that we could only lay N.N.E., which course we kept all night, and in the morning sighted beautiful Grenada, hilly and covered with trees, ahead. The Sailing Directions refer to a westerly current between the Bocas and Grenada of from 1 to 3 miles per hour, but luckily we did not get more than 2 miles per hour, and Grenada was ahead when sighted, and not on the weather bow as I thought quite likely. Before noon we had anchored in the lovely harbour of St. George, one of the most beautiful in the West Indies, which has, moreover, the added advantage of being clear of the track of hurricanes. As there were only three on board and one a mere lad, we started getting canvas off outside the harbour, and then went in quietly under power. It was not advisable to go in with the sails up, as they and the gear are very heavy, and with the small crew it always took a long time to make or take in sail. The Harbour Master, an educated and refined African, who spoke with the accent of Oxford, came off and guided us to where he wanted us to anchor.

"How many are there of you on board?" he asked.

"Three."

46

This struck his boat's crew as a very funny state of affairs, and they so far forgot themselves as to laugh uproariously. The smallness of the crew was always a source of amusement to the harbour police.

The Harbour Master took charge of our letter of introduction to the Governor, and had it sent up to Government House. Very soon afterwards an invitation to an "At Home" taking place that afternoon came down, and we extracted our blue-serge suits, and, in spite of the heat, put them on, creases and all, and went ashore in search of a conveyance. There had been a run on the local Fords, but we managed to track down the owner of one which had not been engaged, and induced him to take us up. Fords suit the conditions in the West Indies very well, and are almost universal.

The Governor and Lady Haddon-Smith received us very kindly, and asked us up to eat our Christmas dinner at Government House, and also to stay there while the ship was in port, but as I never sleep ashore I could not accept this part of the invitation.

On Christmas morning, Mr. Percy Horne, who is famous for having landed a 196-lb. tarpon with a rod after a struggle of four hours, took us to Grande Anse for a bathe. The beach there is fine sand, and the water beautifully clear and warm. After the bathe he produced a Thermos flask, and I expected to be offered a cup of hot tea, but not a bit of it. The flask contained an iced cocktail! I realized that I was in the tropics. In the evening we went up to Government House for the Christmas dinner, which, it is hardly necessary to say, was excellent. I thought of it with regret on the following Christmas Day when I was hove to in a gale of wind, and dined on bully beef, fried potatoes, and mouldy bread. Next day the Governor took us for a drive round the island. He wanted to inspect the roads, in which he is keenly interested, and asked us to go with him. The track runs between palms, and groves of cocoa shrub, or perhaps they should be called trees, and presents a series of the most lovely views. On the way we climbed a mountain of 1,750 feet to visit the Grand Etang, a small lake on the crest. Grenada is certainly a beautiful island, the view over the harbour from

Government House being especially fine. At the time of our visit planters were depressed, owing to a slump in the cocoa market. Cocoa is the chief product, and it seemed that there was temporarily no demand for it, but the previous few years had been good.

On the 29th December we weighed and left for Carriacou, one of the 100 islands and rocks in the Grenadines just north-east of Grenada. While we were laboriously winding in the cable—work which David disliked very much—a boat, containing an elderly negro, came within speaking distance. The negro stood up and took off his hat.

"Sah," he said, "I hope your stay has been pleasant. We consider your visit an honour," and then rowed off, leaving me slightly dazed. However, I recovered myself sufficiently to shout some inadequate reply. The coloured man was always springing surprises on me. I started with the idea that he was a foolish, childish sort of person, but very soon changed that view.

Having got the anchor on deck, and, with infinite labour, hoisted the sails, we left the harbour, with the help of the engine, as there was not a breath stirring. It was also calm under the lee of the island, but once clear of that we had a nice breeze. Disquieting accounts had been given us of the probability of meeting heavy seas off a rock, with the suggestive name of "Kick-'em Jenny," which lay on our course, but we got past with dry decks, and early in the afternoon brought up in Hillsborough Bay off the little pier.

Comparatively few ships visit Carriacou in a year, and those that do are well known by sight. The arrival, therefore, of a strange, unknown ship surprised the Commissioner, and he sent out his District Officer, who is also the Health Officer, the Works Officer, and the Road Surveyor, to find out who we were, and what we wanted. With him came the Customs Officer, and both stayed for tea, while the Commissioner fidgeted about impatiently in his office, looked out of the window and wondered why his Officers did not return to clear up the mystery. In due course telegraphic rays from the Commissioner's brain impinged on his satellites' receptive organs, and they suggested that we should all go ashore and call on the Commissioner. Arming ourselves with a letter from the Governor of Grenada stating who we were and urging, indeed ordering, that every effort be made to find us an able seaman from amongst the whalers of the island, we landed and made our bow to the Commissioner. He considered us as a break in the monotony of official life, and was genuinely glad to see us. Messages were sent all over the island to enquire for a suitable hand, but no one could be found. All the likely ones were away, and we had only one application from a rather insolent negro, who asked in a strong American accent, to join what he called our "marine expedition."

The Commissioner borrowed horses and took us for a ride round the island to a lime-juice factory and up to the highest part, where the hospital is placed, and whence a magnificent view of the surrounding islands is obtained. Broken water, white amidst the beautiful blue of the sea, showed where lay the reefs. Stretching away to the north were islands and detached rocks, as far as the eye could see, each fringed with a white line of breaking surf. Very fair they appeared in the setting sun.

We dined that night with Mr. Cocks, the Works Officer, and next day went with him by sea to Tyrrell Bay, where we gathered oysters from mangroves, and caught some barracouta on the way, and then returned to lunch with him. One of the items served was a pepper-pot. That particular one happened to be new, and had not been going for more than a few days. It was as hot as fire, but a well-matured pot is excellent. I am not quite sure how they are prepared, but I believe that a large casserole is half-filled with hot condiments, chillies, pepper, and so on, and that legs of fowl, pieces of meat, or anything left over are thrown in and the whole lot cooked up daily. We were told that some of these pepper-pots go on for years.

The Commissioner asked us to dinner and a small dance, and David, though unfamiliar with the steps, took the floor with great success. Next day the whole family came on board to tea. The Commissioner showed us how to make it in a way

49

new to us. He added the juice of a lime, sugar, and rum instead of milk. The ladies, however, did not stop to partake of the brew. The slight roll of the ship was too much for some of them, and they had to be landed with speed, most unfortunately not with sufficient speed.

On the 1st January we weighed anchor with the help of Mr. Cocks and his man Ana, and left friendly Carriacou for St. Vincent, 43 miles to the north, passing westward of Union Island, Cannouan, Bequia, and the other islands in the archipelago. The morning was fine, but in the afternoon the wind drew ahead, obliging us to beat, and a heavy rain blew up, blotting everything out. Just at sunset it cleared away and we got into Kingstown Bay after dark. As we sailed in, the Signal Station hoisted two pennants which I could not read, but I took them to be E.C. "what ship is that?" I replied by hoisting the four flags giving her name, and the Station hauled the pennants down. Neither of us could read the other's signal, but honour was satisfied.

Next morning an invitation came down from the Administrator at Government House for us to spend the day there, and shortly afterwards a police-boat came to take us to the pier, where a car was waiting to drive us up.

The Administrator, His Honour R. Popham Lobb, received us cordially, and made us free of the house and grounds, while he attended to some business in the hurricane shelter, which he used as an office. These shelters are fairly common in the West Indies, and the necessity for them gives some idea of what a hurricane is like. We heard tales of trees torn up by the roots, of sheets of corrugated iron blowing about like paper and cutting people in two, and of the contents of a strongly built two-storey house being blown out through the roof by the wind, which forced a shutter and entered at the ground floor. Everything simply goes unless securely bolted down.

While at Kingstown I got rid of a further 2 tons of ballast, making, with the ton taken out in the Canaries, 3 tons dispensed with so far. This was a noticeable improvement, both as regards speed and sea-going qualities. A launch crowded with negroes came to receive the pigs of iron. They wandered about the ship in a spirit of simple curiosity. They had never seen a ship quite like her before. She was, it is true, losing much of her yacht-like appearance. The bright woodwork was oiled instead of being varnished, the masts and spars wanted scraping, also the blocks, and altogether she looked rather weather-worn, but they did not notice that. To them she was a new type, and the last word in smartness.

The negro who did the weighing was an extremely conscientious person. He had been told to get 2 tons, and he wanted that weight, neither more nor less. He was greatly grieved that the weight did not come out exactly and that the addition of a pig brought the total over 2 tons, while its absence made it less, and suggested sorting the lumps. I had had enough, however, of dragging about 140-lb. pieces of iron in sweltering heat, and sent him away with a load of just over 2 tons.

A Mr. George Fraser, whom we had previously met in Grenada, then appeared, and was anxious to take us up the La Soufrière volcano, a climb of over 4,000 feet. He suggested that we should go round and anchor in Chateau Belair Bay, and make the ascent from there. A climb of 4,000 feet, in considerable heat, with the torment of flies and biting insects added, did not appeal very much to either of us, especially as it was more than likely that we should not see anything when at the top, which is nearly always enveloped in cloud, and we excused ourselves. I had an additional reason for not going, as the anchorage there was none too good, and there was no one to leave in charge of the ship except the boy. If anything happened he would be helpless alone, even if he had known what to do. Mr. Fraser was anxious that, if we would not climb the mountain, we should, at any rate, see something of his beautiful island, and with characteristic West Indian kindness arranged with his brother to take us for a drive up the east coast to Georgetown. The road was hilly, and wound and turned about in an extraordinary way. Possibly some ancient Carib, forcing his way through the undergrowth, and working round fallen trees and stones, made the first track, which has been followed ever since. But, though the road was roundabout, it had the advantage that every turn offered a fresh and enchanting view of seashore, fertile valley, or level, cultivated land.

It was a delightful drive, but one cannot live on beautiful scenery. Like Speed, "I am one that am nourished by my victuals and would fain have meat," and when noon came and went, and there were no signs of lunch, I began to make gentle enquiries as to the programme to find out if lunch formed any part of it. Apparently it didn't. The plan seemed to be to drive out as far as we liked, and then drive back, and have lunch some time during the afternoon. There was not an hotel at Georgetown, but Mr. Fraser said he knew a man there who would be glad to give us lunch. We telephoned to say that we were coming, and received a hearty welcome on arrival. Our host was a negro who spoke English very fluently, and I fancy he liked to have someone to talk to, and had lunch put back to enable him to indulge his hobby, as it was an unduly long time making its appearance. However, cocktails finally appeared, and then lunch. As a compliment to us, and a concession to the supposed craving of Europeans for tinned meats, all the items of the lunch came out of tins, except the rice, but they were not less welcome on that account, and filled an aching void very satisfactorily. After lunch we drove back by the same road to Kingstown, and called in at the "Self Help" to buy a few curios. These Self Help places are very general in the West Indies, and one can get light refreshments there and curios and articles of local make. They are run by the white lady residents of the district.

At 4 a.m. next morning the black bumboatman arrived to help us get under way. He brought some Avocado pears, and claimed to have been walking about half the night to find them. With him came two youths, probably his sons. In theory getting under way should have been a simple matter with six to do the work, but actually, beyond heaving in the cable, our assistants were a hindrance, as the night was dark and it was almost impossible to move in any direction without colliding with an invisible black object. Moreover, they, naturally, did not know one rope from another, and simply hauled away when told to do so, without knowing what they were doing, or what was at the other end of the rope. Altogether they were more trouble than they were worth.

The chain of lofty mountains which runs from north to south of the island, with other ranges of densely wooded hills diverging from it to the sea, between which lie fertile valleys, forms a magnificent picture, but has the disadvantage from the sailor's point of view of interfering with the supply of trade wind, as a result of which we had to run the engine until we had cleared the north end. Our little fellow chugged gamely along, and pushed us clear. I dislike engines, but on occasions such as this, they are invaluable, and I would not be without one on any account.

A fine fresh breeze met us as we drew clear, and we laid a course for Castries, St. Lucia, 58 miles from Kingstown, and soon had the two remarkable Pitons in sight. These are conical peaks rising perpendicularly out of the sea to over 2,600 feet and 2,400 feet respectively, and are densely wooded to the tops. The island is mountainous and covered with forests. As we sailed along the coast several native canoes passed under sail. They are hollowed out of a tree-trunk, and the sides are then raised by two narrow planks. Two flat-headed sails are usually carried on bamboo masts without stays or supports. In place of these one of the crew stands on the gunwale to windward of each mast and holds on to a rope made fast to the masthead. As the canoe heels over he leans out, and in this way acts as moving ballast, and as mast shrouds. It seems a haphazard arrangement and rather unsafe, but the negroes are daring sailors, and go out a long way off the land in quite fresh breezes. The canoes are used to take fruit, produce and passengers from one place to another along the coast, and to go out fishing. It is a great sight to see fat, gaudily dressed negresses sailing along in one of these slight canoes.

At 5 p.m. we were off the harbour of Castries, and went in under power, after lowering the sails, and anchored west of the wharves. After a time a black pilot came off, and was very off-hand in his manner at first, not to say insolent, but he altered his tone very soon, and went to the other extreme.

With the pilot came a mulatto detective, who drew me aside

in a mysterious manner and showed me the butt of a revolver under his shirt. He whispered that he was a detective, and during the rest of the interview winked at me in a knowing sort of way when he thought that no one was looking. He seemed a suitable man to whom to confide a bag of mails I had brought from St. Vincent, and a letter of introduction to the Administrator. He took charge of these with ill-concealed joy, carefully hid them inside his shirt, and departed in an atmosphere of mystery, evidently feeling that he was engaged in an important, secret mission.

We spent six very pleasant days at Castries. Word had been sent from Grenada that we were coming and, on the morning after our arrival, Mr. Johnson and Mr. Plummer came off, and took us ashore, where they made us members of the Club, and introduced us to many very nice people. As a result we had a great time, received a lot of hospitality, visited La Vigie, where the old barracks have been made into residential quarters, bathed in the Anse du Choc, and visited the famous Morne Fortuné, which has seen so much fighting between the English and French. Between 1664 and 1817, when it finally became British, St. Lucia was captured six times by the British, and restored by treaty to the French four times. On one occasion, in 1795, the French drove out the British. Most of the fighting centred round the Morne Fortuné, the top of which is still covered with old forts and magazines. There are also large, modern and extremely hideous barracks there, which have never been used. The cost of erecting them was prodigious. The view from the Morne is indescribably beautiful, whichever way one looks, whether south across Cul de Sac Bay and along the coast; inland at the ranges of hills, covered in forest, with deep valleys between; or across the harbour to La Vigie, Anse du Choc, Pigeon Island, with Martinique away in the distance. As fair a picture as one could wish to see. I do not know where it can be matched, even in the crescent of lovely West Indian islands.

One day we took the motor boat to Soufrière. The Administrator had arranged with the magistrate there that he should look after us, but on landing the magistrate met us and said that he had to go on to Vieux Fort to judge some evildoers, but that a planter, Mr. Laffitte, would take us in hand. This gentleman then appeared on horseback and Mrs. Du Boulay kindly sent a horse and trap to take us up to Mr. Laffitte's estate, the Dauphine, 3 miles out. The road winds upwards through groves of coffee, cocoa, and limes. When we were about half-way I happened to look back, and discovered a little black imp hanging on behind.

"Hallo! How did you get there?"

"Me belong Mrs. Du Boulay," he replied briefly.

An excellent lunch awaited us at Mr. Laffitte's house, where Mrs. Laffitte received us and offered a cocktail. The lunch consisted of tunny fish, and avocado-pear salad; chicken with yam, peas, and potatoes; curry and rice; fruit.

We went over the estate, and saw cocoa, coffee, limes, and essential oil being prepared for market. Our trap was then brought out, and we drove to the crater to see the sulphur springs. About half-way down our steed came to a stop, and refused to proceed in spite of our efforts to persuade it to advance. Out we got to try the effect of the human eye, since the cruder method of the whip had failed. It was then discovered that the harness had come adrift. The intelligent beast had noticed that the trap was out of adjustment and was pushing it along sideways, and had stopped until things were put right. Having apologized to the horse and buckled up the harness we got in again, and completed the descent. The negro lad took charge of the trap, and Mr. Laffitte tied his horse to a tree. We then pushed through some undergrowth, and came out on the bed of the crater, where all vegetation ceased. It lies about 1,000 feet above sea-level and is crusted with sulphur, alum, and cinders. In one part there are several boiling springs sending up jets of sulphurous water and steam in dense clouds. An uncanny sort of place. It looked as if it might burst out at any moment. Whilst we were wandering about examining the surroundings it began to rain fairly fast, but Mr. Laffitte did not seem to notice it, and when his attention was called to the fact replied:

"This can hardly be called rain. This is merely a dry drizzle."

Luckily it was soon over, and we then drove back to Soufrière to have tea with Mrs. Du Boulay and to catch the boat back. Quite unintentionally I fear I offended Mrs. Du Boulay, by giving one of her servants a small tip. Our boots were covered with mud on arrival, and he had cleaned them for us. Chancing to meet him as we left I tipped him a small sum, and at the same moment became aware of the lady regarding me with evident disfavour. Apparently I had done the wrong thing, and the best plan seemed to be to retreat to the boat "with all convenient speed," which I did. The underlying idea is very pleasing. As guests, the servants and the house and all in it, were at our disposal, and to make a money present in return for services rendered was to cast a reflection on the hospitality of the hostess. So, at least, I read the position. It is to be regretted that the idea is not more widely spread. The tipping system is essentially rotten.

On the 13th January we weighed our anchor with the help of the Harbour Police, and left, hoisting sails as we went out. Our next port was Fort de France, Martinique, 37 miles to the north. On the way we passed some of the sailing-canoes miles out to sea in a smart breeze, and lumpy sea. It is wonderful the way the negroes handle those frail, unstable craft. In smooth water they are very fast, and in the harbour they had passed us as if we had been anchored, but once outside we went away from them.

We picked up a nice breeze, the constant Trade Wind, off the north end of the island, and made a fast passage to Fort de France, crossing an area which has seen a lot of fighting between English and French frigates during the stormy period of the Islands' history. We also passed the celebrated Diamond Rock, which rises almost straight up to a height of 574 feet, and which was fortified by Admiral Hood in 1803. He placed his ship the *Centurion* alongside the rock, and hoisted the guns up by tackles. It seems an impossible feat, but three long twenty-fours and two eighteens were got into position. For sixteen weeks the garrison caused the French much damage and annoyance, and then stores and ammunition ran out, and they had to surrender.

As we approached the harbour David's cap blew off, and we came round to pick it up, but lost sight of it in the process, and did not see it again until it was abeam. This happened three times, and each time it was not seen until too late. David then stripped, and jumped in after it. Neither of us thought of sharks until he was in the water. Luckily he got back safely. As a matter of fact I did not see a shark all the time I was in the West Indies, though they are fairly numerous.

The Health Officer was waiting for us, and came on board as soon as we had anchored. He was followed by the Customs Officer, who demanded a list in duplicate of all stores on board, down to the salt. He was, however, a very reasonable man, and he gave me to understand that the main thing was the list, and whether it was accurate or not did not greatly matter. In those circumstances I supplied a list in a few minutes of some of the things I thought were probably on board, and everyone was satisfied.

From the sea Fort de France is not an inspiring place, as all that can be seen of the town are the backs of dingy warehouses, amidst palm-trees. On the right of the town Fort St. Louis juts out into the sea. In 1774 when the British captured Martinique, Captain Faulkner of the *Zebra* took this fort by sailing his ship right up alongside it, and climbing in through the embrasures. The men of those days certainly were a wonderful lot. Nothing seemed to be impossible for them to carry through. The capture of the rest of the island at the same time by General Grey was also a magnificent feat. He marched right through the island capturing all forts and redoubts with the bayonet only. He would not allow his men to fire their muskets, and to make sure that they did not he had the flints taken out before starting.

We only stayed one day at Fort de France, where we were received very kindly by the Consul, Mr. Meagher, but coldly by the French authorities. The same official attitude was noticeable in other French ports, and we came to the conclusion that our statement that we were sailing for our own amusement was only half-believed. Sailing around in quite small ships, and doing most of the work oneself, does not seem to be the average Frenchman's idea of pleasure, and the authorities, while always very courteous, were not cordial, and appeared to look at us askance, and left the impression that they were wondering what really lay under it all. The Consul, however, received us with open arms, and took us ashore to lunch. Not to be out-done we invited him to dinner, together with several men to whom he introduced us at lunch.

On leaving Fort de France we sailed along the coast for the ruined city of St. Pierre. The wind was strong, and we got along quite fast under jib, staysail, and mizzen, with the mainsail left stowed, and soon ran off the 13 miles separating the two places. Before it was destroyed by the eruption of Mount Pelée in 1902, when 25,400 people perished in a moment, St. Pierre was one of the most important cities in the West Indies, and from all accounts was a bright, gay, and delightful place, beautifully situated; but the eruption utterly destroyed it, and a second eruption a fortnight later buried a large portion under a flow of mud, and threw down every wall in the remainder not already overthrown. Of all those who were in the city on that dreadful 8th May, only one escaped, and he was a prisoner in a dungeon of the jail. Seventeen vessels were lying at anchor in the Roadstead, but one only, the *Roddam*, a British steamer, got away, and she was nearly capsized when the blast of superheated vapour struck her. All the others were destroyed, and sank where they were. The fact that all these wrecks were in the Bay made me rather chary of going there. Striking a submerged mast would probably mean foundering. However, we both wanted to see the place, and I decided to risk it, but to minimize the chance of striking anything I kept outside the 30-fathom line of soundings until the little wooden jetty, erected since the eruption, was abeam, and then turned 8 points, and went straight in, and anchored quite close to the shore, closer than a steamer would go, to avoid dropping the anchor on to a wreck. On landing at the pier the first thing to strike us was a remarkably well-carved statue of a female figure representing the agony of St. Pierre. The town must have been a fine one with numerous good stone buildings. Lafcadio Hearn describes it as "the sweetest, queerest, darlingest little city in the Antilles," but it is now a scene of utter desolation. Only about 200 people live there, in wooden shanties, and there seems no intention of rebuilding the town.

Our next port was Roseau, Dominica, 35 miles farther north. As we laboriously wound up the cable next morning rain came down in torrents, and lasted for some time, and off the La Perle rock at the north end of the island a heavy squall blew up, and obliged us to stow the mizzen and staysail. While crossing the Dominica Channel we found the sea heavy, and the wind strong from the east, and we experienced several squalls, and a specially heavy one which again compelled us to reduce sail, just south of Scott Head. Columbus discovered the island in 1493 on a Sunday and named it Dominica in consequence. A range of lofty, rugged mountains covered with vegetation runs from north to south, the highest, Mount Diablotin, being 4,747 feet. It is indeed a beautiful island seen from the sea, a mass of tree-covered peaks and deep-green valleys, and it has an additional claim to interest as the only island where pure-blooded descendants of the aboriginal Caribs are to be found.

The water in the regular anchorage was too deep for us, and we were compelled to go uncomfortably close to the beach to get a suitable depth in which to anchor. The Harbour Master came off while I was changing, and his crew announced his arrival by banging on the deck. I rushed up half-dressed, and protesting loudly, but the Harbour Master was not offended at the vigour of my remarks, and came below and had a drink in all good fellowship.

Next morning we landed, and climbed the Morne Bruce guided by a small negro boy. The view from the top is magnificent. Inland one catches a glimpse of the lovely Roseau Valley, and below lie the Botanical Gardens, the red roofs of the town and the blue sea. On the way down we walked round the Botanical Gardens, which must be unique in their way. They seem to contain every native tree and shrub and many foreign ones, and have evidently been planned and laid out by someone who loves the work.

In the afternoon we weighed and proceeded up the coast to

59

Prince Rupert Bay under easy sail. This is the best anchorage in Dominica, but the small and dilapidated town of Portsmouth is said to be unhealthy. A cable ship was lying at anchor sheltering from the weather. There was too much sea outside for her to do any work. Next morning we were under way again bound for Point à Pitre, Guadeloupe, 39 miles northeast. It lay rather out of our way, and our only reason for visiting it was that it was Stéphane's native place, and as we were passing we thought we might as well go in and let him see his friends and relations. As we cleared the north end of Dominica we met a strong wind and a heavy sea, and we had to lower both staysail and mizzen, and leave her to stagger along under the mainsail and jib. We were passing over historic waters, for it was here in the Saints' Passage that the great sea battle between Rodney and De Grasse was fought on the 12th April 1782, which resulted in the destruction or capture of the French ships, and established British mastery of the sea in the West Indies.

The Iles des Saints were left to port, and Marie Galante, named after the ship Columbus was in when he discovered it, to starboard. The latter gave us some shelter from the rough sea. In the early afternoon Gozier Lighthouse appeared ahead, and after a time the Mouchoir Carré buoy was sighted, and we could then bear away for the entrance, which is narrow, but well buoyed. By 2.30 p.m. we were inside, and anchored off the town.

The Health Officer came off and was very brusque in his manner. He could not understand what we were there for. There was no cargo, which in itself was very unusual, not to say suspicious, and apparently we had no business to transact in the town. Then why had we come? There is nothing to attract one in Point à Pitre, and probably yachts never go there, which explains his surprised attitude. He left, apparently much mystified, and presently returned with a policeman, armed with a revolver. This officer was full of tact and very courteous. He refused to come on board in his official capacity, but said he would like to see the ship and would come as a visitor. After his departure the Captain of the Port, a Mulatto, also paid us a visit. He examined the ship and fittings with great interest, but all the time seemed preoccupied, and full of some pleasant secret. At times he almost hugged himself. All at once he beckoned me into the cabin and asked in a whisper if I was a Mason. My reply in the negative disappointed him, but he recovered somewhat on learning that David was one of the fraternity. He told me, with evident joy, that he himself belonged to a large French Lodge, and asked that David be sent for. As it happens David is not a French scholar, and, as the Captain could not speak English, they could only smile at each other when confronted. Still the interview seemed to give the Captain great satisfaction, and he left well pleased with his visit. Before going he asked me to keep a look out for a schooner of about 100 tons, as he wanted to buy such a vessel, and carry passengers and trade between the islands. At the time of our visit communication between the islands was very bad; indeed, it was a difficult matter to get from one island to another.

Next morning we went to the market guided by two little boys, the sons of an American, who had been hanging round the ship since our arrival. It is held in the cemented Place du Marché, and, when we got there was crowded with buyers and sellers. The latter were mostly negresses, clad in brightly coloured print gowns, and turbans of many hues. Each sat by a small stock of vegetables, fruit, etc., and all seemed to be talking at once. The noise was almost deafening. We bought oranges, bananas, and cocoanuts, and returned laden with these to the ship. After lunch we weighed and left the rather smelly, but bright and animated little town, and made for the entrance. We found a small drogher there beating out. She made six boards, before she got clear, but owing to our deep draft and the fact that the engine was running we went out in one apparently to the great surprise of the drogher's skipper. We could see him waving his arms about, and pointing us out to the crew. Outside the harbour the wind was strong and the sea rough, but we could lay the course easily, and by dark had rounded Vieux Fort Point, and were off Basse Terre, where we lost the wind under the lee of the land, and ultimately had to run the engine for a time to get clear. As we were rounding

Vieux Fort Point a small sailing-canoe, filled to overflowing with negroes, had passed heading for Martinique. The negroes are daring sailors and skilful in handling these canoes. I hope they got there safely, but there was a lot of wind and sea, and it seemed a hazardous undertaking in the dark.

The intention was to call in at Montserrat, but when we arrived off the town at 4 a.m. the wind was so strong and the sea heavy, and the anchorage afforded so little protection, besides being very deep, except close in shore, that we decided to miss it, and run on to Nevis, 35 miles to the north-east. On the way we passed the great uninhabited rock of Redonda, which rises from the sea in a rounded dome to a height of 1,000 feet. At 8 a.m. we were nearing Nevis, which has been a British colony since 1628. It is a lofty volcanic island of 20 square miles, and is highly cultivated, but it is bare of trees, and can hardly be said to be beautiful. In fact so little were we impressed with it that we decided to go on yet further to St. Christopher, another 13 miles, which we reached at 10.30 a.m.

As we had recently visited Dominica, where we now learned there was an epidemic of influenza, the Harbour Master rather demurred to giving us pratique until the doctor had seen us, but when the latter came off, he passed us as free from infection. On landing we found the town full of American tourists, who were taking full advantage of the fact that the island was not "dry." An American mine-layer had also just come in, and five others were expected, and the police and inhabitants anticipated a lively time. One of the American tourists, who had been looking on the wine while it was red, stopped me on the pier and asked if I was travelling in the same steamer as he was.

"No," I replied, "I have a little ship in the anchorage."

"Which one?"

I pointed her out, but he was troubled by a multiplying eye, it seemed, and was unable to pick her out from amongst the innumerable ships he saw in the bay. He asked further questions, but I had got tired of him and left him.

St. Christopher, or St. Kitts as it is usually called, is named after Columbus, who was so charmed by its appearance when he discovered it in 1493 that he gave it his own name. It has been a British colony since 1623, and the table-lands at the foot of the lofty hills are richly cultivated. But we did not stop there long; indeed, about this time we did not stop anywhere for very long. Our letters were at Jamaica, and I rather wanted to get mine, and David was also very anxious to get on. We therefore merely got a Bill of Health for Ste Croix, had a scamper round the town, and returned on board. On the way off to the ship we visited a schooner to find out if they had any hands to spare. We still hoped to pick up a good man as we went along. With only three on board, and one of them a youth, we were short-handed. Weighing the anchor and hoisting the sails was very hard work, and when this was done and we were at sea we had very little spare time, as the boy did the cooking and cleaning up, and was not available on deck during the day, so that David and I had to steer, and attend to the sails, etc., which kept us fairly busy. At night each of us took two hours at the tiller and then four hours off.

The schooner had no spare hands, but the mate thought we might very likely find one at Saba, an island famous for its seamen, and as it was on our track we decided to go there next day. Accordingly, we left the bay at 9 a.m. on the following day in a perfect downpour of rain, and headed for Saba, 39 miles distant. The wind was strong once we were clear of the land, and we had to get the topsail down. The sea was also heavy. The correct thing would have been to reef the mainsail, and change to a smaller jib, but as the distance was short we let her go along under the full mainsail and big jib. With a small crew one is tempted to put off undertaking heavy work, such as reefing in a breeze, until the last moment, which is not the least of the disadvantages of being short-handed. The blow which we experienced that day was the tail-end of a big disturbance farther north, we learned afterwards. The wind was from the north-east, right on the beam, and so naturally was the sea. As a result, as the ship staggered along with more sail on than she wanted, the spray was flying over her in sheets, and we were wet to the skin. The Dutch island of St. Eustatius gave some shelter for a time. This sleepy little island, with an import trade of £2,081, and an export trade of £1,031 in 1907, was, for a brief period, the centre of trade in the West Indies, and the beach is even now covered with the remains of the extensive warehouses then put up. It has been a Dutch Colony since 1600, and it rose to importance about the time of the American War of Independence when regulations of all kinds made trade in the West Indies almost impossible. Holland then made St. Eustatius a free port, and all the trade went there as a result. There were often over 100 merchant ships at anchor off the town. For a time all went well, but, instead of sticking to legitimate trade, the islanders went in extensively for contraband to supply the French and American ships and ultimately Rodney sailed up, and captured 150 merchant ships, and all the goods in the warehouses, worth nearly £4,000,000. The whole lot was auctioned on the spot, and after the goods had been removed the island subsided once more into its normal state of calm. But it must have been a feverish time while the boom lasted.

There is no harbour at Saba, but there are two anchorages, on the west and south sides, and we made for the latter, which is the more sheltered with the wind N.E. As we approached we saw a schooner standing off and on, as if unable to decide whether to go in and anchor or not. I did not like the look of the place myself, but did not want to miss the chance of finding a good hand, and stood in for the anchorage marked on the chart. A boat put off from the shore as we approached and hailed us to say that they would lead us to the best spot for anchoring, which proved to be close inshore under a beetling cliff. A more unsuitable-looking spot it would be hard to imagine, but the men in the boat said that it was good holding ground, and that we need not fear dragging ashore. The schooner came in soon afterwards, and anchored a little farther out.

The Harbour Master presently was rowed off, and came alongside on his way to the schooner. We told him that we had come in search of a good hand.

"What would the pay be?" he asked.

Now that was just what we did not know. It might be anywhere from $15 to $90 per month, the English dollar being taken at 5*s.* It depended largely on the colour of the man. At a venture I replied:

"Oh, say $30."

He seemed to think that a satisfactory figure, and went on to the schooner, while we went ashore in a boat which came off. There was a slight surf on the beach, but the boatman got us in unsplashed by waiting outside the line of small breakers until the right moment, and then going in with a rush.

Saba is a remarkable place. It is merely the rim of an extinct volcano, rising above the sea. There is, of course, nothing very remarkable about that, and the extraordinary features of the place are that though it belongs to Holland the people speak English amongst themselves and though it has no harbour, timber, or any conveniences for building ships yet it was at one time famous for its ships and its seamen. The principal village is in a dip in the crater called the Bottom, and with such a name, in Saba, this is naturally 960 feet above sea-level. We climbed up to it along a well-kept path, laid in wide steps, bordered with cactus and aloes, and found the village spread about in no particular order. The postmaster came to meet us. As time hangs rather heavily on his hands, he also runs a navigation class. We spent some time with him. He said that all Saba men go to American ships, where the pay is high, and as they all know something of navigation they mostly do very well.

While we were talking to him a coloured woman brought some lace handkerchiefs for sale, and we bought a few. Presently the Harbour Master appeared, and told us that there was no hope of getting a hand at $30. Indeed, only one was available, and he would only come as master or mate at a big wage, as he was a qualified navigator, and so we returned to the ship. The men who put us off had already heard that our search had been unsuccessful, and asked if we would take a "middle-aged" man. They knew one who would go, as he was unhappy at home owing to a masterful wife. Though I did not feel flattered that my ship should be regarded as merely the lesser of two evils, I asked them to send him along, and next morning we saw an old man tottering down the ravine with the help of a stick.

"There comes the candidate," David said.

"Oh, no," I replied, after inspecting him through the binoculars. "That man must be over eighty. One could hardly describe a man of eighty as middle-aged."

But David was right, he was the candidate. The boatmen lifted him tenderly into a boat, and rowed him off. There he sat with dull and listless eyes, holding his stick between his knees, an old man.

"How old are you? " I asked him.

"About fifty."

"Are you over seventy?"

"About fifty," he muttered, "about fifty."

I told him I was sorry he had had the trouble of coming down, but that he would not suit, and he was rowed back to the beach, and later we saw him crawling slowly up the path towards his unhappy home, and his masterful wife. His attempt to escape to the quiet and peace of the sea had failed, and we were still without a second hand.

Our plan was to leave the anchorage at about 6 p.m. under easy sail, so as to avoid arriving off the island of Ste Croix, our next port, in the dark; but during the morning, the wind came more easterly, and sent a nasty sea into the anchorage, which no longer gave any shelter. At 2 p.m., therefore, we started weighing, and, having finally wound in the cable we got the anchor on board, and then hoisted the sails, using the trysail instead of the mainsail, as the wind was strong, and we did not want to go fast. As it happened it would have been better if we had used the mainsail, since the wind raised a short, vicious sea, which made us roll heavily. The mainsail would have steadied her. Moreover, in spite of the small canvas set, we still went too fast, and made the unlighted east end of the island at 3 a.m. Heavy rain then came on, and we had squalls of wind and rain all the morning. At 11 a.m. we were standing in for Fredericksted Bay under power with most of the sails stowed, when a fierce squall came off the land, which drove us backwards, and we had to get sail on again before we could get ahead. We anchored off the jetty in water so clear that we could see the anchor and cable on the bottom in 3½ fathoms.

Two Customs Officers, two Medical, a pilot, and the son of the British Vice-Consul, Mr. Merwin, came off, a fine bunch of clean-cut Americans, full of energy and go. They were very breezy and pleasant, and sampled our whisky with gusto, drinking it neat, and then drinking water. The island had belonged to America since 1917, when Denmark sold it to her, together with St. John and St. Thomas, and is consequently "dry."

I do not know whether the negroes like the change of masters. Americans are very particular about colour, and one of the Medical Officers apologized to me for not having shaken hands when he came on board, as, at the first glance, he was deceived by my excessive tan, and thought I might have a dash of colour in me. However, he soon saw his mistake, and explained matters, while binding up my hand, which I had cut when thrown down in a heavy roll. As a matter of fact, I had not noticed the omission until he referred to it.

In the afternoon Mr. Merwin junior took us for a drive round the island, through cane and other crops, passing through Christiansted, and back to his house, where we had supper. Next evening we weighed at dusk, and left for Ponce Harbour, Puerto Rico. The wind was light all night, and all the following day, and we did not make Muertos Island off the entrance until long after dark. There is a lighthouse on this island, how-ever, and good leading lights up the harbour, which clear the reefs on both sides of the Channel, and there was no difficulty in going in, the only trouble being to pick a good place for anchoring when we were inside. In the end I merely got out of the line of leading lights, and let go. Early next morning I heard a boat come alongside, and on gaining the deck found an American Customs Officer brooding over the Blue Ensign, fluttering proudly in the breeze.

"Say, Cap," he said, "what sort of a flag do you call that?" He had actually never seen a Blue Ensign before, and did not even know it was a British flag! One would expect a Customs Officer, whose business is with ships, to be able to recognize the flags of other nations, and certainly those of England, whose ships roam every sea, and go to the ends of the earth, but this particular officer did not. He was, in spite of his sketchy knowledge of flags, a pleasant enough young fellow, and a bit of a wag in his way. He chose to think that I was one up on him over the matter of the flag, and decided to equalize matters somehow. Our stores gave him his chance.

"Of course you know that this country is 'dry'," he began, "and it is my business to see that no spirits are introduced. I must search the ship. It is a matter of duty."

Accordingly, he set to work, but did not find any concealed stores of spirits. He locked up all we had shown him, however, and, having thus cut us off from our stock of alcohol, felt that the game was "one all." But he wanted to be one up, and demanded a list of stores, an exact list. While David and Stéphane toiled in the bowels of the ship, and extracted tins from amongst the ballast, I wrote down the results of their researches, and the Customs Officer smoked cigarettes, and smiled. He felt that he held the winning cards. In course of time the list was complete, and a lengthy one it was too.

"That's great," he said. "Will you please make out a copy? All ships entering the port have to supply an exact list of stores—in duplicate." And he smiled once more, a broader smile. He was, as I said, a pleasant young man, but I began to dislike him. And the worst of it was that he had not played all his winning cards even then.

"There will be one or two other forms for you to fill up at the office, when you come ashore, Cap," he said and left, after expressing his pleasure at meeting us.

He was right about the other forms, and I had to sign declarations that I would not take letters or persons away, nor allow anyone to come on board the ship while in port, and I only escaped by a narrow margin having to enter and clear the vessel. The next step was to call on the British Consul, who was very agreeable, and who sent for his car, and drove us round. He also changed our money, and took a lot of trouble to put us in the way of getting stores. Later he paid us a visit on board, and after he had left our pleasant young Customs Officer arrived.

"Did I see someone on board?" he asked.

"Yes. The British Consul."

"You made a declaration this morning that you would not allow anyone to board you."

"It is becoming a bit thick if a British Consul cannot board a British ship without getting someone's permission."

"That's so," he agreed, "and now I want you to do something for me, to take a letter to Santo Domingo."

But I won a trick there, as I reminded him that I had also signed a declaration that I would not take any letters away. But he was several tricks ahead, and could afford to lose one.

After he had gone I rowed over to a barquentine lying astern to see if they had a spare chart of Santo Domingo. The Captain received me very cordially, but seemed a trifle preoccupied, and in the course of conversation it came out that every time he went on shore he had to be on the look-out to avoid being murdered by one of his crew, who had avowed his intention of doing for the captain at the first chance. The strain of being continually on his guard against being knifed or shot was beginning to weary him, and he had reported the matter to the Police.

"After all, that's what they are paid for," he said, "to prevent crime, and now let's see about your chart."

As it happened he had not got one, but he gave me much useful information about the port, and with that I had to be content.

Next morning we left beautiful Puerto Rico with its forest-covered mountains and fertile, green valleys, and took a good wind to Cana Point at the east end of the island of Santo Domingo. There it failed, and we rolled about all day in a calm, and all the next night. There can be few things more trying than rolling about in a small vessel in a calm if there is any swell. There is so much noise that it is often impossible to sleep. The ship is never still, and the booms and gaffs swing to and fro, in spite of all that can be done to keep them quiet, and bring up with a jerk, blocks creak and groan aloft, or bang about on deck, and the sails flap. Altogether it is a miserable time, and the gear wears out five times as fast as with steady sailing, on account of the uneven strain, and constant chafe. However, at 2 a.m. on the following morning we got a breeze again, and by 11 a.m. were nearing the outer anchorage, where all vessels wait for the doctor's visit. A four-masted schooner and three small trading vessels were lying there. They were rolling heavily in the swell which always runs into the bay. We got the sails down, and went on under power. Just as we were about to cross the bows of the schooner the engine stopped, and we began to drift down on to her. David had perhaps forgotten to turn on a tap somewhere. He rushed below, and said he would have it going in no time, but I have little faith in motors, and proceeded, with the boy's help, to get sail on again, and it is lucky I did, as the engine remained coy and refused to respond to David's blandishments. However, with the sails, we managed to clear the schooner, and then, as its services were no longer urgently needed, the engine, naturally, started off almost on its own.

Santo Domingo, or the Island of Misrule, as Treves calls it, has had an unhappy history. Columbus discovered it in 1492 and was so pleased with its appearance that he called it Hispaniola, or New Spain. It was then inhabited by about 2,000,000 Arawaks, but the Spaniards very quickly exterminated the whole lot. It is at present divided into two unequal halves, Haiti and Santo Domingo, the Black and Mulatto Republics, and the population in 1913 was estimated at 2,500,000 and 750,000 respectively.

In 1505 negro slaves were introduced into the island, presumably to replace the Arawaks. The island remained Spanish until 1697, when the French got in, and held the western part. In 1785 the Sovereignty was given to France, but in 1803 they were expelled by the blacks. In 1844 Santo Domingo revolted from Haiti, and established the Mulatto Republic. Since then revolutions, bankruptcies, and general unrest have been the order of the day. It is a fine island, 350 miles long by 150 miles greatest breadth, and is extraordinarily fertile. The *West Indian Pilot* says, "The mountains are richly and heavily timbered, and susceptible of cultivation nearly to their summits, and it is probably the most fertile island in the West Indies, but its commercial prosperity has been completely destroyed by continual revolutions."

Having anchored and cleared up the decks, we had time to look round. High and dry on the beach was an American cruiser which had been blown ashore in a hurricane. The town is full of interest as the oldest settlement in the New World still existing, and also as the alleged burial-place of Columbus—his tomb is in the cathedral, if his remains are not—but we were destined not to see it, except from the sea, as the Health Officer did not come off. During the morning the three trading vessels went up the River Ozama to the anchorage off the town, one after the other, each in tow of three motor-launches working tandem fashion; but we and the schooner remained rolling at anchor in the outer anchorage. Hour followed hour, and still no doctor came. In the afternoon a vessel came out, and the pilot came alongside in his launch on his way back, and said he would fetch the doctor. But we waited in vain. Possibly the authorities hoped that we should get tired of rolling about, and would weigh and go up the river to the town without waiting for the doctor's visit; in which case we should have been subject to a fine of £100, or so we had been told at Puerto Rico.

When, at 4 p.m., the doctor had not turned up, we decided to weigh, and proceed to Jamaica. It was annoying to have reached such an historically interesting city, and then to have to go away without seeing it, but there seemed nothing else for it. We had already been rolling heavily for five hours, and the prospect of a whole night of it, and perhaps all the next day, was very unpleasing, so up came the anchor, and off we went. Getting the anchor on board was a rare job, as the ship was rolling nearly to the gunwales every time. Heaving it up to the surface had not been any trouble, beyond the labour involved—the anchor alone weighs 200 lb.—but lifting it out of the water, and getting it on deck without damaging the copper or side, was the difficulty. As a matter of fact it crashed against the side once or twice before it could be secured. Once it was on the deck up went the sails and we were off before a fresh breeze.

Next morning we were nearing Beata Point Peninsula. The

wind hardened and in three hours we logged 33 miles, which is about the fastest the little ship ever went while I owned her. For the next four hours she reeled off over 10 knots, 40·6 miles. We then passed between Beata and Alta Vela Islands and brought the wind more aft. As a result the speed fell to 8 knots. The run for twenty-four hours was 187 miles or 7¾ knots. I have never been able to get up to 200 miles in twenty-four hours, but on several occasions have done over 180, and once 190 miles. Still 187 miles was not bad, and we hoped to make a quick run to Jamaica. Such calculations are pleasing to make, but they do not always come off. They did not in this case. At dusk we were nearing the Morant Cays, which are three small islets about 10 feet high, surrounded by reefs, on which, the *West India Pilot* says, "the sea constantly breaks." It also adds that "the remains of several wrecks lie on the reef surrounding these Cays." It did not seem to be a nice place near which to wander at night, and I planned to give it a wide berth, and when the boy came to the tiller, cautioned him not to let the ship work to the southward, but at the same time not to let her point north of west, as that would mean bringing her dead before the wind, a dangerous position at any time, but especially so that night as the sea was rough. He promised to be careful, and I went below. Ten minutes later there was a heavy crash on deck, and I heard the boy shouting "Capitaine, Capitaine." I bounded out of my bunk, and up the ladder. He had let her gybe, and the boom lay against the runner, broken in two. It was a heavy spar 26 inches in circumference, but it went like a carrot. This will give some idea of the weight behind it, and what a gybe means in a seaway. Here was a pretty kettle of fish, and to make things worse the spinnaker and topsail were set.

However, it was no use crying over spilt milk and the only thing to do was to clear up the mess, and get the ship in going trim again. David and the boy started in on getting the spinnaker and topsail off while I took the tiller, and kept the wind in the mainsail to prevent it shaking, without bringing it on the beam. The spinnaker was taken in first, and the spinnaker boom placed on deck. During the process one of the boom guys

72

got over the side, and round the propeller. This was not noticed in the dark, and we did not find out what had occurred until later. The topsail was the next thing to take in, and then we were ready to lower the mainsail. While the other two had been at work forward I had been trying to think out some scheme for controlling the aft part of the boom when the halliards were slacked up. Unless it was controlled in some way it would certainly swing about and cause a lot of damage and very likely knock someone overboard, and that someone would be me. Spurred on by the instinct of self-preservation I evolved the scheme of setting up both topping lifts, and then hauling the mainsheet in taut. This held it more or less, but when the halliards were slacked up the broken part landed on deck, and the aft part swung about in spite of everything, and when we found that we could not get the mainsail down with both lifts set taut, and had to slack the lee one, its swing became greater, and so did my activity. The boom seemed to have a grudge against me, and to be trying to get at me, and I was constrained to fall flat on deck from time to time to avoid its attacks.

After much strenuous exertion on everyone's part the sail was finally lowered, and the boom secured to the rail. So far so good, but the work was not finished yet. We had first to clear the decks of the frightful raffle of ropes lying in heaps everywhere, and then to drag the storm trysail from the sail locker, and set it. By the time this was done I was so tired that I could hardly stand, and was not at all pleased to find that it was then my turn to take the tiller for a couple of hours. However, it was all in the day's work, and one does not expect much rest at sea, at any rate in small ships one seldom gets it. Something often happens which one man cannot fix up alone, and the others have to be called. Even a shift of wind usually means another man having to turn out, and as the rule was that I was to be called if any change occurred, I was always the one.

The *Amaryllis* did not like the trysail at all. She considered that not enough sail was being carried, and simply loafed along. I suggested to David that in the circumstances we were justified in starting the motor.

"Good scheme," he said. "I will couple up the shaft," and he dived below for the purpose. Sounds of violent exertion, and muttered exclamations, soon arose, and then ceased, and David appeared, bathed in perspiration.

"Something is holding the propeller shaft. I cannot get the flanges together."

The reason was not far to seek. A rope end was over the side and wound round the propeller hub. Nothing could be done in the dark to clear it and the only thing was to wait for daylight. David, who always rose to emergencies, then stripped and went over the side. He is a very good swimmer and diver, and he tried hard to get the rope clear, going down time and again, but without success, and in the end, after wasting much time, we had to give it up, and proceed as best we could under the trysail. Luckily our port was to leeward and the distance was not great, so that we were bound to get there in a few hours. At 4 p.m. that afternoon land loomed up ahead, and before dark I was able to fix the ship, and knew where we were.

At 10 p.m. we hove to south-west of Morant Point to wait for dawn, as I did not care to attempt the rather complicated entrance to Port Royal in the dark with a crippled ship. Before dawn we let draw, and made for Cow Bay, a few miles east of Plum Point, and as soon as we were in smooth water, or relatively smooth, David prepared for another attempt to clear the propeller. I am a very poor swimmer, and hopeless as a diver, while Stéphane had not enough backbone to do any good, and so the work fell to David, who, as I have said, was always at the level of any emergency, no matter what it was. Just then a canoe came past with two negroes. As a rule negroes are fair divers, and I called them alongside, and asked them to see what they could do. In the interests of economy, and to discourage them from asking too much, David then came on deck in a bathing-suit, ready for the attempt, but the blacks assured us that they could not dive, and so I waved them away, and David lowered himself over the side, armed with a knife, which he had carefully sharpened. In a few seconds he came up, and said that he had cut the rope on one side, and then went down, and cut it on the other, and we pulled the ends on board. Once more David dived, and this time unwound the portion round the hub. Coupling up the shaft only took a minute or so, and the engine was ready for running.

I got the ship under way for Plum Point, and went to the tiller, while David did what was necessary to start the engine, but could not get it to go. There was absolutely no response, not the suggestion of a kick. The ignition seemed to be at fault, and it seemed probable that the batteries were weak. As the motor refused duty, the only thing was to continue to crawl in under what sail we could set, and this we did. The Fates, however, had pity on us and sent along a heavy squall from the S.E. which, even with the reduced canvas, sent us along at a good speed. David saw his opportunity, and put the clutch in. The motor fired at once, and our troubles from the weak batteries were over.

The approaches to Kingston Harbour are much encumbered with reefs and low islets, and there are only two channels available, east and south. Both of these are badly buoyed, and only the east channel is lighted, and of use at night. The harbour itself is formed by a peculiar long, flat tongue of sand covered with mangrove bushes, named the Palisadoes. At the western end of this tongue is Port Royal, the Naval yard, at one time a very busy spot, and even in the days of the buccaneers gay and dissipated, but now deserted and of small importance. Part of it was submerged in the earthquake of 1907, which did a good deal of damage to Port Royal, and destroyed a great part of Kingston, but Fort Charles escaped unharmed save for one cracked wall. Nelson was in command of the Fort in 1779, and there is a tablet in one wall reading: "In this place dwelt Nelson. You who tread his footsteps remember his glory."

From Port Royal, Ships Channel, about 2 miles long, leads between reefs to Kingston Harbour, a fine spacious place, 7 miles long, and 1 mile wide on the average, with depths of from 6 to 10 fathoms.

We had passed Plum Point, and were in East Channel when the squall blew up, and enabled us to start the motor, and by the time it had screamed itself away we were close to Gun and Rackum Cays, between which lies the Channel, about 200 yards wide at that point. After passing through we rounded Beacon Shoal and were off Port Royal, and ready for the doctor to come on board, examine our Bill of Health, and give permission to proceed to the harbour. There were several vessels at anchor awaiting his visit, and it seemed likely that it would be some time before our turn came. In the ordinary way this would not have mattered, but as things were we dared not stop the engine as it would be impossible to start it again; so we chased his launch about, and, moreover, succeeded in cutting him off, and inducing him to come on board. He was a very conscientious man, and he was rather upset to find that the Bill of Health was made out for Santo Domingo, and not for Jamaica, but we persuaded him that this was quite in order as we had not landed. He then made a careful copy of all the ports we had visited since leaving England, a lengthy business. As he wrote a thought struck him, and he said to me:

"By the way, your wife and little boy are here, and have been making searching enquiries for the ship."

"But I am not married," I replied.

"Oh, that is strange. She must refer to this ship, as yachts seldom or never come here, and she has exactly described the vessel, and the people on board."

Strong in the knowledge of a blameless past I refused to accept a wife and little boy, and then David intervened and said they might be his.

"But," I objected, "you told me that they were in Egypt."

"So I did, but I have since suggested to my wife that she should come out here."

I did some rapid thinking, and in a prophetic vision saw the *Amaryllis* leaving Kingston Harbour without David. And that is what actually happened.

For the first two days after our arrival he continued to live on board, and then he joined his wife at the hotel, and the ship knew him no more. Urgent business, he explained, compelled him to give up the trip, and to return to Ireland.

This was rather a jar, as not only did I lose a very pleasant companion, and a useful hand on board, but, left in this way with a small ship and a smaller boy as the sole crew, I was faced with the prospect of having to abandon the whole thing, and sell the ship for what she would fetch, unless I could find a suitable companion. To this task I applied myself in the intervals of re-fitting the ship, and arranging for a new boom to replace the one broken. There was no difficulty about the latter, but getting hold of a suitable mate was another matter. Only two men were serious in their offers to join, and one of them was far too sick to undertake such a trip. His doctor refused to sanction it, and caused me to be warned in a roundabout way that if I accepted the candidate I should certainly be called upon to read the Burial Service at sea. The second man was very anxious to leave Jamaica, but he knew nothing of ships or the sea, and always left such a pronounced odour of alcohol behind him after a visit on board that I turned him down.

In the meantime I was having a very pleasant time, and by the kindness of various people was made a member of the Liguanea, Jamaica, and Yacht Clubs. I also went a drive with David, his wife, and child right across the island, passing through Spanish Town, the old capital of the island; the lovely defile of Bogwalk; up to Moneague, where we had breakfast; down to Ocho Rios on the north coast, where we bathed off a beautiful sandy beach, and then had a fresh-water bath under a waterfall; and so on to St. Ann's. No lunch could be had there at the time we wanted it, and so we turned east, and drove along the coast to Port Maria, and lunched there. The scenery was magnificent with the blue sea on the one hand fringed with the graceful cocoanut palm, and on the other spacious valleys and undulating and well-wooded ground running back to the central ridges of the Blue Mountains. Jamaica offers every kind of scenery, while the climate, according to the *Pilot* varying "greatly with the altitude and situation is, in general, pleasant, healthful and salubrious." The mean temperature varies from 78·8 at the coast to 55·78 at 7,400 feet.

From Port Maria we drove along the north side to Annotta Bay, and then turned inland once more, and made for Kingston, passing through the lovely Castleton Gardens on the way. The drive, through the most entrancing scenery, was delightful, and the only unpleasant feature was the fact that I had to pay for burning a hole in the hood with a spark from my pipe. Though the point was not actually proved, I have no doubt that my pipe was responsible for the fact that as we drove quietly through a village the hood started smouldering vigorously. Excited shouts from all around warned the black chauffeur, and he stopped the car. The residents flocked joyously to the spot and beat the smouldering hood and also poured water from kerosene tins all over each other and the car, and had quite a jolly time, to say nothing of obtaining a subject of conversation for the rest of the year. But it was rather an expensive day for me, as half the hire of the car was £7 10s. and repairs to the hood were £4 extra.

During my stay at Kingston a fine two-masted schooner yacht, the *Haswell*, designed by Herresoff, came in from Toronto. She carried a crew of six, besides the owner and his son, and was most beautifully finished, and kept like a new pin. She quite took the shine out of the *Amaryllis*.

The owner suggested that we should make a tour round the island together, but there was too much for me to do, and I had to refuse very reluctantly. Before he started on his trip back to Toronto he came and asked permission to photograph my ship, which he considered worthy of record on the grounds that she is an interesting relic of the past!

Time went on, and still no suitable companion appeared. It became clear that I had to make up my mind whether to sell the ship, and give up the trip, or to hire another man, and go on with only the two forward hands, until I could pick up a companion somewhere on the way. A sailmaker who had done some work for me, and who took a keen interest in the trip, offered to get me a young San Blas Indian from Central America, one he knew and had had on board his ship before he gave up the sea and settled on shore. He described this Indian as a good seaman, and said that most San Blas men made excellent sailors.

It seemed a pity to give up the trip so soon, and I agreed to ship him, and to go on with him and Stéphane.

Two days before we sailed the sailmaker brought off the Indian, Sam, and a small valise containing the latter's slender wardrobe, and all his earthly belongings. Sam is very short, about 5 feet, but sturdily built. He is copper-coloured, with a heavy, impassive face, and straight black hair, and he looks very much like an Esquimau. His knowledge of English was slight, almost negligible, but he could speak Spanish after a fashion, and so was able to talk to, and occasionally quarrel with, Stéphane. Taking us all round we were a most amazing ship's company to sail across the Pacific, one white man, a savage, and a French lad with a dash of colour in him! We had not even a common language. The two lads used Spanish, while I spoke to Stéphane in French, and to Sam in English. Unfortunately I could not always understand the guttural noises Sam made when speaking what he imagined was English, and I do not think he understood me very often. At times Stéphane had to be called in as interpreter. It seemed that Sam could express himself more readily in Spanish than in English, and when he and I utterly failed to understand each other Stéphane came to the rescue, and turned Sam's Spanish into French. But this was always the last resource, as Sam rather fancied himself as an English scholar, and I did not want to hurt his feelings. In the main things ran along very smoothly in spite of everything. Sam was quite a good seaman up to a certain point, but he could not read the compass, and was unable to learn the names of the points. He could steer all right by the wind when beating, but when steering a compass course I had always to make sure that he understood which point to keep her on. Once he had grasped that he never made a mistake.

His real name is Waltarda, but he had taken the sailmaker's name to save trouble, and was signed on as Sam Bodden, age unknown but believed to be nineteen.

I prepared to leave about the middle of March. A day or so before we sailed the stores came alongside in a boat manned by two negroes.

"Are you the steward?" said one of them to me.

"Yes. Also deckhand, bos'un, mate, engineer, doctor on occasion, navigator, and skipper. Likewise owner. At the moment I am the steward, so pass up the stores."

He was quite overcome. One man, one job, seemed to be his motto.

On the 14th March, after five weeks at Kingston, we weighed, and made for the Ship Channel. Two or three friends put off in various craft to wish us good luck, and the *Kellerig*, at anchor in the stream, hoisted T D L, i.e. "Wish you a pleasant voyage," as we approached. I was too busy in helping to get the anchor on board and secured, and the sails, and running aft at intervals to steady the helm, to make a suitable reply by flags, but I shouted my acknowledgments as we went by.

The dignity of our departure was much marred by Sam's clothes. He had appeared on deck that morning in his working rig of a pair of shorts, and a shirt which bore a strong family likeness to a lady's camisole, and which was very much too small for his sturdy body. It split in the back as we were heaving in, and during the process of hoisting the sails it split in several other places. It soon ceased to be a garment, and became a collection of ragged ribbons of cloth attached to a collar, fluttering in the breeze around his copper-coloured body. For the credit of the ship I had to suspend all operations while I found him an old stiff-fronted shirt. He accepted it in silence and retired below to put it on. In a few minutes he returned wearing the shirt, in the front of which he had inserted two gold studs, and gravely went on with the work. He was a very sedate young man, and seldom smiled. Like most American Indians he was silent and taciturn, not to say morose. At times he did not reply when I gave him an order, and I put him down as sullen, and hustled him about a bit, but I now believe that very often he did not understand the order, and that his apparent sullenness was really his natural manner.

After safely negotiating the twisty Ship Channel, we passed Port Royal drowsing in the sun, and left by the badly buoyed South Channel.

A nice easterly breeze kept with us all the way to Colon, and we made a fairly fast passage in spite of a heavy beam sea. The daily runs were 165, 158, and 155 miles. At noon on the 17th March land was by observation 35 miles distant, and during the afternoon the hills south of Point Manzanillo loomed up through the mist. At 6 p.m. the lighthouse on the Point was abeam, and at 10 p.m. we were off the entrance to the harbour. However, I did not go in that night as I was so tired and sleepy that I could hardly keep my eyes open, and I knew that going in would mean at least an hour's hard work, with the probability of having to keep awake for a further hour or so to receive officials, and fill up forms. I therefore decided to heave to outside for the night, get some sleep, and go in at dawn. Accordingly we rounded up, and got the headsails to weather, and then started to get the topsail off. The breeze was fresh, and as soon as the halliard was started the sail behaved like an unchained devil, and slatted violently about. All three of us got on to the tack, and ultimately succeeded in dragging the sail half down, and then it stuck and nothing that we could do would move it. Plainly something was foul aloft, and Sam went up to see what had happened. A lot of guttural noises were heard and then these ceased, and on looking up I could not see any signs of Sam. Where on earth had he got to? He certainly had not fallen into the sea, or we should have heard the splash. Just then the noises started again from the end of the gaff, and there he was right out at the very end, holding on with his feet as best he could, and working desperately with his hands at the topsail sheet which had taken a turn round the end of the gaff. After a time he got it clear, and we were able to haul the sail down. When he got back on deck I patted him on the shoulder and said "Bueno marinero," whereat he chuckled, and his heavy face lit up for a moment. It would have been better to get the topsail off before we rounded up, but I had not realized that the wind was so strong.

Next morning we sailed into the fine harbour of Colon between the mole-heads of the breakwaters, and lowered sails. Before this operation was complete four powerful sea-going motor-boats came alongside, and as each was as big as the *Amaryllis* we disappeared from view in the crowd, and only the masts remained to show that we were still there. The Customs Officer was the first on board, and then came the Medical Officer, the Official Measurer, and the Pilot, each arriving in a different motor-boat. They all treated the affair as rather a joke, especially the pilot, who was "tickled to death" as he said, at having to conduct a vessel of 28 tons to an anchorage. However, the rule of the port that no vessel shall move about without a pilot admits of no exceptions, and for the first time since he became a pilot he steered the ship himself, and steered her, moreover, with a tiller instead of a wheel.

Now that the breakwaters are built Colon is a good harbour, but it had an evil name before they were there on account of the extraordinary speed with which a heavy sea would get up when a "norther" was blowing farther up the coast. There are cases on record when ships alongside the wharves have not had time to cast off their hawsers, and have been obliged to cut them and get away to sea, and ships at anchor have slipped their cables and gone out as there was too much sea to permit of the anchor being hove up without damage to the ship.

I spent four days at Colon, and thanks to the kindness of the British Consul, Mr. W. Ewing, had a most delightful time. Major Pepper, of the U.S. Army, whom I met at a dinner-party, asked both of us to visit his camp in the jungle. We accordingly drove to Gatun Locks, and embarked in a launch which was to take the Major to the camp. The track lay for 19 miles through the tree-tops of a forest which was submerged when the Locks were made. A number of natives were then living in clearings in the forest, and the authorities had had great difficulty in getting them to move. They laughed at the idea that the forest would be submerged. The messengers explained that the Locks would hold back the water until it reached the tops of the trees, but the natives replied that the Locks were miles away, and remained unconvinced. When the Locks were completed the water was raised very slowly to give them time to move off. All the trees are now dead, but many remain standing with the tops still above water. It was a weird experience, zigzagging about amongst tree-tops. At times the branches were within a foot or two on each side. The channel is very intricate. At frequent intervals are finger-posts nailed to trees at the more critical points, but usually all one could see were branches sticking out of the water, amidst which the native helmsman steered confidently. After a time the banks closed in, and eventually we entered a narrow arm much encumbered with trees at the head of which was a cloud of smoke.

"That smoke seems mighty close to my camp," the Major remarked, and he was right, it was mighty close, in fact right up to it, a forest fire. The launch hauled in alongside the bank below the camp, and we landed, and climbed the bank to where stood the tents on a ridge. Dense clouds of pungent smoke enveloped them, and sparks flew about in showers. Occasionally a tent started smouldering. Little tongues of flame, the advance guard of the fire, crept along the ground to the sound of crackling twigs. Farther back whole trees roared ablaze over a wide front. The officers and men of the detachment had been up all night trying to stop the advance by a series of counter fires, burning patches of undergrowth so that the main body of flame would not have anything to feed on. Their eyes were red and streaming, and they all looked more or less singed. When we arrived they had been driven right back to the tents, and some of them were then packing up the camp in case they had to abandon it. The Major, however, was in no way disturbed. While he went to survey the position with his officers, all of them mopping their eyes and brushing occasional sparks off their uniforms as they walked, Ewing and I searched for the camp kitchen. It was then after 2 p.m., and both of us had had an early and very light breakfast, and nothing since, and felt famished.

We wandered about in the smoke amongst the tents, and in the end found the kitchen, but the cook was away fighting the fire, and we could not find any food. A native hut was visible a short distance away, and we made for it in the hopes of getting something there. It was a very primitive abode, and consisted merely of a leaf roof supported on uprights. There were no walls, and fowls and cows shared it with the Indians. Two or three men lolled about, but they had nothing to offer in the way of food, and were not greatly interested in the matter. We therefore returned to the camp, and after successfully resisting the temptation of borrowing some bananas lying on a camp bed in one of the tents, asked an officer for some biscuits. He at once sent for a couple of tins of hard tack, but we would only accept one, and embarked with the Major and a detachment of troops in pleasant anticipation of something to chew. The Major had decided that the fire was "under control" and that there was no need for him to remain. He was perhaps right, and it was under control, though it did not seem to be to the layman. On the contrary it seemed to be going strong, with nothing to check it.

Once the launch was under way Ewing and I opened our tin and found it full of maggots. What fools we were not to have taken both tins! Too late. Ewing soon became so weak from the want of food that he could not talk and went to sleep, on the principle of "qui dort dine," while I did my best to converse with the Major, a man of iron, who appeared to feel no hunger. He told me that he often had to go exploring for days at a time, and frequently went without food for long periods, and I quite believe it. He had seen much service in Cuba, and Manila, and had led a very eventful life, but he was reticent, and information had to be dragged out of him. Eventually we arrived back at the Locks, and as soon as the Major had seen the troops disembarked, and on their way to barracks, he took us round to his house, where we sat and chatted to his family for a time, and then had a most welcome supper. Curiously enough neither of us then felt in the least bit hungry, but once we had got started on the supper our appetites revived, and we both did remarkably well.

I spent the next day in getting in stores, which the American authorities very kindly allowed me to draw from their Commissary, also a few charts, and paying bills, and then the question of tolls for passing through the Canal arose.

"I have a warrant from the British Admiralty to fly the Blue Ensign," I said to the Collector, "and as you are aware"—I don't think he was as a matter of fact—"vessels flying that Ensign are always treated by the courtesy of foreign Governments as warships. The *Renown*, with the Prince on board, has recently passed through. What rate did she pay? I am in the same class."

"Fifty cents per ton, but I shall have to see the Port Captain before letting you through at that figure."

The Captain knew that the Blue Ensign usually carried privileges, but as he gazed through his window at the *Amaryllis*, looking very small in the distance, he hesitated over letting her through at 50 cents.

"You can't call that little thing a warship," he decided, but he agreed to the rate of 75 cents, which at 8 tons net worked out to $6, not an exorbitant figure.

At 6 a.m. next morning the Canal Pilot, and two canal hands, negroes, came on board, and we weighed, and made for the Gatun Locks, 4 miles distant, up a dredged channel. I had persuaded the Consul to come through the Canal with me, and he had joined the previous evening, and had slept on board. The engine chugged away manfully, but it took an hour to reach the Locks. At Gatun there are three pairs of locks arranged in series, and ships enter the first, and are raised a certain height, and then pass into the second, and are again raised, and also in the third, the total rise being 85 feet. No ships are allowed to use their engines once they are in a lock, and they are towed through by locomotives running on the sides. The reason for this is, of course, that the ship's engines might not be stopped in time to prevent the ship hitting the gates, and damaging them. We were, however, allowed to pass from lock to lock under our own power, as the canal authorities had no fear that we should damage the gates even if we hit them.

These Locks are very impressive, not only on account of their size, though that is great, but also on account of the silence in which things are done. As we neared the first a large arrow on a pedestal swung over to show us which lock to enter. We passed in, sent our lines ashore, and were pulled to the end to make way for a British steamer. The *Amaryllis* seemed to cause the people on her bridge a good deal of amusement. We could see them pointing at us and laughing. No doubt in that huge setting we did look rather small. As soon as she was in, and secured, the great gates silently closed, and then the water started swirling round, and bubbling as it was let into the lock through pipes laid along the bottom. As soon as the right height was reached the swirling ceased, and the gates into the second lock opened and we passed in. Again the process was repeated, the gates closed behind us, the water swirled, and then became quiet, and silently the gates into the third lock opened and again we passed on. At each lock there is a control house containing a working model of the Locks and the man in charge sees in the model the exact height of the water in each Lock, and can regulate things, and open and close the gates without even looking out of the window.

The very efficient way in which everything in the Canal Zone is done is very impressive. The Canal, with all connected with it, is the great work of a great people, while the courtesy shown me and the kindness I received from all the officials could not have been exceeded. As an instance, I found at Colon that an order had been sent to the motor-boat shed that a boat was to be at my disposal to take me on board at any hour of the day or night.

On leaving the third Lock we passed into Gatun Lake. The steamer which had come through with us, overtook us and, as she went by, dipped her ensign, a salute which the Pilot acknowledged, as I was busy trying to tighten up the clutch, which was slipping. The Consul looked on, and gave me moral support. Neither he nor I knew anything about clutches, nor how to tighten them, but there was a lever which looked as if it might have something to do with the job, and I slacked a lock nut on it, and gave a screw a quarter turn. Luckily this was the right thing to do, and the clutch slipped no more.

The channel from Gatun to Pedro Miguel Locks is 33 miles long, and passes through a number of beautifully wooded islands, the summits of what were hills before the Canal was made. Towards the end it passes through the famous Culebra Cut. Dredging and excavating work is always going on there, as the bed has a tendency to fill up. Just before the *Renown* went through a rock was discovered in the centre. It was blown up by a charge of two tons of dynamite. It seems a terrific quantity, but they said it was not out of the way. Possibly the Pilot was trading on my credulity, though I do not think so. He was a pleasant, cheerful, young man, and was much amused at sailing through the Cut, a thing he had never done before. At about 4 p.m. we entered Pedro Miguel Locks, which are two single locks side by side, and we were lowered 30 feet. This time we had the lock all to ourselves, and the *Amaryllis*, alone in a space big enough to take the *Renown* and then leave a bit over, appeared extremely small. It almost seemed that an apology was due to the authorities for putting them to the trouble of working the Lock for our sole benefit, especially as they were doing it for nothing. Our tolls came to $6, but the Pilot was paid $10, so that they lost $4 over him, and working the Locks was pure loss. As we passed out several of the officials came to the end, and shouted good wishes. The last Lock, Miraflores, is only 1½ miles from Pedro Miguel Locks. Again we were lowered 55 feet and on leaving it were in water from the Pacific.

I spent several days at Balboa, which adjoins old Panama city built in 1518 and destroyed in 1673 by the buccaneer, Morgan, the Welshman, in his celebrated raid. From all accounts it was a noble city, and from it started the famous Gold Road to Cruces, along which passed the mule trains bearing gold from Peru for Spain.

While we were there it looked as if the crew would disappear, as Sam said that the ship was too small, and Stéphane's mother lived in the city, and it seemed possible that he would want to stay with her. Moreover, he and Sam did not get on any too well, and had already had one or two quarrels. Stéphane found his mother after some trouble, but she advised him to stay where he was, as things were very slack in Panama. Sam also refused to leave. He said that he had signed on for New Zealand and would go there, though he thought the ship too small, at least that is what I think he meant.

Things undoubtedly were slack in Panama. The wharves in the fine spacious harbour of Balboa were lined with every loading and unloading device, but they all stood idle. No ships were alongside discharging or taking in cargo. Moreover, the Canal people were cutting down expenses and paying off hands every week. Quite a number of these young Americans offered to join me, but none of them knew anything of sailing, and their outlook on life was very different from mine, and I refused to risk it. A vegetarian pacifist, with rather pronounced pro-German views for a pacifist, also appeared. He wanted to go to Tahiti to found a colony of vegetarians there. He seemed a harmless enough person, but wanted a special diet of tapioca and similar foods, which he proposed to prepare himself, and I thought he would probably prove a nuisance in the end. Moreover, he could not satisfy me that the French would let him land in Tahiti when we got there. The prospect of having to sail him and his sloppy messes about the South Sea for an indefinite period did not appeal to me, and in addition I did not like some of his views. I therefore refused his application, and made preparations for leaving with only the two lads. Before leaving, however, the hull had to be scrubbed. It had not been touched since leaving England, and was getting foul. The *Amaryllis* is too deep and sharp in build to be beached, and the only slip in the West Indies, at Jamaica, is too small to take her. Furthermore, in the West Indies, the rise is only about 2 or 3 feet, so that it was not feasible to put her alongside a quay and let her dry out, and so there had not been a chance of cleaning. It would have been possible to put her in dry dock at Colon or at Balboa, but I should have had to pay as much as a 10,000-ton ship, and I refrained. At Balboa, however, there is a Yacht Club, and they told me that I might be able to get alongside a quay there, the spring range being 16 feet. I therefore drove out to examine the place, and interviewed the Yacht Club secretary, who was a nursing mother. She told me that no yachts ever went alongside the quay, but came on to the beach and were there propped up by legs. I was about to explain that this would be too risky in my case, when lusty yells from an inner chamber, uttered apparently by an infant demanding nourishment or other attention, caused her to depart hurriedly. Left alone I went out on to the quay to have a look round. A shipwright working on a boat told me that a fair amount of swell usually came in at high water, and this added to the fact that there was only just ten feet of water at the quay decided me not to attempt to clean her there. The Harbour Master, Mr. McEvoy, then suggested that I called in at the Pearl Islands and got native divers, who can dive to 40 feet, to do the work. This seemed to be the only way out of the difficulty and I decided to act on the suggestion.

Accordingly, we filled the water-tanks, took in stores, and got ready to sail on the 29th March. Before leaving, however, I had to get a Bill of Health for the Marquesas, and another one for the Galapagos. The former belong to France, and the latter to Ecuador. There was no difficulty over the former, but the Ecuadorian Consul stoutly refused to give me one for the Galapagos and insisted on my going to Guayaquil and getting one there. He could not speak English, and I could not speak Spanish, and before long we reached a deadlock. He then pulled out his watch and pointed to two o'clock, and made signs asking me to return at that hour. On leaving his office I went round to the British Chargé d'Affaires, and got him to telephone enquiring the reasons for refusing the Bill of Health. No definite reply was made. At 2 p.m. I went back, and found an interpreter in attendance, a coloured man who said that he was a British subject, whereupon we both rose from our chairs and shook hands solemnly. He then proceeded to question me very cleverly as to my reasons for visiting the islands. I explained that the distance from Galapagos to the Marquesas is over 3,000 miles, and that my last chance of filling up with water would be at San Cristobal Island. All I wanted was water.

"Solamente agua?" interjected the Consul.

"Solamente agua," I replied.

I could see that the interpreter was convinced that I had no ulterior motive, and he finally persuaded the Consul that a Bill of Health might be given safely, and in the end the Consul sat down and made one out to the accompaniment of many sighs and shakings of the head. I never saw anyone do anything with less enthusiasm. He might have been signing his own death warrant. Perhaps he expected to get sacked for giving it. As I walked away a possible explanation of his mysterious conduct occurred to me. He had probably put me down as a treasure hunter. Ralph Stock had visited the islands the previous year, and had written an account of his trip, and in it had stated that an old man in San Cristobal Island knew where some treasure was hidden in one of the islands. The

Consul evidently thought I was after it, and tried to prevent me from going there. Still a small ship with one white man and two coloured boys on board did not look like a well-organized treasure-hunting expedition, and in the end he had given way.

The next thing was to get some French money for the Marquesas. On the advice of the Bank I took a dollar draft on New York to be exchanged against francs at Nukuhiva. By taking this draft I was assured that I should gain considerably over the exchange. I then called at the Treasury office to pay for stores supplied, and got a severe shock, as they told me that I had to pay $100 for having a stern line made fast to one of the harbour buoys. $100 with the £ at 15s.! Luckily the Consul had come over from Colon to spend the week-end with me, and we both went to the Port Captain, who at once caused the charge to be cancelled, as being quite unreasonable in my case. He, however, mentioned casually that I should have to pay $25 for a pilot to take me out of harbour.

"But I do not want a pilot," I objected.

"Of course not, and I do not intend to send one, but you will have to pay the fee all the same." And I had to too.

CHAPTER III

SOUTH SEA ISLANDS

On the 29th March we weighed anchor and left the harbour. It took a long time to get the sails up as we were so short-handed, and the ship was outside the harbour channel before the last one was set. As a matter of fact they were useless, as not an air stirred. A flat calm prevailed in the bay. Still with the help of the engine we gradually drew away from the coast, and opened up the City of Panama which as the *South America Pilot* truly says "has a noble appearance from the sea; the churches, towers, and houses, showing above the line of fortifications, stand out from the dark hills inland with an air of

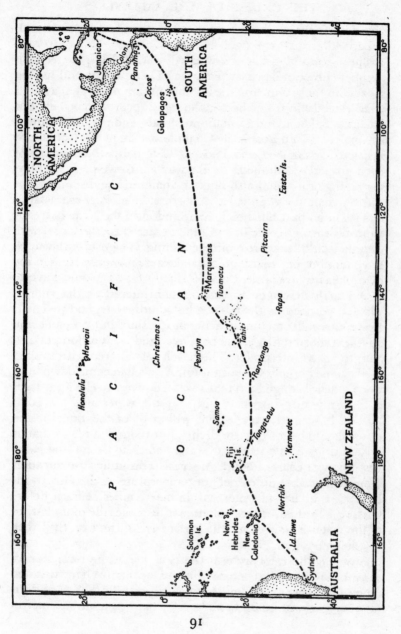

grandeur to which there is no equal on the west coast of South America."

The beautiful and well-wooded Perlas Islas, sixteen in number, lie 30 miles from Panama. There are several fishing villages in the group, and the inhabitants are mostly engaged in pearl-shell fishing. The best anchorage appeared to be between Pacheca, Saboga, and Contadora Islands, and the best channel by which to approach it Contadora Channel. Rocks are suspected in Saboga and Pacheca Channels, which have not been properly examined. On the way across we passed several swimming crabs, and also sighted whales in the distance.

At 5 p.m. we rounded the north side of Pacheca Island, and stood on past Bartholomew Island until the Near Islet and Saboga bearings came on, and then entered by the Contadora Channel, and anchored off the fishing village of Saboga. A large number of pelicans, most awkward, ungainly birds, were flying heavily about.

Our arrival seemed to excite much interest in the village, which is perched on the top of a hill amidst trees, and we could see groups collecting and gazing at the ship, but no one came off. Next morning I got the boat over and went ashore, taking Sam to act as interpreter. The beach was littered with broken shells, some of them very beautiful. A few men came down, and I explained through Sam that I wanted divers to clean the hull, but, to my surprise, they said that the water was too cold, "frio!" It seemed strange that within 8° of the Equator the water should be too cold for diving, but I found out later that at certain times a cold stream of water comes up from Cape Horn past the west coast of South America. This same stream causes some remarkable differences of temperature at the Galapagos Islands in bodies of water within a few miles of each other. On one side of Albemarle Island, for instance, the temperature of the water 1 foot below the surface is 80°, and on the other side less than 60°.

Anyway, there we were at the Islas Perlas, and apparently as far off as ever from getting the hull cleaned. What was to be done? The choice seemed to be to go back to Balboa and go into dry dock, or go on to Galapagos on the chance of finding divers there. The former was very expensive, and the latter very uncertain, not to say improbable. Still, I decided to chance it, and at noon weighed, and left the anchorage. The wind outside was very light and the sun very hot. The area between Panama and the Galapagos is usually windless and so we found it. Day after day there was a light breeze for a few hours, and then long periods of calm, during which we ran the engine. The heat in the absence of wind, was great, and the deck was too hot to touch, while the brasswork was unapproachable.

Slowly we crawled along, occasionally sighting a whale afar off. Sharks also showed up at intervals, and swimming snakes. Often, at night, there was much lightning in all directions, but the general rule was beautiful quiet nights, with brilliant stars, the lower ones throwing tracks of light on the calm sea. It was very pleasant to sit at the tiller, and drink in the beauty of the night, while the ship rolled lazily to a slight swell, and the sails swung to and fro, and blocks lifted and fell on deck with a soft thud. Very peaceful and pleasant, if one was not too tired to appreciate it, but it meant slow progress. Strangely enough when seven days out it became cold, though we were within 2° of the Equator, and I had to put on extra clothes. We were probably passing over a cold body of water from Cape Horn. On the 9th April we crossed the line, and marked the event by eating a Christmas pudding sent by my sister, and having an extra jam issue. Both the boys were very fond of jam, which they ate with a spoon. A pot went at one meal. On the same day Sam caught a dolphin, 4 feet long. He got it on board very cleverly. The deck immediately became the scene of great confusion. The fish, the line, and Sam were all mixed up together.

"Iron, iron," he shouted excitedly, and I gave him the clutch lever, with which he ultimately stunned the fish with blows on the head, though it was very active and put up a good show. We had some of it for supper. It tasted rather like cod, but salter. This was one of the half-dozen fish we caught at sea. A line was usually trailed astern, but we had little success. Altogether perhaps a dozen were hooked, but they were big fish and usually broke the line before we could stop the ship.

In the afternoon San Cristobal Island was, by observation, 60 miles away, and Sam went aloft before dark to see if it was in sight, but could not make it out. However, it showed up through the haze next morning at 9 a.m. At noon the wind fell, and I started the engine in a hopeless attempt to get to Puerto Chico before dark. Off the east end of the island a schooner, flying the Ecuador flag, came by. Those on board seemed much concerned by our presence, and waved us away. One man was particularly energetic, and stood on the cabin top, and waved us off the face of the earth. He made it clear that he wanted us to sail away, but I merely waved my arm in reply, and went on. Apparently, he had also heard of treasure and, like the Consul, concluded that I was after it. What interested me at the moment, however, was not treasure, but what I was going to do at dusk, as it was clear that, in spite of a strong current which was sweeping us along, we could not reach the anchorage until long after sunset. To attempt to enter at night would be rather hazardous, owing to the Schiavoni Reef, which lies across the entrance. It is true that a lamp on a post at the head of the Bay is lit at dark as a guide through the pass, but the Chart says that it must not be relied on. If we went on and it happened to be out we should probably get ashore on the reef before we knew where we were, while if we were lucky enough to miss that the current would carry us away from the island, and, in the total calm reigning, it would be a hard matter to get back. The best thing seemed to be to bring up off the coast for the night. Bassa Point anchorage appeared a suitable spot for the purpose, and we made for it. It was dark before we reached it, and, lying under the black mass of the land, it was very hard to identify. Kicker Rock, which we passed at sunset was one guide, and the sound of the surf on Bassa Point, where the sea breaks heavily, was another, and in the end we brought up safely in 5 fathoms.

Inspired by his success of the previous day, Sam started fishing at dawn next morning, but only hooked a shark. There did not seem to be room on our small deck for a 4-foot shark and ourselves, and we did not attempt to get it on board. In order to get rid of it, and retrieve our hook, Sam dragged it slowly to the surface, and I shot it with a revolver. As it was pulled up to meet its doom the shadowy forms of its mates could be seen swimming round in circles. They knew that the unlucky fish was in trouble of some sort, and were waiting a chance of eating it. Not very sporting on their part. As soon as we had recovered our hook we weighed, and made for Puerto Chico. Heavy rollers had started forming a short distance farther down the coast, and I was anxious to get clear. These rollers are most terrifying things. Out of a smooth sea a mound of water 5 or 6 feet high suddenly rears itself, and rolls in on the beach gathering speed as it nears it, and finally breaks in a welter of foam. They are distinct from the ordinary surf on a beach, as they start much farther out. The Galapagos are subject to them, but usually from July to November only. An hour and a half later we had entered by the pass between Lido Point and Schiavoni Reef, and had anchored in wonderfully clear water off the crazy little pier. The lighthouse keeper and another Ecuadorian came off to find out who we were, and while they were still on board the élite of the settlement, the manager of the sugar factory and his bookkeeper rode down from Progresso, five miles inland, and also came on board. They seemed much interested in the trip and examined everything on board most carefully, but conversation was a bit difficult and without Stéphane as interpreter would have been impossible. However, with his help, we did manage to converse after a style. They evidently treated our arrival as an excuse for taking a holiday, and remained on board all the morning drinking neat gin. Under its mollifying influence they urged me to remain at least a week, and promised to send horses next morning to take me up for lunch.

At 8 a.m. next day Stéphane and I were on the beach, awaiting the arrival of our steeds. The lighthouse-keeper took advantage of the delay in their appearance to get me interested in his lamp, with a view to extracting a chimney from me. We mounted a ladder to the platform, supported on an iron pedestal, insecurely braced by rusty chains. The lamp itself was an ordinary paraffin lamp, and the chimney simply a pattern of cracks. He explained that he had no spare chimney. Could I, in the interests of shipping generally, let him have one? I would see if there was one on board of the right size. Another thing, could I let him have some linseed oil to mix with paint for his boat? Before he could think of anything else to ask me the horses arrived, two horses and half a dozen peons. My steed had a finely plaited leather bridle, and ornamented brass stirrups shaped like a shoe, into which unfortunately I could only get the extreme tip of my boot. We mounted, but two seconds later only one of us was on horseback, as Stéphane had fallen off. The peons ran to his assistance, and got him mounted again. Our host then arrived, and the cavalcade started.

Masses of lava and cactus plants bordered the track, and the bed was filled with half-buried lava boulders. It seemed an impossible path for horses, but they ambled on without difficulty. I gave mine his head, as he knew the road better than I did. After a time it was noticed that our interpreter had disappeared, and we went back to find him. He soon hove in sight mounted behind a peon, who was looking after the horse, while Stéphane devoted himself to holding on. It seemed that he had found it impossible to attend to the horse, and also remain in the saddle, and after a few falls had mounted behind a peon. As we neared the settlement we passed through a grove of fruit trees, and then past the dilapidated sugar factory, and finally arrived at the house, a large one-storied building, built of wood plastered with mud. At the back a wide verandah looked out over the sea. It was littered with scrap iron, empty bottles, and other oddments. The ground floor was divided into two stores, and at the end of the outer room was an office. Thither we were conducted, and sat down. Conversation languished. At times someone made a remark which Stéphane translated into French. I replied, and he translated my remarks into Spanish. A silence usually ensued, while we looked at each other, until someone else made another remark. Various people came in and were introduced, amongst them the local magistrate, to whom I made a rather unfortunate remark in saying that I supposed he had little to do. A constrained silence ensued, and after his departure, they told me that he had recently been very busy, as two officials had had a dispute over a matter of bookkeeping, and had fired at each other with revolvers. One was killed, but before he went down he got three bullets into his opponent, who was at that moment on his way to Guayaquil in the schooner we had passed off the east end of the island. He was in a serious condition, and not expected to arrive alive. The schooner, by the way, had been three days at sea when we passed her, and in that time had only made good 25 miles, on account of the light wind, and strong adverse current. On one occasion, they said, two schooners from Guayaquil were carried past the island, and were three weeks in sight of the port before they succeeded in crawling in.

At length lunch put an end to a dull morning, and after it we walked round the settlement. The huts were simply thatched shacks with any kind of wall, boards, bits of corrugated iron, or thatch, but they all had an upper chamber in which the families slept. The ground floors were filthy and swarmed with fowls and dogs. Heaps of old tins, bottles, and rubbish lay around. They presented an appearance of awful squalor. We then went for a ride inland with the manager and a youth. Stéphane's horsemanship improved rapidly, and he cantered about without falling off once. After leaving the village we passed through groves of guavas, and patches of sugar cane, and then came to open hilly country. Large herds of cattle roamed about. We rode for miles amongst the hills, and climbed the highest crater, in the centre of which was a fresh-water lake. The view from the top was very fine, and we could see many of the islands of the group, with the imposing mass of Albemarle Island away in the distance. All the islands are purely volcanic, and the northern sides are more or less barren. There are said to be 2,000 craters amongst them. The group takes its name from the Giant Tortoise, which is still to be found there.

I was glad to get back to the village, and still more glad to be back on board, as my ankles ached so from the uncomfortable stirrups that I had to do the last part without them. Before parting from Señor Escobar, I asked him to send down some water, as, in spite of what the Sailing Directions state, there is none to be had at the anchorage.

Next morning we started to clean the hull as best we could with long-handled brushes, but it was not a satisfactory job. Still, it was the best we could do, as no divers were to be had. Presently a frightful clattering announced the arrival of the water-cart, which came bumping down from Progrésso. I went ashore with the boys, and the casks, and was horrified to find that the water had been emptied into a dirty pit. It was the colour of mud, or coffee, and looked quite undrinkable. The peons were astounded at the uproar I made and protested that it was good water. The lighthouse-keeper was also surprised and said he used it himself. He made the valuable suggestion that I should wait four or five days to see if it would settle, which, he thought, might happen if a cow or a pony did not walk into the pit, and stir it up again. Señor Escobar then rode up and said that he had done the best he could for me, and that no other water was to be had. The inside of the water cart certainly was a bit rusty, but that would not matter, nor, he thought, would the addition of a little mud. I was very unwilling to start on a passage of over 3,000 miles with half the water of doubtful quality, but as none other was to be had there seemed no choice, and I filled up the 100-gallon tank from the other two, and then filled up the two with the muddy water, adding some chloride of lime to discourage bacteria, and so had 100 gallons of good and 100 gallons of doubtful water. Unless disaster overtook us 100 gallons ought to see us through, and as a matter of fact 45 gallons was all we used, or just over $\frac{1}{2}$ gallon per head *per diem* for drinking and cooking. That is how it actually worked out, but on these long passages one never knows what may happen. The loss of a spar, for instance, would greatly prolong the time taken, and then every drop of water would be wanted.

Next morning, the 14th April, after the arrival of bread, eggs, and potatoes, which I had ordered, we started to weigh anchor. The cable came in very slowly. We strained and tugged at the capstan handle, and seemed to be heaving up the bed of the ocean. On looking over the side I saw the anchor suspended upside down with festoons of cable hanging from both flukes and round the stock. It was what one might call a really foul anchor. There was nothing for it but to heave it out of the water and dislodge the bights of cable, which we did with great difficulty and then left the bay under power, passing on the way out the wreck of the Australian steamer *Carawa*, which was lost on Schiavoni Reef. The sails were hoisted by degrees as we went along, and at last we had fairly started on the long passage to the Marquesas.

Short-handed and what crew there was young and inexperienced, half the water of doubtful quality, and no one to speak to were not ideal conditions for a trip of 3,057 miles, but there had been no choice, and I was committed to it. As a matter of fact, I was, by that time, used to being alone, except for the lads. The position was not without its compensations, though, of course, it would have been better to have someone for company and in case of accidents.

The first two days were calm, and we fanned and drifted slowly along past the islands. Our slow progress made me rather anxious about water, and I took the handles off all the pumps and each morning drew water for the day, keeping a record of how much was used. Fresh water was used only for cooking and drinking. We washed in salt water, or perhaps I should say went through the motions of washing in salt water, and it was also used for washing up the crockery. Our baths consisted of buckets of salt water drawn from the sea.

Life became very simple, and consisted mainly in eating, sleeping, and steering. The ordinary routine was as follows: Breakfast at 7 a.m., dinner at noon, tea at 3.30 p.m., and supper at 7 p.m. These were the nominal hours, but, as Stéphane had the vaguest idea of time, meals often appeared an hour or so sooner or later. Between 7 a.m. and 8 a.m. I took a sight, while Sam steered, and another one at noon. After working out the first sight I steered while Sam slept. In the afternoon Sam steered, and I had a nap. Stéphane did the cooking and lamps, and work below, and did nothing much on deck during the day beyond helping to shift sails. The first night watch started after supper, until 10 p.m., when the helmsman was relieved and went below. At midnight the helmsman was again changed and also at 2 a.m. In this way each of us had two hours at the tiller and four hours off. Each was called twice each night, rather tiring work, but we usually had a nap during the day, and so managed to get enough sleep. The cooking was very plain. Breakfast consisted of eggs, while these lasted, coffee, bread or biscuit, butter, and jam. For dinner there were three standard dishes, pomme de terre, macaroni, or riz mélange. The potatoes, macaroni, or rice, according to which was to be used, were first boiled, onions were sliced and fried, and a tin of bully beef was minced. All these ingredients, together with a tin of tomatoes, a spoonful of Bovril, and two spoonfuls of Worcestershire sauce, were mixed together and warmed up, and the dish was ready. It served for dinner, supper, and at times breakfast next day. Occasionally dry hash, rissoles, or curry varied the menu, and at rare intervals fish, when we were lucky enough to hook or land one. A line was always towing astern, but we seldom caught anything.

And so one day followed another in pleasing, uneventful monotony. The weather was mostly fine. Occasionally, how-ever, there were days of continuous rain and squalls, varied by others when the wind was light and the ship rolled heavily in a very troublesome swell, with the boom jerking to and fro, and shaking the ship. In one rain squall the spinnaker, which is made of light stuff, cotton and silk mixed, split in two, and it took me nearly two days to repair it with a table cloth cut into strips, as there was nothing else at all suitable on board. Time did not hang heavily on my hands. As a matter of fact, I was usually very busy and had no time for reading even. A small sailing-ship wants as much looking after as a harem, and there was always something to do about the decks. She was probably the most silent ship sailing the seas. I never spoke except to give an order, and the two lads quarrelled every now and then and would not speak to each other, or even feed together, for days at a time. Occasionally I had to intervene in these rows, and always found Sam in the wrong. He was a morose and uncouth person, a regular savage, and was inclined to bully Stéphane, who resented this hotly. In the intervals between quarrels the two were quite friendly and chatted together in Spanish as if there had never been a cloud between them. In the main, however, she was a silent ship and forged ahead day and night to the soothing sound of water swishing past the bow, the creak of the gaff-jaws, a rope rattling on the sails, or the thud of a block, but rarely to the sound of the human voice.

One day it occurred to me that if I fell over the side, or anything happened to me, the lads would be in rather a fix. Neither ever knew where he was, or where he was going, or how long it would probably take to get there. These matters they were content to leave to the white man, who would tell them what course to steer, what sails to set, and how to trim them, and they would eventually arrive at their port. So it had always been so far, and so, presumably, it always would be. In order to provide for the chance of my being disabled I asked Sam what he would do if I fell overboard. He was steering at the time, and he continued steering for a minute or two without any expression at all on his heavy face. Then he smiled and spoke.

"Sir Cap, I go back."

He always addressed me as "Sir Cap," perhaps because he thought "Sir" unsuitable when speaking to his skipper, while "Cap" alone sounded a bit off-hand, so he combined the two.

Going back would not, however, be an easy matter, as the wind would be dead ahead, and I told him to keep her away, full and bye, to the north-east, by so doing they would be sure to make the coast of North America, sooner or later. It would be safer for them to do so, than to try and find an island in the Pacific and possibly get involved amongst reefs. From that time I showed Stéphane, who is a very intelligent lad, the ship's position on the chart every two days, and also noted in the margin the course to aim at for the homeward trip should it be necessary.

When we were over 2,000 miles from the coast a white column appeared at dawn to the northward. It looked like a lighthouse, but proved to be a full-rigged ship following the sailing track from San Francisco to Cape Horn. She made a fine picture with all her towering mass of canvas showing white against the blue sky. The wind was light, and she was in sight all day. At dusk she passed under our stern two miles away. It is very pleasant to meet a ship at sea. It gives the feeling of companionship. She was, however, the only ship we met away from the land between Panama and Sydney.

On 9th May the long trip was drawing to a close, and land was, by observations, due next morning. At dawn on the 10th Hood Island—named after Lord Hood, then a midshipman in the *Resolution*, Captain Cook, who first sighted it in 1774—lay to port, with Ua Huka one point to starboard. A light breeze carried us slowly along and as the day drew on it became clear that we should not be able to make Nukuhiva, our port, which lies farther west, before dark, and I decided to anchor for the night under the lee of Ua Huka, in Shavay Bay. As we sailed along the south side of the island its beauty was very striking. In the centre is a line of high hills with ridges running down to the sea. The valleys between these ridges were a mass of luxuriant vegetation, very pleasing to the eye. We rounded Hemeni Islet, and stood on into Shavay Bay, but when the soundings should have been 10 fathoms, according to the chart, we were getting over 22 fathoms. It was impossible to anchor in such a depth, and I got the sails down and proceeded slowly along the coast under power, with Stéphane aloft to look out for rocks under water. On the north side of Tetutu Point a small bay with 7 fathoms was shown and we made for it and brought up.

It was quite pleasant to be anchored for a change after twenty-six days at sea, even though it was not a good anchorage on account of the swell running in, which made us roll more than if we had been under way. On Tetutu Point was a horse, and several goats were climbing about the cliffs, but no natives appeared. Next day we sailed across to Nukuhiva and anchored in Taï o Haé Bay. This island is very mountainous and even more beautiful than Ua Huka. On the beach were a few houses standing amidst the graceful cocoanut trees and a small pier ran out into the sea. Our arrival can hardly be said to have created a stir, but it excited some interest, and we could see a few natives and a white man preparing to launch a whaleboat. In due course they rowed off to enquire who we were and a splendid native also appeared in a catamaran canoe with outrigger. The white man was a Britisher named Bob McKetterick, manager for a French trading company. He would not come on board until he had sent up to the representative of the French Government, a gendarme living in a house near the old Fort. As a matter of fact, I had expected to find the Resident and the seat of Government at Taï o Haé, as stated in the Sailing Directions, but learned that he had installed himself and the seat of government in Hiva Oa Island, to escape the attacks of the small black "nono" fly, which seems peculiar to Nukuhiva, and which, though diminutive in size, has a wonderfully hard bite. The gendarme was having a siesta and sent back a message that everything was probably all right and that McKetterick could board us. The native, clad in a singlet and shorts, with flowers in his hair, also came on board, and we all had a cup of tea together. McKetterick said that there were six white men in the island, the gendarme, a priest, a missionary, two traders, and himself. At the moment there were also three Americans living the simple life and an American botanist and his wife. There was, however, no bank and my draft on New York was a drug in the market, as no one had the slightest idea what the rate of exchange was. The fact that I had no money did not matter in the least, I was told. I was going on to Papeeté? Yes. Then nothing could be more simple. All the three traders had their chief station there, and I could get what stores I wanted and pay for them on arrival at Papeeté. *Voilà!*

Next day when I landed to call on the gendarme I met the three simple-life men on the Pier. Two of them were Swede-Americans and one was Italian-American, and they were absolutely fed up with the simple life. The Italian was covered with the red marks of nono-fly bites. They asked me to take them to Tahiti. It seemed that they had been lured to the Marquesas by a mendacious account of the conditions of life there, but found things very different from what they were led to expect. On arrival they had been obliged to sleep under the verandah of the missionary's house, but finally found a disused shed lying back from the path in dense undergrowth and had taken posesssion of it. They asked me to see it, and we waded through vegetation and decayed cocoanuts towards it. It was an appalling edifice falling into utter ruin. It rains daily in the Marquesas, and the rain-water came through the leaf roof in several places. The earth floor had been cleared of most of the decayed vegetation, but still seemed to be the home of innumerable insects. In the circumstances, the simple life no longer attracted them and they wanted to return to civilization. A diet of an occasional fish, bananas, and cocoanuts was all very well, but they felt that a change would do them good. I left them mooning aimlessly round their shack and went in search of McKetterick. He took me round to call on the Lady Superior of the French Mission. She was a charming old lady, eighty-two years old, but full of life and vigour. She deplored the fact that she had no wine to offer us, as the Mission was no longer supported officially and was simply hanging on as best it could, but sent out for some young cocoanuts. The native who brought them sliced off the tops with his long knife, and we drank the delicious contents from the shell. She told us that the natives were dying out fast and in the last fifty years had diminished 90 per cent. Lung trouble, possibly caused by wearing clothes, seemed to be one of the chief causes of the decrease, and an epidemic of influenza had been very fatal. In the old days they oiled their skin and when they got wet it did not matter, but now that they wear clothes, which are often wet with rain, they get chills. Further, their chief interests in life in the past were fighting another tribe and dancing. Civilization frowned on these diversions, and the natives have lost interest in life. It looks as if the race were doomed, a deplorable thing as they are a fine people, tall and well built and with pleasant features, always smiling and courteous and very fond of singing and of flowers, which they wear in chaplets round their heads and necks. As we walked away from the Mission we met a splendid native coming along the path, singing to himself. He wore flowers round his hat and carried a knife about 30 inches long. As he passed he raised his hat in salutation and smiled.

"That is a prisoner," said McKetterick, "but as there is no prison, he cannot, of course, be locked up, and so he lives in his hut and works for a few hours daily on clearing the path."

He had been convicted of making an alcoholic drink from a cocoanut palm. How this is done I do not know, but it is apparently illegal. It seems a bit rough on the native that civilization should step in, take his island from him, and then punish him for following his ancient customs, but it is really in his own interest, as the orgies which used to take place were a bit above the limit, and did him a lot of harm.

We were seven days at Nukuhiva, but I did not spend much time ashore as there was a lot to do on board. The fresh-water tanks had to be cleaned out and refilled, and the gear overhauled, and the sails repaired, all of which took time. The hull was also scrubbed by two native divers. They wore diving-glasses of native make. The glass is held in water and cut with scissors to fit the wooden rims, which are bound tightly to the head. They can see quite well under water with these on. Shaping the glass in water with scissors is a system of their own. I have never tried it, but they say it works quite well.

One day I had lunch with McKetterick in a room behind his store. Before lunch his carpenter, a splendid man clad only in shorts, cut my hair and then prepared the meal, which consisted of an omelette, fried fish, large fresh-water prawns, tea, and cake. It was a change of diet, and I thoroughly enjoyed it. Two nice little native boys waited on us. After lunch we walked up the Pakiu Valley through plantations of bananas and cocoanuts, taro and bread fruit. A stream ran down alongside the path amidst huge boulders. About a mile up the valley, the sides of which are covered with a mass of dense vegetation, is a spring of mineral water very pleasant to the taste. A beautiful island is Nukuhiva.

On my return the simple-life men waited on me in a body to beg me to take them away, and on my refusal, each of them came secretly to urge me to take him at least, even if I left the other two. They were a bunch of tough-looking citizens, and it occurred to me that if I took them they might easily drop me over the side one night and go off with the ship. Similar things have been done, and the South Seas seemed the right setting for such deeds. There have been many strange happenings in that part of the world in the past. Though times have changed and conditions are hardly favourable for daring, lawless acts to-day, I was not taking any chances.

There is a very remarkable waterfall in the island, but I could not get away to see it. The bed of the stream is said to be several yards wide, and the water is precipitated from a rock 2,000 feet high. I was very much handicapped all along, in getting away to see the natural curiosities of the places visited by the fact that there was no reliable person to leave in charge of the ship while I was away. As a result I could never be absent from the ship for more than a few hours at a time. Moreover, there was always a lot of repair work to do to the sails and gear, which I had either to do myself or else to super-intend closely. What I wanted was a good Britisher of the fisherman type to act as mate, but as he was not there I had to fill the position myself.

On the 18th May I bade farewell to Professor and Mrs. Brown, the botanists, who were collecting specimens for an American Museum, took charge of the letters which the settlers wanted to have posted in Papeeté, got a Bill of Health from the gendarme, weighed anchor with the assistance of McKet-terick and one of his boys, and beat out of the bay. As we neared the entrance the wind came in violent gusts from all directions, and, still further to complicate matters, the wire on which the staysail sheet travelled parted and the sail blew out before the wind. It was a strenuous time. I could not leave the tiller on account of the frequent shifts of wind, but the boys managed to drag the sail down. They were both powerful lads, and Sam always shone if he had a straightforward job to tackle, one that he understood. He had been seven years at sea, and up to a certain point was a good seaman.

Eventually we managed to beat out of the Bay and had time to fix a new wire for the staysail sheet. The wind was fresh and the sea rough, and as the course to Tahiti brought the swell right on the beam she rolled heavily, and things were very uncomfortable on board. The cabin table swung to and fro, and at meal times my plate was at one moment under my chin and the next at my knees. It was not easy to remain on the settee and avoid being thrown over the table. Taking sights was also very difficult. By strict attention to the business on hand one could stand upright on deck, but it was a distinct feat of balancing. When, however, it became a question of looking through a sextant the difficulties were enormously increased, and it was practically impossible to keep the sun in the field long enough to get a proper sight. The best I could do was to take a series of snap-shots at it. A further difficulty arose when I was taking a sight with the sun off the meridian. In that case it is necessary to note the exact second at which the sight is taken, and it is customary to have someone standing by with a watch to note the moment when the observer takes the sight and shouts "Stop." Neither of the lads could be trusted to do this, and I was obliged to hold the watch in the palm of my hand, and glance at it as soon as I got the sight. The results worked out very well on the whole, but the affair was beset with difficulties.

The run from Nukuhiva to Papeeté is 757 miles, and the track leads through the Tuamotu Archipelago. The Tahitians called it Paumotu or Submissive Islands from the fact that they used to go over, when they had nothing better on hand, and bully the inhabitants. There are seventy-eight islands, not including a few odd ones to the south-east, spread over fifteen degrees of longitude. With three exceptions they are all atolls, or low circular coral islands surrounding a central lagoon. The group is often called the Dangerous Archipelago by seamen, as all the islands are low and very hard to see, especially at night, the winds are variable and the currents irregular and unknown, while the area has not been at all properly surveyed. Pearl shells are found in the lagoons of these atolls, and the natives, men and women, are expert divers, but the French authorities do not allow indiscriminate diving. They decide which lagoons are to be fished, and when this is to take place the atolls selected, usually peaceful and populated sparsely, if at all, suddenly burst forth into a state of intense activity. Chinese store-keepers flock from Tahiti with their wares and erect makeshift stores, and Jewish and other pearl dealers arrive in swarms. Neighbouring atolls send divers in canoes, and for the time being the island is so densely crowded that there is hardly room to lie down to sleep. Cinema shows, of course, arrive with the crowd, and at night electric light blazes on these remote Pacific strands which until recently knew only the soft light of the moon and stars. It seems a desecration, but the natives probably enjoy the excitement, which is about all they get out of it, as the bulk of the results of their labours under water seems to go into the pockets of the traders and dealers.

Sailing-ships bound for Tahiti often go round the group to avoid getting mixed up with them in the dark. Others pass between them, and I decided to do so too, as it is shorter, if I found that I could get between Rangiroa and Arutua in daylight. If this was not possible I proposed to stand away W.N.W. and go round them. At noon on the third day out we were by observation 100 miles from Manihi. At dusk I managed to fix the position of the ship by three star sights. At midnight we were 35 miles away. I did not quite like rushing through the night so near low islands, but felt fairly confident that we were clear and hardened my heart and went on. At 7 a.m. next morning Ahü Island should lie on the beam 12 miles away and Stéphane went aloft, and could just see the tops of trees. It looked as if we might be able to get through in daylight if the wind held, which, however, it did not do. It eased during the afternoon and threw me into great perplexity as to what had better be done. I decided to put on all the light sails that would draw and stand on until the last minute in the hope of sighting Rangiroa before dark. Just before sunset I went aloft and could see Rangiroa plainly and also the trees on Arutua. There was then no further cause for anxiety and we could stand away for Tahiti.

At noon next day the island hove in sight 65 miles away. This is a great distance, but it has been seen 90 miles off. At sunset we were still nearly 20 miles away, and, as the Sailing Directions said that the leading lights through the Pass in the

reef had been destroyed when the Germans bombarded
Papeeté, I hove to off Venus Point to wait for dawn. As a
matter of fact, the lights have been replaced and I could have
gone in that night if I had only known this, and saved myself
from the humiliation of sailing past the place and having to
come back to it, which was what I did next morning. We let
draw at dawn and sailed along the coast. With the rising sun on
it, causing fine shadow effects on the mountains, the island
looked strangely beautiful. The centre is a mass of towering,
fantastically shaped peaks, amidst which nestled Le Diadème
summits. Ridges run down to the sea, enclosing fertile, wooded
valleys, and on the lowlands bordering the beach were groves
of cocoanut-palms and banana-trees. With white beaches and
the fringing reef a mass of white foam in the foreground it was
a fairy picture, and I was so taken up with it that I paid
scant attention to pilotage. Outside the barrier reef there are
no dangers to trouble one, and I just let her go along clear of
the coral, expecting soon to see a considerable town. Presently
the spires of two churches, and a few tin roofs appeared amidst
the trees, with a few ships at anchor. I took these to be Taunoa
and went on, only to realize soon afterwards that we had
opened up the south side of the island and what I had taken
for Taunoa was really Papeeté. A bearing of the east side of
Murea Island confirmed this, and the only thing to do was to
come round and beat back. Luckily, the distance was not great
and we were soon off the break in the reef which forms the
Pass into the fine natural harbour of Papeeté. On each side of
the gap great seas rolled majestically along and broke with a
roar on the reef, pouring over them in masses of milk-white
foam, but the Pass itself was clearly defined by the still water
and we entered without trouble. The passage from Nukuhiva
took four and a half days which they said was unusually fast
and has not often been beaten.

The little town is strung out pleasantly along the beach
fronting the harbour. The houses, mostly built of wood, nestle
amidst trees and are more or less invisible from the sea. On the
eastern side are the wharf and the business quarter. With the
exception of a few big European stores, all the retail trade is

done by Chinese, that extremely industrious and well-conducted race. The Tahitians themselves appear to be concerned chiefly with plantation work and fishing.

As in duty bound I called on the British Consul, who was an American. Why this should be when there were plenty of suitable British about seems strange. I also cashed my famous draft on New York, and lost frs. 250 over the exchange, instead of gaining as the wily banker had assured me I should do. Perhaps, however, it was the manager of the firm which cashed it who was wily, though he sent to the Bank for the rate of exchange and all seemed in order. He was an American with a strangely impassive face, and a very low voice. From time to time he called people from various parts of the large store, and never raised his voice, yet they never failed to hear him. It was most peculiar. At his office I met a Mr. Young, who had studied the history and traditions of the Islands, and who was a fund of information on everything connected with them. He told me yarns of treasure concealed in the Islands which were quite fascinating, and he had also collected a lot of information about the lost continent of Atlantis. Up to then I had always regarded the theory as a pure fable, and I was astounded at the quantity of evidence of its probable existence at one time.

That night I treated myself to a dinner at the Hôtel du Diadème, kept by a native from Mauritius named Louis, and usually called Louis the Fourteenth by way of compliment. It was served on a wide verandah and was the first decent meal I had had since leaving Panama, with the exception of the lunch at McKetterick's. It was very pleasant to sit in the tropic night with palm-trees around the verandah at a table which was not swinging to and fro, and which was furnished, moreover, with a bottle of very fair *vin ordinaire*, and be waited on by a sleek Chinaman who knew his job. Little Stéphane was in process of becoming a smart seaman, but waiting at table is not a necessary part of the rôle, at any rate it was not his forte, while his cooking left much to be desired.

At first it seemed likely that my stay would be dull, as I knew no one, but the aspect of affairs changed next day when I saw a handsome, alert-looking individual gingerly paddling himself off from the beach in a native outrigger canoe. He succeeded in getting alongside, and transferring himself safely to the ship.

"My name is Hemus, Harry Hemus of Auckland," he said. "I saw the Blue Ensign, and I have come off to enquire whether I can be of any assistance."

That was the start of a friendship which I trust will endure. After him came Mr. Hoole and his brother and also Mr. Draper, and finally I got to know most, if not all, of the Britons in the place. I also met Mr. F. N. Abercrombie, a big, large-hearted, broad-gauge American. Every evening I dined at the Diadème, usually with Mr. Hemus. It is, or was, a cheery little place, well run by Louis and his capable wife. There was a room next to the kitchen, across the yard, in which Louis kept his spirits and liqueurs, and the hotel habitués used to foregather there every evening before dinner and mix themselves cocktails and *aperitifs* of various kinds. Louis sometimes came and officiated, but if he were not there we served ourselves and told him later what we had had, a free-and-easy way of doing things quite in keeping with the place.

During my stay of a fortnight, Mr. Hemus and I drove out along a beautiful road bordered by cocoanut, mango, banana-trees, and luxuriant tropical plants to Venus Point, where Cook observed the transit of Venus in 1769. The tamarind-tree which he then planted still stands, and the stone which he placed in the ground with a meridian line cut across it is also there, surrounded by a railing. He was a marvellously accurate astronomer and navigator, and in spite of the crudeness of his instruments the longitude he deduced from his observations only differs 37" from the longitude now fixed for the spot. As a matter of fact, he was not the first European to find the island, as the Spaniard, Quiros, probably sighted it in 1606, and in 1767 Captain Wallis of the *Dolphin* landed and took possession in the name of George III. This, however, did not prevent the French from annexing it in 1844. The extent of their possessions in the Pacific is surprising, the Marquesas, Tuamotu Archipelago, Society Islands, Austral Islands, New Caledonia, and the Loyalty group belonging to them, and they also exercise joint control with England in the New Hebrides. Tahiti is also connected with the Mutiny of the *Bounty* in 1789. She arrived in October 1788 to collect bread-fruit-trees and take them to the West Indies. Six months later she sailed, and the mutiny occurred very soon after her departure. As is well known, Bligh and eighteen others were turned adrift in a 23-foot boat, and made their amazing trip through uncharted waters to Timor, 3,600 miles away in forty-two days. The mutineers first took the *Bounty* to the Austral Islands and then returned to Tahiti, where some were left, and finally finished up at Pitcairn Island.

In company with the two Mr. Hooles I went out in the dinghy to the reef to see the curious fish to be found there. I had never imagined that such weird fish existed. They were of all colours and shapes. Some were deep blue, others light blue or vivid green, orange or yellow; some were striped lengthwise, others cross-wise; some seemed to be all head and no body to speak of, others all tail. A wonderful collection of strange little fish.

On 11th June I bade farewell to the cheerful little town of Papeeté and sailed over to Murea, which is one of the most beautiful islands, if not the most beautiful, I have ever seen. It is much broken up into peaks, and is densely wooded on the slopes and in the valleys. One of the peaks, Monaputa, has a large hole right through it near the summit. The shores are fringed with masses of cocoanut-palm-trees, and oranges, guavas, and every kind of tropical fruit grow in the valleys.

On this trip I had two passengers, Mr. and Mrs. Draper, who had been invited over to spend a few days with a friend in the island. The distance is only 18 miles, and we were soon off the Pass which leads to Papetoai Bay. On each side the seas thundered on the reef in the most awe-inspiring way, but the still water showed where lay the channel and a still better mark was the wreck of a small French gunboat, the *Kerseint*, on the edge of the starboard-hand reef. She managed to pile herself up there in broad daylight and fine, clear weather, to the great surprise of the natives, who revenged themselves for being compelled to help salve the guns without pay by making a song of the affair, not, I gathered, very complimentary to the captain.

We came to anchor in a little bight off Urufara near the head of the Bay, and my passengers left with their friend who had come to meet them. They had gone to Tahiti originally in company with several others, all provided with spades, rakes, hoes, and other agricultural instruments, with the idea of getting hold of some land and working it as a community. None of them, it seemed, knew anything about the matter, and on their arrival various difficulties arose, and the scheme fell through. The organizer returned home, one of the colonists took up some land and did well, while of the others some went on to New Zealand and others remained waiting for something to turn up.

Murea is hardly the place where one would expect to find one of England's leading airmen living in seclusion, with a Chinaman as cook and servant, yet Captain Gilmour, R.A.F., the youthful host of Mr. and Mrs. Draper, stands high on the list of British "aces," with thirty-four German aeroplanes officially credited to him. Maybe after the intense excitement and strain of air-fighting he finds the quiet of Murea an agreeable change. His house lies a few yards back from the path running through the little village of Papetoai. It is a one-storey wooden building raised off the ground on piles. Steps lead to the verandah, on to which open a bedroom at each side, with a reception-room in the centre, behind which again is the dining-room. At the back, away from the house, is the leaf-hut kitchen presided over by the Chinaman. I dined with Gilmour several times, landing on the beach in Urufara Cove and walking for just over a mile to his place. The road ran through groves of cocoanut-trees, past a few native houses, and finally emerged in the long, straggling village of Papetoai. The natives I met always greeted me in passing with the customary polite salutation of "Urahna," and the little boys took off their little hats. A very courteous, delightful race. The walks back to the ship when the moon was well up were indescribably beautiful. The soft light on the palm-trees and the graceful shadows on the path almost suggested that I was walking in fairyland. It was not always so, however, as I have waded back in an absolute deluge with the path under water. As a matter of fact, the weather just then was not all that could be desired, and at times the wind was very strong and there was a lot of heavy rain.

At first, however, it was fine, and the Drapers, Gilmour, and I made various excursions and gathered a bagful of oranges from an ex-German plantation, fished in the bay, and incidentally ruined the gears of my outboard motor by running on a reef in the dinghy, and attempted to pass from Papetoai Bay to Cook Bay through a tunnel which is said to run under the Rotui Mountain. In the past it was used as a place of refuge during hostile attacks. The entrance is half-way up a cliff. It is very low and can only be entered by wriggling through on one's stomach. A colony of the largest cockroaches I have ever seen inhabited the first few yards of the entrance. After about 50 feet it was possible to proceed in a stooping position, and ultimately there was enough head-room to stand upright. We went on for a few hundred yards and then the cave branched off into three passages. We took the central one, but could not go far along it, as the air was foul and breathing became difficult. We therefore returned before the conditions became too bad. At the other end of the tunnel, in Cook Bay, there is said to be a large cave containing an ancient canoe and a skeleton, but we could not find the entrance, and the natives either did not know where it was themselves, or pretended ignorance.

Four days after my arrival Mr. Abercrombie also came across from Papeeté, and for lack of an hotel took up his abode in the house of a native named Mahina. I saw a good deal of him and often lunched or dined with him at Mahina's house. The cooking arrangements of the establishment were very crude, but Mahina's wife turned out some wonderful meals, omelettes, deliciously fried fish, curried fowl and rice, fried bananas, bread fruit, a mixture of taro and bananas called "poy," fruit, with the milk of young cocoanuts to drink, and a bowl of excellent native coffee and cocoanut cream to wind up with. The meals were served on the verandah, and a bunch of

Mahina's children—he had a large and complicated family—
were always in attendance. They never took their eyes off Mr.
Abercrombie. Never had they seen such a fine big man, nor
one so kind-hearted, and they simply worshipped him. After
dinner they usually sang native songs to him and sang most
tunefully too.

One day we hired a pony and trap with the intention of
driving round the island, a distance of about 27 miles. It could
easily be done in a day they said, but our pony thought otherwise, and nothing would induce him to move faster than a walk.
There was plenty of time to admire the scenery, but by noon
we had only done about nine miles and were at Marepa. At
that rate it would take two days to get round, and we gave up
the plan and interested ourselves in the subject of lunch. There
is a store at Marepa, kept, of course, by some Chinamen, and
we entered, and expressed a desire for food. "Can do," said
John, and sent some of his countrymen out of the back room
which was lined with cases of vanilla. He spread a paper on
the table by way of tablecloth and set forth the meal, sardines,
bread, and tea. One fork and one spoon was all he could do in
the way of cutlery, and Abercrombie ate his sardines with the
fork, while I used the spoon, under the careful observation of
six cats.

At intervals during the drive the harness broke, but the
owner with admirable foresight had supplied several lengths
of rope, and with these we effected the necessary repairs and
ultimately got safely back.

Next day a hard wind blew down the valley at the head of
the bay, and as it swung the ship rather too near to a reef to
be pleasant I weighed anchor and shifted the ship farther to
windward. On letting go again the third shackle caught in the
compressor and opened out, and away went the cable, 45
fathoms of it, like a flash. I had never used so much chain
before, and so had not noticed that the third shackle had been
put on the wrong way round. The ship was then in a very
awkward position, as the motor was unable to drive her against
the strong puffs coming down the valley and we were gradually
losing ground, and getting nearer to the reef. The only thing

to do was to get some sail on to hold her up to windward while we got the second anchor ready. For an hour I beat about the bay under staysail and mizzen, while the two lads, working like Trojans, got out a spare length of chain and shackled it on. To add to our troubles the strop of the mizzen sheet block parted, and the sail had to be lowered while a temporary repair was being made. In the end we got her safely anchored once more, and then the search for the lost anchor and cable began. When the chain parted I had taken a rapid bearing of the end of a Chinaman's hut in line with a cocoanut-tree, and of a point of land, and so had a rough idea where the anchor lay. The first thing was to get hold of a grapnel, or a substitute, as there was nothing suitable on board. Mr. Philip lent me a small boat anchor, but we had no success that day.

Next morning I hired some natives to help in the boat and they rowed to and fro all day towing the anchor, but failed to hook the cable. Two other natives also paddled around in canoes towing a makeshift grapnel made of a bunch of fish-hooks. I promised them 50 frs. if they found it. They had no luck either, nor did we do any better next day, though the search went on without cessation, but on the third day the boat party hooked something with the boat anchor, and it was clearly the cable, as they could raise it a few feet, and it then became too heavy to lift any farther. We therefore shifted the ship to the spot, and took out the kedge anchor on a long wire and dropped it well on the other side of the chain. Twice it was hove in without result, but the third time we got a bite, and when the anchor appeared on the surface links of the missing cable lay across one fluke. A wire was at once shackled on to avoid losing the chain again in case it slipped over the fluke, and the question then arose as to how we were to get the loose end on board. One of the natives, Hemu, solved the difficulty by seizing the end of a rope and dropping off the bowsprit vertically into the water feet first. A few bubbles came up and marked the spot where he had disappeared, and then up shot his head and he swam to the boat. He had made the rope fast to the chain about 5 fathoms down. There was then no further difficulty, as we were able to hoist this and an equal length up to the cross-trees on the jib halliards, secure the cable at the rail, lower the bight to the deck, and repeat the process until the loose end came up. This was shackled on to the rest of the cable and all that remained to do was to heave up the second anchor. This turned out to be a terrible business. The spare bit of chain used is very heavy and, moreover, it was rather too big for the gypsies of the capstan, and with four men straining at the handles and two hauling on the chain we could only get in about a foot in a minute. All our assistants said that they had never worked so hard in their lives, and they were probably right. However, they were quite cheery about it, and as I paid them well they left in great good humour.

My original intention had been to remain only two or three days at Murea, but Gilmour thought that he might be able to go with me to Rarotonga if I waited a little longer, and as I was having a very pleasant time I did so.

While we lay at anchor waiting for him to come to a decision, poor Sam fell from grace, indeed he fell twice. On the first occasion he went ashore in the afternoon, was asked to a "houla" dance, and did not come back all night. In the ordinary way this would not have mattered very much, but on that particular night it rained in torrents and blew very hard from the north, in heavy squalls. The ship lay with her stern within 50 yards of a reef, and if the anchor had started dragging in one of the squalls, we should have been ashore before anything could have been done. Had Sam been on board I should have hove short on the cable and let go another anchor, but with only Stéphane and myself, I did not care to attempt this, and all I could do was to remain up, ready to steam to the anchor at the first signs of its dragging. In the small hours the wind ceased and I was able to turn in.

On the second occasion of Sam's fall from virtue, he went ashore and came back very drunk. He spoke to me very earnestly, but unintelligibly, and then suddenly remembered that he wanted to buy some clothes.

"You can't buy clothes here, Sam," I said, "and in any case you must not go ashore now. You had better turn in and sleep for a bit."

"Must buy working shirt, Sir Cap. I swim," and he threw off his clothes.

"Plenty shark here, Sam. They eat you."

"Shark no eat Sam. You bet me? You bet me?"

The only thing left seemed to be to knock him down, but first I tried guile.

"All right," I said, "by and by you go ashore. Now we set up the main shrouds. Get me the grease and some marline."

Sam at once became the sailor and started tacking along the deck for the grease pot. On the way he fell full length. This surprised him very much, and he returned on hands and knees and examined the deck to see what had tripped him. Eventually he reeled back with the pot, and we set to work. He hauled vigorously on anything given him, and repeated all my orders in a loud voice, apparently under the impression that he was in charge of a gang of men. Every now and then he fell down, but always scrambled to his feet full of energy. The arrival of Abercrombie on board created a diversion, and Sam forgot the shrouds to boast what a fine seaman he was, and also forgot about his working shirt, so that after a time I got him to turn in and the incident closed.

In the end Gilmour found that he would not be able to go, and I arranged to leave on the 29th June. On the evening before my departure I went round for a last dinner with Abercrombie. After the meal some of Mahina's children came up to the table and silently crowned us with wreaths made of shells. The thing was done so naturally and gracefully that we were both greatly pleased at the little attention. Abercrombie wore his all the evening, and looked quite dignified in it, but I had to take mine off as he said that with it on I reminded him strongly of a low comedian he had seen in New York.

Next morning Mahina appeared on the beach with a cart, and hailed us. He had brought a present of drinking cocoanuts, bananas, and a bag of oranges and paw-paws, for which he would not accept any return.

"You come long way," he said. "You got no house, no land. I got house, land, fruit. You no got, I got, I give you."

I managed to smuggle two large tins of biscuits and some

candles into his house, things I knew that he wanted, though it seemed a pity to do so, as it detracted to some extent from his act of genuine kindness.

As we passed out through the gap in the reef I saw Abercrombie on the beach, surrounded by a crowd of Mahina's children, waving a pareo, or loin-cloth, on a long pole. A bit of a send-off, no matter on how modest a scale, is always a pleasant thing. It is nice to think that those one is leaving wish one well, and a few shouted farewells make all the difference.

The wind was very light all day, and it was late in the afternoon before the beautiful island had faded from sight, and we were fairly started on the 605-mile trip to Rarotonga, a trip which was the reverse of enjoyable.

On the evening of the second day it breezed up hard from the E.N.E., and I had to call the lads and get the topsail off at 10 p.m. It rained heavily at intervals next day, and there was much lightning for six hours during the night. On the 2nd July rain fell all day, but not a breath of air stirred. We remained stationary, rolling to an easterly swell. I was wet to the skin all the time, as I did not like to leave the deck for the reason that the barometer was behaving irregularly. In those latitudes the barometer should keep its level, with a slight rise from 4 a.m. to 10 a.m. and a corresponding slight drop from 10 a.m. to 4 p.m., when the movement is repeated. If it fails to carry out this routine (fails to rise when it should, or drop when it should, and remains steady) trouble is on the way for a certainty, while if it moves the wrong way, as it did that day, then look out. I looked out and remained looking out all day, wet and chilled and marvelling why, since there was no need, I should endure all the discomfort and bother inseparable from long cruises in small vessels. A steady trickle of cold rain-water down one's spine continued for several hours is apt to give a gloomy tinge to one's thoughts, and by the evening I had come to the conclusion that the French are right and that such trips are pure folly.

Just before dark a light air came from the north, and at 6 p.m. the clouds lifted over the sun and revealed a most poisonous-looking sunset. I came to the conclusion that there would be trouble of some sort during the night, and that with our small crew it would be better to be a bit beforehand, and so gave the order to lower the mainsail. As things turned out this was quite a sound thing to have done, since a hard wind sprang up soon afterwards which would have made the work of lowering the sail then very difficult. As it was, we were relatively comfortable, and there was enough wind to keep her going along under the mizzen and staysail. The wind worked gradually to the left, and at 9 p.m. it was blowing downright hard from the N.W. As we could then no longer steer our course I hove to on the port tack under the second jib and mizzen, and went below to read up what the "book of the words" had to say about revolving storms. After the turmoil on deck it was extraordinary how quiet things were below. The lamp and the table swung gently to the roll, but the motion of the ship was remarkably easy considering that the sea was by then fairly heavy. According to the "Concise Rules for Revolving Storms," since the ship was in the Southern Hemisphere, and the wind had shifted to the left, she was in the left-hand or dangerous semicircle, and the right thing to do was to remain hove to on the port tack and wait for better times. That is the rule for hurricanes, and though the wind had nothing like hurricane force and was no stronger than a moderate gale, if so strong, yet it was of a revolving nature and no doubt the rule would apply. I, therefore, left her hove to. She drifted bodily to leeward owing to the small extent of canvas showing, but rode the waves very quietly. Some spray came on board, but no heavy water. The watches were, of course, kept as if we had been sailing, but all the man on deck had to do was to hold on, look out for passing craft, and report if anything carried away.

No doubt the lads merely considered it a miserable time which had to be endured, but I must say that, in spite of feeling very tired, I found a curious fascination in sitting on the deck of the storm-tossed little craft and watching how confidently and easily she met the big waves that came rolling up seemingly full of menace. It was a wild scene. Overhead the clouds scudded low and fast. The wind whistled through the rigging, and all round were sudden gleams of light where the crests of the waves broke into lines of white foam. Next morning the wind had got round to S.W. and was still blowing hard, but the barometer had plucked up its spirits and was evidently trying to "resume ordinary routine." After breakfast we set the trysail and started off again. At noon the result of two sights, taken under very difficult conditions, showed that we had lost ground and were twelve miles farther east than we had been the previous noon. There was nothing surprising about this as we must have made a lot of leeway during the night. It was, at any rate, a better result than that obtained by a schooner also making for Rarotonga from the east. We heard when we got there that instead of heaving to she ran for it, and in the morning was over 100 miles to leeward.

On the 5th July we were nearing Rarotonga, and I hoped to get in before dark. At 2 p.m. Sam reported land on the port beam. This was most surprising, as in the first place land was not due, and in the second it was on the beam instead of ahead. Still it seemed to be there, high land showing through the clouds. We altered course to head for it and ran on for an hour and a half, and then it simply disappeared, having been merely cloud with the appearance of land. We had been absolutely taken in and had destroyed our chance of getting to Rarotonga that night. Just before dark, however, we got near enough to sight it, through rain clouds, but the two little harbours are only holes in the reef, and it is not possible to enter after dark. The only thing to do was to heave to and wait for the dawn. This we did and passed an uncomfortable night, as the wind was high and the sea rough, and it rained most of the time. At daylight next morning we let draw and ran down towards the island, and before long sighted it again. A few minutes later a rain storm blew up, so heavy that it was impossible to see 100 yards, and we had to heave to again until it had passed and we were able to go on once more. When opposite to Avarua we hoisted the flag for the doctor and beat to and fro until he came out. A nasty swell ran into the little harbour, and a schooner which was lying there, moored to anchors on the reef, was plunging heavily.

THE CRUISE OF THE AMARYLLIS

The Sailing Directions have a high opinion of Rarotonga as a place of residence and state that "the climate as a tropical island is probably the healthiest and finest in the world," but think very little of Avarua as a harbour, remarking briefly that "it has an evil reputation," and "no vessel of 100 tons can enter." The remains of the wreck of an iron steamer on the reef just westward of the entrance gave point to the "evil reputation" part, while as regards entering, though the *Amaryllis* is not 100 tons, it was plain that she could not enter unless the schooner came out first, as not only did the latter take up most of the harbour, but she had lines out right across the entrance.

There remained Avatiu as a possibility.

After standing off and on for about an hour we saw a fine whaleboat come off with the doctor and ran in to save them a long pull against a lumpy sea. They got alongside with some difficulty as the *Amaryllis* was dancing about and so was the whaleboat, and I handed the doctor some letters I had brought from Papeeté. I told him that I did not like the look of the harbour, and should proceed.

"There are no ships in Avatiu, and none are expected," he replied. "It is not at all a bad harbour with this wind. Let me lend you one of my crew. You must have local knowledge, as you cannot lie at anchor and must moor to anchors on the reef."

I accepted the offer, as all three of us were very tired and needed a rest, and I did not want to go on if it could be avoided. One of his crew accordingly scrambled on board, and we sailed on to Avatiu, about half a mile farther on and stood on and off until some natives appeared on the beach. Sails were then lowered and we made for the entrance under power. The pass is only 70 yards wide and, with the sea breaking on the reef on each side, did not look very inviting.

"Good harbour inside," said the native who had noticed me regarding the entrance with apparent disfavour.

"It does not seem to have an inside," I replied.

"You see. Fine harbour."

As soon as we had got past the line of breakers and were,

seemingly, about to run right on to the beach, our pilot seized the anchor and threw it over the side, knocking part of the rail off in the process. This brought her up with such a sudden jerk that for a moment I thought we had hit the coral. She swung rapidly round. Natives were already swimming off for warps with which they returned to the reefs, dived and made the ends fast to anchors placed there for the purpose. After some hauling in and slacking out of warps the ship was finally dragged into the right position and after the cable had been unshackled from the anchor and the end taken ashore with infinite toil by Teka, who I thought would get drowned or knocked to pieces by the surf in the process, and shackled to an anchor on the reef, a wire led from the other bow, two warps from each quarter and two more from the stern, she was declared by the natives to be well and truly moored. The youth of the place regarded our arrival with unfeigned delight. Not only was she a yacht, and therefore an unusual type and so an object of interest, but she made such a splendid diving platform. Every afternoon during our stay they came off, a bright, merry crowd, and swam round, or sat happily on deck for hours. The noise they made was most distracting, but they plainly meant no offence, and I concealed my feelings as best I could.

Rarotonga is a small island, only 6 miles long, and is very beautiful. Inland the mountains rise up in pinnacles and fantastic peaks, covered with luxuriant vegetation. The valleys and slopes are carefully cultivated, and the natives are a fine type, rather darker in appearance than the Tahitians, but equally cheerful. The island is administered by New Zealand, and I gathered that the inhabitants do not congratulate themselves on the fact. They seemed to think that they are over-administered.

Next morning I paid a courtesy call on the Deputy Commissioner, but he sent out word that he was too busy to see me, which one would naturally expect a Deputy Commissioner for an island the size of Rarotonga to be, and asked me to call some other day. Everyone else, however, received me with the usual kindness. Mr. Mathews invited me frequently to his house, as did Mr. Morris and others. Living so much alone and feeding indifferently, I appreciated a little social intercourse very keenly and, to at least an equal extent, a good meal.

On the third day after my arrival the *Tahiti* anchored off Avarua, with Mr. Abercrombie and a Mr. Jewett on board. They came to see me, and we went for a drive round the island and were much struck with the beauty of the scenery, the high degree of cultivation of the available land, and the neat and well-cared-for appearance of the houses. The drive right round the island is only about 20 miles, and on our return we lunched together at the little hotel. It could hardly be called a good lunch, at any rate Mr. Jewett did not think much of it, since he remarked as he stepped into the boat with Mr. Abercrombie to return to the *Tahiti*:

"As regards the lunch, you will no doubt agree with me that at least the salt was excellent."

Next day the natives came off, dived down, cast off or unshackled the various lines and chains holding us, and we crawled out of the diminutive harbour under power, hoisting the sails outside and shaped a course for Nukualofa, in the Tonga group, 860 miles distant. Again we had a very uncomfortable trip. The weather, which should have been fine at that time of year, seemed to have gone to pieces. As a matter of fact, it was of an unusual type everywhere we went. On the second day out the barometer moved the wrong way in the evening. The wind was then blowing strongly from the east and the sea was rough. We seemed to be in for more trouble, and I hove to and put two reefs in the mainsail to be on the safe side. The wind gradually worked round to north and blew harder than ever. This shift of wind naturally raised a very confused sea, and great waves rolled along in all directions frequently running at right angles to each other, and piling themselves past in masses of white-crested water. The *Amaryllis* staggered on through all this upheaval, rolling and pitching in a way which reduced conditions on board to a state of intolerable discomfort. Loose articles hurled themselves about the cabins as if they had been endowed with life and had become demented. Moving about below resolved itself into crawling from place to place holding on to pieces of furniture. Sleep, of course, was out of the question, but I lay down and wedged myself into my bunk as best I could, after seeing the ship settled on to the course, to try and get some rest.

I soon heard Sam shouting for me. On gaining the deck I found that a furious squall was on us. Vivid lightning was flashing all round, and loud peals of thunder rolled overhead. The wind was screaming, and the force was extraordinary. It tore at my clothes as if trying to rip them off. The air was full of flying scud, blown bodily off the tops of the waves, mingled with heavy spray and rain, and there was such an uproar going on and I was so battered with the water which flew over the ship in sheets, and hustled by the wind, that I could hardly think. Instinctively, however, I felt that something must be done at once to ease the pressure, and that the only way to do this was to run before the wind. I therefore took the helm from Sam and put it up. He resigned it with evident relief and sat on deck beside me quite dazed and be-wildered. As soon as she was before the wind, dashing along at a great pace, I shouted in Sam's ear to go and rouse Stéphane and get the staysail down, and then to take the boom tackle off, and added a quite unnecessary warning that he was not to let himself be blown overboard. He crawled forward, and the sound of slatting canvas soon arose to be followed by silence. The lads then appeared indistinctly through the flying scud working at the tackle. They got this off and secured, handed themselves aft, and crouched on deck near the tiller. My plan was to heave to at the first sign of the squall easing, before the sea had time to get up. So far the weight of wind had flattened the sea, but it would probably rise very fast as soon as there was less wind. After about half an hour, and when I was just beginning to wonder whether we had not got mixed up with the start of a hurricane, arrived by some chance in the off season, the wind lulled slightly and I shouted to the lads to haul in the main sheet while I put the helm down. Round she came in a fine sweep and was soon hove to, and riding like a sea-gull. Every now and then she did an extra plunge, and in one of these the wire bobstay fall parted, but nothing could be done to repair it at the moment. When this happened it seemed possible that the topmast would be the next to go, but it was a fine spar and came through without damage. The squall finally screamed itself away and left a fresh breeze behind it. Lightning continued flashing at intervals, but there were no more heavy puffs of wind. Slowly the hours passed, but at length the eastern sky became lighter and lighter, the ropes and gear about the deck gradually took form, and quietly and imperceptibly it was dawn.

"Joy cometh in the morning." This, of course, depends largely on how the previous night has been spent, but at any rate in small ships, lurching about in rough seas, the morning usually brings comfort, even though no one has slept. For one thing it is a great advantage to be able to see what one is doing, should it be necessary to alter sails, or if any gear gives way. Making repairs in the dark is a lengthy, unsatisfactory, and at times a risky business. Then, on rough nights, the weather always seems more threatening than it does in daylight. The sea seems bigger and more vicious, and it is often difficult to see squalls approaching, and they may arrive unexpectedly and cause a lot of annoyance and trouble.

At dawn we made a temporary repair of the bobstay. This was not an easy thing to do, since Sam and I had to get out along the bowsprit and as the ship plunged, were taken under water once or twice. Luckily the water was warm, but we had to hold on with hands and legs to avoid being torn off whenever the bowsprit dipped.

The wind took two days to get back to its proper quarter, S.E., and fell very light as it slowly worked round, leaving us rolling in a diabolical sea. My heart ached for my poor tortured little ship as the boom swung to and fro, bursting tackles at intervals and straightening out the tail hooks of blocks, and making the ship shiver. In the end the wind got back to S.E. and blew fresh. Even running before the wind she could hardly carry the topsail, and it had to come off. Next day, the 14th July, the barometer started to rise, when it should have been dipping, and as, in addition, the sky looked stormy we hove to and double reefed the mainsail.

There is plenty of variety in cruising, especially in long-distance cruising, and there is usually something to the fore to occupy one's attention. If it is not the weather, then it is something else. On this occasion the weather gave me one subject for thought and the navigation gave me another, as the track to Nukualofa lay between two reefs marked on the chart "P.D." which means "Position Doubtful," the official way of saying that no one knows exactly where they are. The first, Harans Reef, was passed at night by Mr. Harans, of the *Thomas Dickenson* in 1842. He reported that the sea was breaking furiously over it for two ship's lengths. What a scene there must have been on board the *Thomas Dickenson* that night, eighty years ago, when the urgent shout went out "Breakers ahead!" What a trampling about the decks as the hands rushed to throw the coils of the sheets and braces off the pins, and trim the sails to the loud, shouted orders of the mate, while the "old man," outwardly calm though with a heart sinking with anxiety, had the helm put hard over. As the ship wallowed slowly round through what seemed an eternity on to the new course and there was time to look around, one can imagine that group of men standing silently on deck, watching, and calculating their chances. Tense moments those. A matter of life or death to all hands. The *Thomas Dickenson* surged past that tumbled mass of furiously breaking seas to safety, but there might be other reefs about, and all hands would be on the alert gazing into the darkness for the rest of the night. It is quite likely that it was not until the day dawned in glorious sunshine and the strain of anxious watching was over that anyone thought of the actual time when the reef was passed. This might have to be estimated and, in consequence, the position of the reef estimated too. As a result the survey ship sent out to search for it would very likely be looking in the wrong place and fail to find it, and the legend "P.D." would appear on the charts.

Sixty miles to the north-west is Buffon Reef, also "P.D." The French barque *Buffon* came across it at 2 a.m. one morning in 1880 and was very nearly wrecked.

As the only thing certain about a "P.D." reef is that it is *not* in the position given it on the chart, the question arose as to how best to avoid two reefs which were known to be somewhere in the neighbourhood, though the exact spot was doubtful. One way, of course, would be to pass 100 miles north or south. That should be a safe margin, but in the end I decided to sail between them, in spite of the fact that it would be night when we got there. Both the reefs are small, and it seemed probable that we should be able to clear them even if we came across them. I warned the lads to keep a sharp look-out for broken water when on watch, but as a matter of fact the conditions for sighting reefs were particularly bad that night on account of the heavy wind, which caused the seas to break in all directions, so that white-crested waves were to be seen everywhere.

The ship rolled and staggered along before the strong wind, and every now and then heavy spray fell on board, and the boom end dipped in the water and came out again with a sickening jerk. I began to wonder whether the gear would stand the strain. It was an unrestful time, and as we rushed on through the windy night I must admit that I felt some anxiety about the reefs and did not sleep well, as I did not know what sort of a look-out the lads were keeping. If they as much as moved their feet on deck I started up, but except that a flying fish, during my watch, hit me on the chest and gave me rather a jar, nothing unusual happened, and by dawn we were well past all danger.

Next day we crossed the Calendar Line in $172\frac{1}{2}°$ West Longitude, and put the date on one day. The date actually alters, of course, at the 180th meridian, but as a matter of convenience the line has been modified so as to bring under the same date all the islands in one group.

On the following day Eua and later Eua Iki Islands lying off the entrance to the Nukualofa Channel in Tongatabu hove in sight, but it was dark before we were up to the latter and we hove to until dawn.

The Tonga group numbers over 100 islands of all sizes surrounded by a perfect maze of reefs, and earthquakes are frequent among them. Islands have been thrown up and, after

a time, have disappeared again. The group was discovered in
1643 by the great Dutch navigator, Tasman. It is now ruled by
a Queen and Prince Consort under British protection. The
natives are Polynesian of a fine type, the most alert mentally in
the Pacific. As a matter of fact, they consider themselves
equal, if not superior, to white men. In the past they were
mighty fighters, and have held their own against the whites,
while none of the inhabitants of neighbouring groups could
stand up to them. It is characteristic of them that they will not
do manual work unless highly paid, and ships coming to discharge or load cargo bring their own gangs of labourers from
other islands to do this work.

As soon as it was light we let draw and ran for the entrance
to Biha Channel, leaving the little island of Eua Iki and its
waving cocoanut-trees to port. On the starboard hand going
in is a large horseshoe reef about 13 miles long on which the sea
breaks heavily. Dotted along its length are a number of small,
wooded islands. To the south of the entrance lies the low island
of Tongatabu, a mass of trees and vegetation. As we entered
the channel in the early morning with the sun behind us, the
fertile island to the south, fringed with a line of white breakers,
and the reef to the north, a mass of foam relieved by the
tree-covered islets with a foreground of beautifully blue spark-
ling water, made an entrancing picture, and I was in the right
frame of mind to enjoy it, as I had actually had eight hours
sleep on end. The two lads had shared the watches between
them, guessing that I was rather tired after the harassing
passage of seven days.

Biha Channel has a noble entrance 2 miles wide, but as one
advances the reefs on each side close in, until off the Narrows,
7 miles along, it is only one third of a mile across. It then takes a
right-angle turn and decreases still further in width to 400 yards
for half a mile, after which it opens into the large expanse of
reef-encumbered water fronting Nukualofa.

After we had anchored, the doctor, a young Australian, came
off and took our temperatures, for some reason. Stéphane's
was found to be sub-normal. This could not have been caused
by want of nourishment, as he has an enormous appetite and

eats more than anyone I have ever met. There seems no limit to what he can stow away. He is really a great trencherman.

I spent a few pleasant days at Nukualofa and, as usual, was very kindly received. My first act was call on the Consul, Mr. C. de F. Pennefather, to give an account of myself. I found this an advisable thing to do everywhere. It is unusual for a small vessel to blow in with one white man and two coloured lads on board, no cargo and no apparent reason for being there, and a visit to the British Representative to explain my presence seemed the right thing to do and appeared to be appreciated. At any rate I was always, with the one exception of Rarotonga, received most kindly and sympathetically. During my stay Mr. Wallace drove me out to his plantation and to the Blow Holes. The road at first was very good and ran through some fine cocoanut plantations. After a time we turned off up a rough track until we reached his estate. On the way he stopped to give instructions in pidgin-English to one of his hands, a Solomon Islander with a mop of fuzzy hair rising a foot from his scalp. The subject matter appeared to be cows, but that was all I could gather, though the "boy" seemed to understand well enough.

Farther on we came across another native, with bloodstained arms and hands, about to cook a pig. He had dug a small trench and had made a wood fire in it, in which he had heated stones. He then covered these with banana leaves, put the pig on top, put more leaves over it, and heaped earth on the lot. We left him adding the finishing touches and drove on through one or two "fighting villages," still surrounded by the remains of stockades, to the Blow Holes. These lie on the south side of the island and are indescribably beautiful. A reef of coral fringes the shore and a heavy surf always breaks on it. Holes and crevices have been worn in the coral in the course of time, and as the great rollers hurl themselves on the reef columns of water and spray are shot up into the air. With the sun low down in the west the play of colours in the driven spray is marvellously lovely, absolutely fascinating, a riot of dancing rainbows. I could have stayed for hours, but the day was nearly ended and we had to get back. There is another very remarkable object of interest in Tongatabu, some huge stones, exactly similar to those of Stonehenge, but mortised together. There is no record of who erected them. The point is full of interest, but it is, like the origin of many other wonderful monuments and buildings in some of the South Sea Islands, shrouded in impenetrable mystery.

That night I dined at the little boarding-house and found on the verandah a piano which had once stood in the saloon of the *Amaryllis* when she was at home. It seems strange that one should take a little ship, sail half-way round the world, and find at an out-of-the-way place like Nukualofa a piece of furniture which had once, years before, formed part of the fittings of one's vessel when she was in England. The fact seemed extraordinary, but the explanation is simple enough, as the then owner of *Amaryllis* exchanged pianos with the owner of a little vessel which had then wandered to Nukualofa and there been sold. The piano had been taken out and bought by the boarding-house, and there it was still, when I dined there.

Next day a good many natives came on board to see the ship. One of them brought a present of oranges, and in return I gave him a chart of the group of islands. He was greatly delighted, and examined it with keen interest. I thought I had given him a useful present, but after a time he looked up and asked:

"Which land, which water?" So it looks as if that chart was wasted.

The Prince Consort Tugi also honoured me with a visit. He had himself rowed off with a Mr. Wall in a small dinghy. The wind was strong, the Prince is a big man, and the dinghy was small, and for a time it was doubtful whether the oarsman, an indifferent performer, would succeed in reaching the ship. I was uncertain as to what was Court etiquette in the circumstances. Should one stand by and see a Prince blown down the coast, or should one organize a rescue party, and tow him up to the ship? Luckily his crew succeeded, by dint of great efforts, in getting alongside, so that point did not actually arise.

The Prince speaks excellent English and told me that he preferred England to the Continent, in spite of the fact that when in England he was mistaken for Jack Johnson, the pugilist. He asked many questions about the various places I had visited, and promised to send me a piece of native tapa cloth, made from the bark of a tree. It is hammered out with wooden mallets and stamped in coloured patterns. It is very light and extremely warm as a covering. As wall tapestry it is very effective.

That night the great social event of the year, a dance at the Club, took place. I received an invitation and went. I am not a dancer, and was wandering aimlessly about when the Secretary, Mr. Wallace, came up and said:

"By the way, have you met the Queen?"

"No."

"Then let me introduce you," and before I knew what had happened I was presented to Her Majesty, without having had time to think of suitable things to say to a Queen. She is a large, portly young woman, quite unaffected and pleasant and is said to be very capable. Like her husband she speaks English fluently. She received me graciously, and asked a few questions about the ship, and then someone else intervened and I managed to fade away towards the supper-table, where there was a really excellent spread. The ladies of the Colony had plainly gone all out over the sweets, salads, and other good things.

Next morning when I came ashore I met Mr. Tippit, the Harbour Master, who took me round to the equivalent of a public-house, and gave me some kava to drink. The yangona root from which this is made used to be macerated in the mouth by the local damsels before steeping, but it is now ground up. The drink has a clean, medicinal flavour, and is rather bitter. Taken in excess it is said to weaken the legs, but has no effect on the brain. I cannot say that I liked it. As we left the hut he said:

"I see you are sailing to-morrow."

"Oh, am I?" I replied. "I did not know it."

"Well, there is a notice in the Post Office that you are sailing to-morrow with mails for Suva."

And then I remembered that Mr. Denny, Assistant Post-

132

master, who is a Scot, had asked me on arrival how long I was stopping and whether I would take a bag of mails to Suva when I left. I had replied off-hand that I expected to remain two or three days. He had taken this more literally than I meant it, and by adding three days to the date had arrived at my sailing day. As everyone seemed to expect me to go I arranged to leave on the 24th July, so as not to disappoint them too much. On the evening before my departure I went round to the Club to take leave of the members and met Mr. Jiobe Kaho, Minister of Police, who promised me a piece of tapa cloth, as that promised by Prince Tugi had not turned up. At midnight a policeman in a boat collided violently with the ship, and handed up a piece of cloth from Mr. Jiobe Kaho, and next morning after we had weighed anchor and were hoisting sails I found a very polite Tongan on the deck with another piece from the Prince. Being very busy at the time, I simply gave him a few shillings and thanked him, and bundled him back into the boat. It occurred to me afterwards that he may have been a noble, but he did not seem offended at the tip, so I hope no harm was done.

As we were bound to Suva, 404 miles to the westward, we passed out through the Egeria Channel, leaving the lovely little island of Atata on the port hand and an extensive reef on which the sea always breaks on the starboard hand. The water in the channel is so clear that the bottom shows up distinctly in 36 feet of water, and it looked as if the ship might go aground at any moment. A mile beyond the north end of Atata is the break in the reef which forms the Pass, 800 yards wide, plainly marked by the still water.

The wind was light for the first two days, and progress was slow, but on the third day the wind came strong from the north. For an hour we logged 10 miles, and then the barometer started falling very fast, and the wind shifted to N.N.W. and blew harder. I came to the conclusion that we were in for more trouble and had the mainsail lowered. Lowering a mainsail in a strong wind and heavy sea is not an easy matter even in a well-manned ship, but when, as in our case, the canvas and spars are heavy and the crew very small it is an awkward business and degenerates into a regular fight. Luckily the two lads were very strong and as active as monkeys, and we succeeded in getting it down and secured without damage. As it turned out the wind was at its height when the sail was lowered, and during the afternoon it gradually fell away. At 5 p.m. we therefore lowered the trysail, which had replaced the mainsail, and re-hoisted the latter. Rain started and continued steadily until the early morning and the wind worked round to S.W. This meant sailing "full and bye," or, in other words, close-hauled, but with the sails kept nicely full of wind.

At noon next day we crossed the 180th meridian and passed from West to East longitude. The date had already been changed on the Calendar Line, and there was nothing more to be done in that respect.

The wind kept ahead, and we had to beat up to Suva, leaving Matuku Island to starboard and Kandavu to port. At dawn Viti Levu, discovered by Tasman in 1643, of which Suva is the chief port, was in sight ahead, but frequent rain storms blotted out the land from time to time, and I had great difficulty in fixing the ship, and could not tell whether Suva was to windward or to leeward. The only thing was to stand on close hauled until something could be identified. Ultimately what looked like a wreck could be made out and then the old pile Nasilai Reef Lighthouse. We stood on until close to the reef, and then came round and sailed along just clear of it. Like most of these islands, Viti Levu is wonderfully beautiful from the sea. Inland are masses of peaks, heaped about in confusion, and at their foot all is green. Along the beach are a few houses standing amidst the waving cocoanut-trees, and away from the coast is the fringing reef, on which the swell hurls itself from one year's end to another. Surf breaking on a reef is a strangely fascinating and rather awe-inspiring sight. At intervals we passed openings leading to channels inside the outer line of reef by which it would have been possible to gain Suva harbour in smooth water, but I did not care to attempt them as I had no large-scale chart and they are intricate. Yet the early navigators, with no charts at all, used to work their unhandy ships into many such places in a way which now seems almost impossible. They were real seamen, those tough old shell-backs. Sailing in these then quite unknown seas must have been thrilling work. A keen-sighted man must have been aloft, day and night, on the look-out for seas breaking on a reef, or discoloured water over a shoal. At dark they probably reduced sail and dodged slowly along, or else hove to until daylight. When they came across land in the course of their wanderings they would coast slowly along outside the reefs until an opening appeared, and then send a boat in to take soundings and find out if there were any suitable anchorages. If the report were favourable the ship would be brought in with boats ahead to tow her round if necessary. It must have been exciting, anxious work, and to the dangers from reefs must be added the chance of trouble from the natives, many of them fierce and warlike. How amazed the latter must have been at the sight of the first European ship, with its lofty spars and great hulk compared with their own canoes! Their minds would be filled with wonder, fear, and consternation at the incredible sight. It is not surprising that they were full of suspicion and that conflicts with the whites occurred at times. Their hostile attitude must have added greatly to the difficulties and dangers of exploration, but nothing daunted those old sea-dogs.

Suva does a considerable shipping trade—and the harbour is well lighted and buoyed for the convenience of steamers, and there is no difficulty about entering. By 3 p.m. on the 28th July we had passed through the gap in the reef on the line of the leading beacons, and were inside the harbour. A launch came bounding along to meet me with Mr. Twentyman, the Harbour Master, on board, and after him came Dr. Calment in another launch. With their help we got the sails down and made for an anchorage under power. It is delightful to make a new port and again lie quietly at anchor after a few days rolling about at sea. With the sails stowed and the decks cleared up everything is strangely quiet and peaceful about the ship, while the shore looks most enticing. This is especially so in the case of the fine harbour of Suva. To the north and north-west lies a range of mountains with jagged peaks and densely wooded slopes, to the south is the protecting line of reef, while to the east is the busy town and behind it red-roofed dwelling-houses are dotted about amidst the trees. When the sun is setting, the colours and shadows amongst the hills are wonderful, all purple and gold.

That evening I had my first experience of reporters, as Mr. Able, editor of a local paper, rowed himself off in a very unstable dinghy to interview me. He complained bitterly that I was not sufficiently communicative, but he made quite a long article out of the little I told him.

Next day I called on the Colonial Secretary, Mr. R. D. Stewart, and while I was sitting in his office, a splendid native clad in a sulu, or loin cloth, came in with a bowl of kava. He went down on one knee in front of me, which threw me into a mild panic, and offered the bowl, clapping his hands when I took it.

"What do I do now?" I asked Mr. Stewart.

"Drink it," he replied, so I drank it, and returned the bowl to the still kneeling native. The proper thing, in ceremonious kava drinking, is to throw the empty bowl down, giving it a spin.

I stayed at Suva several weeks, waiting for the start of the spring in Australia, and also for Mr. Abercrombie to join me, and got to know quite a number of people, amongst them Mr. Tommy Horne, who had then been forty years in Fiji and who is blood brother to a chief and has great influence with the natives, and Mr. A. J. Soutar at whose house I dined frequently. His servants were all Indian coolies, and the cook was quite a magician in his way and turned out excellent dinners of several courses on an absurdly small stove. He steadily refused to have a bigger one. After dinner, when he and the house boys were ready to go home, they always came on to the verandah and salaamed. For some reason women are never used as servants, and all the housework is done by men and boys, usually Indians. There are over 60,000 Indians in the Fiji Islands and about 90,000 Fijians. The splendid Fijian, a model of physical beauty with his fuzzy hair standing a foot from his scalp, resembling a Guardsman's busby, despises the Indian, while the latter deems himself of a superior race. As a result they keep strictly apart and do not intermarry. The Fijian is a very attractive fellow, very courteous and good-natured and apparently quite happy. One frequently meets two Fijians walking along the street holding each other's hands. They seem to have a strong sense of humour. One day a small trading cutter anchored near us. Next day the crew weighed the anchor and started towing her to the wharf, but the wind was strong and she went astern instead of ahead and finally collided with another cutter, but no bad language was used. On the contrary, the skipper and crew of the second cutter laughed heartily, and evidently thought it was a most amusing affair. The Fijians are also fond of singing, and crews going off to their ships at night usually sang as they rowed, one man singing the verse and the rest joining in the chorus, which always stopped very abruptly on the same note. Not very long ago they were cannibals and said to be very treacherous, but now they are modest in all their ways and polite. A remarkable change and in a very short time.

Time passed very pleasantly in an uneventful way. I made an excursion by launch inside the reef to Nausori on the river Rewa, returning by car, and Mr. Tommy Horne also took me for drives in the neighbourhood to places whence magnificent views of mountains, fertile valleys, and the sea could be obtained. I played golf on probably the most mountainous course in the world and lunched with the acting Governor in a native-built house put up temporarily while Government House, destroyed by lightning, is being re-built. The supports inside were covered with plaited work, and the general effect was most striking and pleasing.

Mr. Barker took me round to his father-in-law, Mr. Turner's museum, which is crammed full, overfilled in fact, with a very valuable collection of native implements and work and curiosities of all sorts. He has also one of the large sailing double canoes, not now made. It was specially built for him in 1912 from the last available model. The main canoe is 50 feet long, and the outrigger one is 42 feet. Both are hollowed from tree-trunks, and all the fittings are lashed together, not nailed. A platform connects the two, and on it is a small bamboo hut.

The foot of the mast rests on a saddle-shaped step, and the mast itself is canted forward and stayed in that position. The sail is made of matting. As the outrigger of a sailing-canoe must always be to windward, it is not possible when beating to tack in the ordinary way, and the natives get over the difficulty by having a steering oar at each end and canting the mast the other way, swinging the sail round, and turning what was bow on one board into the stern on the next one. While the sail is being shifted and the mast canted the helmsman pulls in the steering oar he has been using, runs to the other end of the canoe and puts out the other one, and off they go on the new tack. Mr. Turner has built a special shed for this magnificent model. He stoutly maintained that these canoes are the finest sea-boats in the world. By special request I did not express an opinion.

Suva is a wet spot. It has two seasons, the "wet" and the "rainy" seasons, and boasts the world's record for rainfall—over 26 inches in twenty-four hours. But, all the same, it is a pleasant, healthy place. When it was not raining I usually went ashore in the evening to the Fiji Club, where the seniors met, or to the Defence Club mostly patronized by the juniors, and afterwards dined either at someone's house—everyone was very hospitable—or at the Grand Pacific Hotel, and once or twice at Macdonald's. At the Club they told me of two great bluffs which Fiji brought off during the war, the first, the capture of Von Lucknow, being surely one of the biggest on record. This is the tale as I heard it:

Von Lucknow was commander of the *Seeadler*, a small German cruiser wrecked in the East Pacific during the war. When his ship was lost he started off with a few hands in the motor boat and reached Rarotonga. More fortunate than I was, he arrived there at a moment when the Deputy Commissioner was at leisure and free to see him. Von Lucknow represented himself and his party to this official as a Danish scientific expedition. It did not occur to the Deputy Commissioner that it was in the least strange that scientists should arrive from the other side of the world in a ship's motor boat, and he received Von Lucknow graciously and arranged for supplies of fuel, water, and provisions. The natives, however, were not so easily deceived, and openly stated that all was not right and that the boat was full of arms. In the end they obliged the Deputy Commissioner to take action. He invited Von Lucknow to the Residency to explain away the absurd doubts as to the genuineness of the scientific expedition. Von Lucknow's reply, very naturally, was to slip his moorings and get away to sea, leaving the Deputy Commissioner full of amazement. Von Lucknow went west and reached the Fiji Islands. He arrived in rough weather, but succeeded in taking the boat through a gap in the fringing reef of one of the eastern islands. The natives received him well, but were doubtful as to his *bona fides*. A contingent from Fiji had gone to the war, and the natives said to each other, "These men are our enemies." That night a cutter went across to Levuka with the news. A police-officer, Hill, was there with a few native police. He knew that Von Lucknow's party were well armed with machine-guns, rifles, revolvers, and grenades, while he had only one revolver and his police had no weapons, yet he never hesitated, but commandeered a small fruit steamer in the harbour, put his police on board and pushed out. Think of the amazing audacity of starting off, practically unarmed, to capture a fully armed party of desperate men! It was a magnificent act, for which I trust he was adequately rewarded. Next morning the steamer went in through the Pass. Von Lucknow saw her come in and prepared to leave by another opening, but before he could get away a boat dropped from the steamer's davits, Police-officer Hill and his merry men bundled into her and rowed towards the motor boat. The sturdy Fijian police bent to the oars, and the boat shot across the water. Von Lucknow was by then under way, but Hill stood up and shouted to him that the game was up and summoned him to surrender. Von Lucknow was completely deceived. It never occurred to him as a possibility that unarmed men could behave so boldly. He jumped to the conclusion that the ship carried guns, in fact he thought he could see them under some canvas covers on the fo'c'sle head. He surrendered. His annoyance when he learned the real state of affairs was, naturally, very great. Later he was taken to New Zealand, whence he and his party escaped and went off with a scow. He was a good sportsman, was Von Lucknow.

In the other case the Governor was the hero. He had reason to believe that the *Scharnhorst* and *Gneisenau* were steaming to pay him a visit, which, as a matter of fact, they were doing. Suva was not fortified, and, since he could not resist by force, he fell back on guile and sent himself a wireless message, purporting to come from the Commanding Officer of H.M.S. *Australia*, that the ship would be in harbour at dawn. To this message he himself sent a reply inviting the Commanding Officer, and such other officers as could be spared from duty, to breakfast on their arrival.

The *Scharnhorst* and her consort were particularly anxious not to meet the *Australia*, and on taking in these messages, they prudently turned and fled, and Suva was saved.

On the 9th September Mr. Abercrombie arrived by the *Tofua* and brought a side of bacon, an excellent Australian Stilton, a case of claret, and other things. I had first met him in Tahiti, and it was then arranged that he should join me at Suva for the trip to Sydney. He is not a young man and had never sailed before, but he was very anxious to make the passage, though I warned him that we should almost certainly meet bad weather. He is not, however, easily turned from his purpose—a man with a name like that would not be—and my description of the conditions of life in a small ship during bad weather left him unmoved. He was anxious for the experience and, as I was very glad of his company, the arrangement stood.

On the 10th September we weighed and left the harbour with two reefs in the mainsail, as the "Trades" were strong, saluting H.M.S. *Chatham* as we went out.

We went south of Mbengha Island and north of Kandavu. The former is the home of the fire-walkers. Some of the inhabitants can walk bare-footed with impunity on stones almost white hot. They only do this on some great occasion, such as the visit of the Prince of Wales. They also did it for Lord Jellicoe when he was there. The stones are heated until they crack, and are then raked out of the fire and arranged in a circle.

The walkers go round this on the stones. Leaves are then put on the latter, and a religious ceremony takes place in the smoke which arises.

For the first two days the wind was strong and the sea heavy. At intervals heavy spray came on board, and one lot went through the skylight, which I had incautiously left slightly open, into my bunk. It is very unpleasant to sleep on a soaked mattress, and as a rule if a bunk gets wet it remains wet, as there is no chance of drying things. However, on the third day conditions improved, and we were able to set the whole mainsail and even the topsail. Abercrombie claimed to be enjoying the trip. He took an interest in the cooking and revealed himself as an accomplished chef. It was a hobby of his, he said. For the first few days, however, he could not do much, as he kept on falling about in the fo'c'sle owing to the violent motion. He is a tall, heavy man, and when he fell he usually smashed something and nearly crushed Stéphane to death once or twice. He takes a delight in cooking, and on one occasion cooked a dinner for twelve friends, a real dinner too, of several courses. While on board he made a tomato sauce which I shall never forget. It was a great sauce, and, after it had finished its career as such, what was left appeared as an excellent tomato soup. If Fate had decreed that he was to be a cook he would have been one of the best cooks in the world. The enormous appetites of the two lads at times upset his plans, and caused him much annoyance. He, on one occasion, decided on a dish for supper which required, as one ingredient, cold potatoes. At noon he accordingly had a large potful of potatoes boiled, but when supper-time came and he went to prepare the dish, no potatoes were left. The two had eaten the whole lot at noon in addition to a generous quantity of meat and vegetables, bread and cheese. Abercrombie was quite staggered and much put out. He did not get over it for a couple of hours. It seemed to him utterly impossible that they could have eaten all those potatoes. I was rather surprised too, though I had long known that as a trencherman Stéphane had a very high standard.

Stéphane went up 100 per cent. in his own estimation when he saw that Abercrombie, for whom he had a deep admiration, could cook. Hitherto he had rather despised himself for being cook, but when he found that such a fine big man was well versed in the art he thought a lot more of his job. At the same time he never really liked the work and he never shone as a chef.

On the 14th September we were nearing New Caledonia. Cook was the first to discover the island in 1774. He sailed N.W. but when he found reefs extending far beyond the end of the land, he came back and, after dodging about for a day or two, took his ships inside the reef on the north coast and anchored off Pudieu Island. Subsequently he sailed S.E. and anchored off Amère Island, south of Havannah Pass, in the centre of a network of detached reefs. It is still called Cook's Anchorage, but it is amazing that he was able to get in there. The risks the early navigators of these parts had to run were appalling.

The usual route for Nouméa, our port, from the east is through the Havannah Channel, but I had not been able to get a chart and was obliged to come round past the Isles of Pines and enter by the Bulari Pass, an awkward approach, as a continuous line of reefs juts out for 40 miles from the mainland at the south-east end, and I had to come round them.

I took a number of observations to fix the ship and felt fairly sure of her position, but I did not altogether like sailing on through the night towards such a mass of reef. However, nothing untoward happened, and at dawn I altered in for Bulari Pass. The water soon became smooth, and I knew we were under the lee of the reefs. At 10 a.m. high land loomed up through the mist, and at noon Amédée Lighthouse appeared. The wind had been strong all the morning but tailed off at noon, and by the time we reached Bulari Pass it was light and very nearly ahead. However, we got in very comfortably, and I was sitting at the tiller drinking a cup of tea and congratulating myself on having managed to get in through the Pass when the wind fell right away to a flat calm. Not an air stirred. This was very disconcerting, as a mile inside the Pass is Tabu Reef, and the current was setting us that way. I watched the small lighthouse on the reef for a few minutes and it certainly seemed to be getting nearer. There was no time to be lost. The engine must be started at once. I went below and got it going. It ran valiantly for a minute, and then stopped. Again I hurriedly dived below and restarted it, and again it ran for a short time and then stopped once more. There was no time to find out what was the matter with it. We were by then quite close to the reef, and the only way of preventing the ship from drifting on to it was to let go the anchor. Sam and Stéphane had got his ready in anticipation, and at the word hove it over, but it was too late; before it could bring the ship up the keel aft had touched. The sails were immediately lowered, the boat hoisted out, and the kedge anchor, attached to 40 fathoms of wire, taken out broad on the bow.

And then began a period of heavy toil at the capstan to drag the ship off. Both Sam and Stéphane rose nobly to the occasion and worked like heroes, while Abercrombie's help was invaluable. Luckily the water was as smooth as a mill-pond and she was not bumping, but we had drifted on with the very last of the flood stream and already the water was beginning to fall. Unless we could get her off quickly, before the water had fallen too far, she would not come off that tide, and if she did not and the sea got up before the next high water she would bump to pieces. We strained and tugged at the capstan, but could not shift her an inch. It seemed a hopeless business, and I looked on the ship as lost. But help was at hand. The light-house-keeper on Amédée Island had seen us drift on to the reef, and he manned a whaleboat with five natives and rowed over. The extra weight of six people forward, all shouting in French or pidgin-French, and the extra strain on the capstan both tended to depress the bow and raise the stern. Slowly, very slowly, almost imperceptibly, the bow moved round and then, to my infinite relief, the seemingly impossible happened and she slid off into deep water. I felt like dancing on the deck, but restrained myself. The ship was not yet out of trouble. She was still very close to the reef, and it was necessary to move her well clear. As there was no wind and the engine still refused duty, the best way seemed to be to tow her off. The natives accordingly manned the whaleboat and chattering volubly started in, but they could not get her ahead against the ebb current and the ominous roar of the surf on To Reef sounded nearer and nearer. We were clear of one reef, but drifting on to another one. Night had long since fallen, and in the darkness the sound of the breakers was very daunting. Just as I was preparing to anchor again, as the only way of saving the ship, a light air came off the land and we were able to make sail and crawl slowly ahead. I was truly thankful to feel the ship once more under way, even though progress was so slight. Still we were advancing, and leaving To Reef. The thunder of the surf grew less and less, and in the course of time we arrived at an anchorage off Amédée Island at 10 p.m., the Frenchman at the tiller. When he gave the word we let go and were once more safely anchored. He refused any suggestion of compensation either for himself or his crew, and said he only came to lend a hand and was glad to have been of assistance. His men suggested a drink, and I was about to serve out whisky all round, when I happened to catch the Frenchman's eye. He shook his head slightly. Natives are easily upset by quite a small quantity of alcohol, and the law which forbids its supply to them is sound. I did not mind what the law was and was about to give them a drink, but as the Frenchman disapproved, and they were his men, I refrained, and gave them all the French money I had instead, not a large sum.

Next day we anchored off Nouméa and annoyed the authorities very much by hoisting the Ensign at the mast head instead of "Q" flag. By the International Code this flag means "I am subject to quarantine, but have a clean Bill of Health." The French, however, seem to regard it as merely a request for the doctor to come off and give pratique. On the other hand, the Dutch were horrified when I hoisted it in their territory and implored me to haul it down quickly. There seems no generally recognized way by which a ship can show that she has come from a foreign port. I usually hoist "Q" flag now, and if the local people do not like it I haul it down.

New Caledonia is in the main barren, though portions of it are fertile, and the view from the sea is gloomy and uninviting.

It is, however, rich in timber and minerals. Nouméa is also a very depressing, squalid town. At one time it was a big convict settlement with about 10,000 convicts in prison there, but of recent years no more have been sent. The steady daily cursing of 10,000 men seems to have cast a blight on the place from which it has never recovered, and even to-day it still seems the abode of horror. One meets poor, broken-down old men wandering aimlessly about the streets, or sitting on the benches in the Place, *libérés*, ex-convicts who have served their time. There are quite a number of them about, with their spirit so crushed out of them that they have never had the heart to make a fresh start elsewhere when released from prison. They probably were a fairly bad bunch in their time, but they now seem so helpless and hopeless that one could not help feeling sorry for them.

No, Nouméa certainly cannot be called an attractive place, but we remained there for twelve days to allow the equinox to pass. Captain Fletcher of the S.S. *Navua* had strongly urged me to be in port about that time, as, from his experience, there was then always bad weather at sea.

Nouméa, however, has its bright spots, and one of them is the British Consul, Mr. Dunlop, and his charming family. The three little children are quite delightful, and it was a great pleasure to go up to the Consulate for lunch, dinner, or tea. Another bright spot was the Vice-Consul, Mr. Johnston, who has lived in Nouméa for many years, but who has never troubled to acquire a knowledge of French grammar, and simply takes English sentences and turns them bodily into French. He is much esteemed by the Frenchmen, in spite of the liberties he takes with their language, and is unanimously elected vice-president of their Club every year.

While we were waiting for the equinox to pass, H.M.A.S. *Melbourne* came in, with Admiral Dumaresq on board, on its way to Sydney from a trip round the islands. As she took up an anchorage she fired a salute, to which the French gunboat, *Aldebaran*, replied, and then a fort also followed suit. The *Melbourne*, not to be outdone, fired another salute and did some more as the Governor went on board, and yet again when the Consul paid his call. Altogether it was rather a noisy afternoon.

Next day an officer from the *Melbourne*, Lieutenant Collins, called with cards from Captain Cumberlege, and Commander Ward-Hunt, and offers of any assistance required. Lieutenant Collins, no doubt with a mental vision of the owner of the yacht reclining on deck in an easy chair, while a steward in a white suit with brass buttons tendered iced drinks, had got himself up for the visit and put on his sword. But when he stepped on board he found a different state of affairs. The owner, attired in a filthy singlet and dirty pair of trousers, and with a hole in the toe of one of his shoes, arms and hands covered with grease from the engine, was summoned from below, where he had been investigating the inside of the motor, to receive the visitor, and appeared with a spanner in one hand and a lump of cotton waste in the other. The contrast between what he had anticipated and what he found must have been rather a surprise to Lieutenant Collins, but it is difficult to catch a pukka Naval Officer off his guard, and he did not give a sign that he had expected to find anything different. Still, the sword was rather a difficulty.

Next day a regatta was held in honour of the visit of the warship. Every ship in the harbour was "dressed" with flags, and the general effect was gay and festive. The Frenchmen were keenly interested in the sailing races, and the crews of the competing boats were very excited and some of them danced about the decks and shouted to relieve their feelings. In ordinary racing, of course, everyone keeps as low and as still as possible, but the Frenchmen cared nothing for that sort of thing. They were out to enjoy themselves, and they certainly seemed to be doing so. The *Melbourne* entered some whalers and a gig in the sailing races, but they were open boats and had not the beam or draft of their competitors, and they did no good. In the rowing race the Admiral's gig went right away from the service whalers of the *Aldebaran* and won easily. The race was not much of a test, as the gig was a vastly superior boat to the whalers. While the regatta was on, the *Melbourne* had a children's tea-party on board. The Admiral very kindly sent a launch with an invitation for us to go on board, but unluckily we could not do so. I went across next morning, however, to get the correct Greenwich time for rating the chronometers. Most of the officers were still turned in, as they had attended a dance and supper given by the Governor the previous evening. The supper started at 2 a.m. and lasted until after 4 a.m., and it was daylight before they got back on board. Captain Cumberlege heard that I was there and sent for me to his cabin. He had just turned out, and at the moment of my arrival he was wearing a towel round his middle to which, by way of completing his costume, he added a vest. Naval Post Captains rather fill me with awe, and especially was this so in the case of one with the great reputation of Captain Cumberlege, but this delightfully unceremonious way of receiving me put me quite at my ease and the memory of Lieut. Collins's sword faded away, and I remained an hour talking ships and listening to his account of Tucopia, San Cristobal, and the other islands he had just visited. The Admiral invited us to lunch and later came on board, and we dined in the Ward Room in the evening.

Next day we prepared to sail, but first went alongside the wharf for water. The *Melbourne* was also alongside coaling, and as we were on the point of starting Commander Ward-Hunt came to see us off, and with him came a Chief Petty Officer and two Petty Officers who had volunteered to help hoist the sails. I was delighted at this little act of courtesy, and felt that the Australian Navy wished us well, and that we were leaving the harbour under their protection.

Once we were outside we found the wind strong, and when north of Thisbe Reef we hove to and double reefed the mainsail. In the midst of the operation the S.S. *Pacifique* passed on her way to Sydney by the Bulari Pass. She dipped her ensign in salutation, and I had to knock off reefing while I acknowledged it. Again we passed Tabu Reef, but under vastly different conditions. On the way in we had drifted ingloriously on to it in a stark calm, but on the way out we went by at a good speed with a fine, hearty E.S.E. wind driving us along. I shook my fist at it as we went by, though, as a matter of fact, it had done us little damage. On our arrival at Nouméa, Mr. Johnston had arranged for a Loyalty native, Goa, a splendid specimen of a man, to go down and examine the hull. The report had been that, beyond three sheets of copper rubbed and crinkled, there was nothing wrong. It had been a lucky escape. Things might easily have been different.

CHAPTER IV

AUSTRALIAN AND NEW ZEALAND WATERS

For the first three days the weather was delightful. A fine S.E. breeze pushed us along at a good speed. Abercrombie had brought away a lot of fillet of steak, chops, and vegetables, and as he saw to the cooking of these we fared like princes. On the afternoon of the 1st October, however, a change took place in the weather. The barometer did not rise, and at dusk the sky looked full of wind. At midnight it was blowing fairly hard and I had to turn the lads out and get the topsail off and the mizzen stowed. This sufficed for a time, but at 3 a.m. it was clear that we must reef the mainsail. Again the lads had to turn out, and Abercrombie also came on deck to lend a hand. The night was dark, and it was raining and blowing hard. He was not at all used to small ships, and he found moving about the decks an awkward and dangerous business, but he hauled lustily on any rope given him without knowing in the least what was at the other end, and rendered yeoman service. It took one and a half hours of hard work to get the reefs in and the ship once more under way, and by then everyone was, of course, wet to the skin. That sort of thing, however, is part of a seaman's life in a sailing-ship, and no one thinks anything of it.

The wind was strong next day until the afternoon, when it eased for a time and shifted from N.W. to S.W., and then back to N.W. At 7 p.m. it shifted again to west and started to blow in earnest. There was too much wind and the sea was too heavy and confused to make it advisable to sail the ship, and the only thing to do was to heave to and let her dodge quietly along. During the night the wind gradually worked up to the force of a moderate gale and shifted to S.W. Dawn broke on a wild scene. Great white-crested seas came sweeping up, one after the other, full of menace, and the air was thick with spindrift blown off the tops of the waves. The pressure of the wind was extraordinary. It howled in the rigging and, in the squalls which followed each other at shorter and shorter intervals, the sound rose to a scream of diabolical rage. As each sea approached it seemed as if it must come bodily on board and sweep everything off the decks, but the little ship was playing a game which she thoroughly understood, and rose gallantly to meet each onrush, slid down into the trough, and was ready for the next one. Occasionally an irregular wave would catch her on the beam and pour over her in torrents of water, but these had not the weight of the regular seas and were not dangerous. They, however, made things very uncomfortable below, where absolute chaos reigned, as each time one arrived a certain amount of water squirted in through the skylights, or got down the hatches.

Taking sights became more or less of a farce. Spray flew over the ship in continuous sheets and wetted the sextant, and the motion was so violent that I found it a hard matter to wedge myself in anywhere with safety, while huge waves heaved up at short intervals and blotted out the horizon. It was important, however, to fix the ship's position, as we were in the neighbourhood of the dangerous Middleton Reef, which lies about 300 miles from the Australian coast and which has caused the loss of many a stout ship, as has also Elizabeth Reef some way farther south. By sticking to it I eventually got results which I thought were probably about right. These put us 80 miles north of the Middleton Reef, and as we were then heading directly for it, I decided to get on to the other tack, and at noon brought her round to west. There was then not the smallest cause for anxiety on the score of navigation, as there was plenty of sea-room, and the only likelihood of trouble lay in the chance of some of the gear giving way under the tremendous strain placed on it, or of being run down.

It was an unrestful time. A condition of intolerable discomfort reigned below. Everything was wet, and loose articles slithered about or lay in heaps; the chairs fell over; and the cushions shot off the settees. Moving about resolved itself into rushes from one fixed bit of furniture to another. It was difficult to remain seated even, unless wedged in, and we were thrown about in our bunks to such an extent that sleep became impossible. Abercrombie confided in me afterwards that he was convinced that nothing put together by the hands of man could possibly survive the buffeting about the ship was experiencing, but his manner gave not the slightest indication of his thoughts. He sat in the saloon quite his ordinary, cheerful self, swaying to the roll of the ship, with his feet against the legs of the table, and playing hundreds of games of patience. At the back of his mind, however, lay the conviction that sooner or later the mast would go, ropes part, sails blow away, or the hull come to pieces. These thoughts occurred to him as he lay sleepless in his bunk. Quite unintentionally I added to his misgivings by remarking that the ship was behaving magnificently, and that I anticipated no trouble as long as the rudder held. He had thought of everything that might happen, but had overlooked the rudder. My words caused him quite a jar, he told me later, but he gave no sign of this at the time. For a man who was convinced that the ship was in a serious position and unlikely to come safely through his manner was simply wonderful. I had not the slightest idea that he was in any way less confident that all was well than I was.

And still the wind screamed and howled, and great seas, any one of which would have caused the ship to founder if it could only have got on board, swept up relentlessly in an endless procession, and still the gallant little ship, a speck in that great waste of heaving water, fought her way gamely on, buried in spray and flying scud, but unwearied and unscathed.

On the afternoon of the second day the climax of the storm was approaching. One squall followed another at such short intervals as to be almost continuous. The turmoil and uproar on deck and the pressure of the wind almost dazed one. The time had plainly come to reduce sail still further, and we took in the last reef in the mainsail and stowed the staysail. As night drew on I began to doubt whether even the close-reefed mainsail would stand, and prepared to ride to a sea-anchor should it blow away; but at 2 a.m. on the third day the squalls seemed to be getting less frequent. As soon as I was sure that this was so, and that the worst was over, I promptly turned into my bunk, which like everything else below was dripping wet, to get a little sleep. As a matter of fact we were all getting tired. Abercrombie could not sleep, as he was unused to the violent motion and could not give to the sway of the ship, but lay with tense muscles. I could not sleep properly either, though I dozed off from time to time, as I was always listening for the sounds of some fresh development, or scheming ways of carrying on should anything give way. The two lads probably got more rest than either of us. To them the gale, and its attendant discomforts, were merely very unpleasant incidents to be endured as cheerfully as possible. No special sense of responsibility weighed on them, and when they came off duty they took off their wet clothes, turned in, and got what sleep they could. Stéphane, of course, in addition to his turn on deck, had to do the cooking, and rose nobly to the occasion. He always managed to prepare something and would usually burst into the saloon, slap the dish on the table, and then fling himself on to something solid and hold on like grim death. It is a mystery to me how he did any cooking at all, but he never failed to warm up something, while Abercrombie's Stilton and claret rounded off the meals very pleasantly.

Once the centre of the storm had passed, conditions improved fairly fast and we were able to make sail during the morning of the 5th October, after having been hove to for sixty hours. During the whole of that time no one had been at the tiller. The ship had steered herself with the tiller lashed slightly down. By the evening the wind had fallen very light, there was not enough of it to keep the sails quiet and the ship rolled heavily in the confused sea left by the gale.

At noon on the following day the land was, by observation, 45 miles off, and at 4 p.m. we got our first sight of the great Australian Continent, and by 7 p.m. we were near enough to make out the light at Cape Byron. The wind kept light all that night and the following day and night, and we rolled about most of the time without steerage way, drifting south on the strong coast current. Several whales appeared in the distance from time to time. There was a lot of whaling done along the coast at one time, but I believe there is only one station left now. Abercrombie spent hours trying to photograph an albatross on the wing. They are difficult to snap, as they are very fast, but he did get some results.

On the night of the 8th October we fell in with a terrible thunderstorm. I had no idea there could be such thunder and lightning, and Abercrombie, who had spent years in South America where thunderstorms are severe, said that he had never seen anything like it. The flashes were all round us and were practically continuous, and the whole sea was lit up for appreciable periods at a time. I half-expected the ship would be struck. The thunder made her quiver, and every now and then rain came down in torrents. At one moment there would be a flat calm and the next a furious squall. Luckily I had double reefed the mainsail in the afternoon as the barometer was then falling very fast and there was a peculiar look about the sky, a strange haze, and purple clouds hung over the land. The wind shifted continually in the squalls, and I was at the tiller all night, and most uncomfortable it was too, as I was wet through and very cold—a night of torture. In the early morning a frightful uproar and slatting of canvas arose forward. I could not leave the tiller, but shouted to the lads to see what was the matter. They were on deck in a second, but by then the sound had ceased and one of them crawled aft to tell me that the jib had blown away and that the wire topmast fore-stay had parted also. Luckily the topmast stood. I could not leave the tiller, with the wind shifting about as it was doing, to see about repairing the stay, but we managed to fix it up at daylight.

All the next day we had frequent squalls which often obliged me to run before them, as a result of which we were well off the land by dark. The weather then improved and the wind settled down from the west and blew fairly hard. A nasty sea got up and we had a very unpleasant time beating in to the land. It was very cold on deck, and things were uncomfortable below. As a matter of fact in rough weather comfort is unknown in small ships. Things usually get wet, and often one cannot sleep owing to the motion, while the falling about and general unrest are very tiring.

However, our sufferings were nearly over for a time. We were gradually working in to the coast. Land showed up again soon after noon, and by 5 p.m. we were off Norah Head. I stood close in to get smooth water and then came round for the run down the coast. Even under the land the wind was fairly strong and bitterly cold, and though the mainsail was still double reefed the little ship got along very fast and put the covering board in once or twice. There was a full moon that night, a good breeze and smooth water, and it was a delightful sail. I was, however, too tired to appreciate it properly, and, while I dozed in the saloon and the two lads slept for'd, Abercrombie steered and thoroughly enjoyed doing so. "This repays me for much that I have suffered during the trip," he said.

By midnight we were off the famous Heads of Sydney Harbour and stood right across before coming round to beat in. I had no chart of the entrance, but the Navigating Officer of the Government ship *Pioneer*, at Suva, had very kindly made me a tracing, which of course was quite as good, and we worked in without trouble, in spite of the fact that I could not pick out the second leading light through the Heads. At 1 a.m. on the 11th October, 1921, just over one year and one month from England, we anchored in Watson's Bay, in the splendid harbour of Sydney, surely the finest in the world. After seeing all right on deck, I went below.

"Well, George," said Abercrombie, "it has been a great trip. I have led a quiet life and nothing like it has ever happened to me before, and I would not part with the memory of it for a million dollars. But if someone were to come down that ladder and put a million dollars on the table and say that to earn them I must go through it again, I should say, 'No.' My peace of mind is more to me than money."

From this I inferred that he had had enough of cruising in small sailing-ships for the moment. And I do not blame him. Rough weather reduces things to a state of intolerable discomfort in small ships, and makes life a misery.

Next morning the doctor came off, and as soon as he had gone I weighed anchor and made for Rushcutter's Bay under power. The Customs launch and also the Police-launch came to meet us and followed us to the anchorage. While I was filling up the forms in the saloon, nine reporters and photographers came off and I had a fearful time with them. As a matter of fact I was not used to reporters and at first refused to have anything to do with them. They were very insistent, however, and said that the Sydney people were interested in the trip and wanted to know something about it. I therefore gave them a few facts and they made the most of them. It would have been much better if I had been more open with them and not left so much to their imagination. The fault was mine and I must say that, considering how little they had to go on, they treated me with every consideration.

Next day we weighed and went across to Neutral Bay to a buoy which the Royal Sydney Yacht Squadron very kindly placed at my disposal. The wind was fairly fresh, and the engine would hardly drive her against it. However, we did advance, but so slowly that Admiral Dumaresq, who was going off to his ship, thought that we had broken down and came alongside to ask whether we wanted a tow. To have been towed across Sydney harbour by an Admiral would have been a noteworthy finish to the outward trip, and the temptation to accept his very kind offer was great, but I decided that it would not be the thing to do and assured him that we were going ahead and expected to reach the other side eventually.

A few days later the ship went on to Sandeman's slip for examination of the copper. It was found that three sheets had been rubbed when we grounded on Tabu Reef at Nouméa and had to be replaced, but that was all. The felt under the damaged plates had not even been disturbed.

While the ship was on the slip I went with Abercrombie and Dr. Fiaschi to Melbourne to see the Cup Race and backed all the horses with nautical names, but they all let me down. I also went with Mr. McCansh and a party to the wonderful Jenolan Caves in the Blue Mountains, a most delightful trip; visited the National Park with Mr. Allen; and spent a weekend on the Hawkesbury River with Mr. Reeks, and having done these things it became necessary to decide on future plans.

No amateur to join me as a sailing partner was forthcoming, at least none that I knew, though people wrote to me from all parts of Australia asking to be allowed to join. I, however, judged it too risky to start on a long trip with a total stranger, though my last experiment in that direction—the original crew —had been very successful. Complete compatibility, for want of a better word, of temperament is essential in the circumstances. Sam, too, became insistent on getting into a bigger ship, but the fact that he was coloured raised insurmountable difficulties. With no sailing partner to be had, and half the crew anxious to leave, the best way out seemed to be to sell the ship, my original intention, and this I tried to do. A few half-hearted enquiries were made, but only one man was in earnest, and we could not agree over the price. He started from the point of view that a ship forty years old ought to be cheap, while I argued that a good little ship, however old, which had come half-way round the world ought to fetch a fair price. So the matter fell through and I decided to see what could be done in New Zealand, and started on re-fitting the ship for the trip.

While these matters were in progress I was having a delightful time. All the Yacht Clubs in Sydney, and others in different parts of Australia, made me an honorary member during my stay, and I got to know quite a number of people and everyone was extremely kind and hospitable. One of the first men to come on board when I arrived had been ex-Able Seaman A. J. Dawes with whom I had been shipmates in "Q"-ships. He had seen my name in the papers and at once came to see me, arriving at 11 p.m. His visit gave me great pleasure, and he came back next day and we spent hours talking over old times. I remembered that the one thing that had worried him during the War had been the question of how he was to induce the

Admiralty to send a piano which he had bought out to Australia with him when he would be demobilized. Mines, shells, torpedoes and bombs, of which he had had his share, he accepted as part of the game. They did not bother him greatly, but the thought of the difficulties of getting the piano out was a constant worry. I enquired after this piano and learned that by successful strategy—which I must not give away—he had gained his object.

At length, after two very pleasant months, the ship was ready to sail, and I fixed on Saturday, 17th December, 1921, as the day of departure. Sydney is by no means a cheap place for fitting out a ship, owing to short hours and high wages, and I had done what was necessary but no more, and even so had spent a considerable sum. Moreover, by the laws of the Commonwealth, yachts, whatever ensign they may be entitled to fly, are classed as merchant ships and are required to enter and clear at the Customs. It is usual to class yachts flying the White or the Blue Ensign as warships and not merchant ships and to excuse them from Customs formalities, but in Australia only ships actually on Government work are exempted. I had, therefore, to supply a list of all stores on board on my arrival and pay duty on any which had been used while in port. Unluckily I lost the copy of the original list, and when I went to clear the ship got into such difficulties that I had to have recourse to the services of a professional. Mr. George Wall, of Loftus Street, earned my gratitude by taking the matter in hand. After an infinity of trouble he straightened things out. His clerk was running about most of the day, and the final papers came for signature at 10 p.m. on the last evening, but Mr. Wall would not accept a farthing for his services. He was interested in the trip and anxious to help me. Kindness so genuine leaves a deep impression, and when I think of the beautiful harbour of Sydney and of the friends I left in Australia I always think of Mr. Wall and his kind efforts on my behalf.

On the morning of the 17th December we slipped the moorings and made for Watson's Bay under power to be medically examined, shouted farewells from people in Careening Cove cheering us on our way. At that time there was plague in Sydney, and the ship had to be disinfected before leaving. This was done the day before we sailed. The Port Doctor gave us a certificate that we were not suffering from plague, for which I was charged £2 2s. to my great annoyance, and we then hoisted sail and left.

We were all sorry to go. We had been received most cordially, almost enthusiastically, and during our stay had been treated with every kindness and courtesy. The two lads had had the time of their lives. They had been photographed and put on the "Pictures," and they used to go regularly to see themselves on the screen. Stéphane had also taken advantage of the opportunity to learn English and could speak it fairly well by the time we came away, while Sam had on one occasion got royally drunk and had nearly been drowned. He fell into the water twice, and the second time was dug out with an oar with great difficulty by Stéphane and Mr. Taylor. They got him ashore, and as he was violent they tied his feet together and lashed them to a post and sent for me. I had to leave my dinner at the soup stage and go down. Luckily Sam recognized me and a broad smile appeared.

"Ah, here Sir Cap," he said and became quiet.

I took him on board, got him into his bunk and gave him castor-oil and then dined on a tin of sardines. Sam regretted these departed joys and also regretted finding himself committed to another trip, one of over 1,200 miles, in a ship which he thought was too small. So that, in one way or another, we were all sorry to move on.

It was not a pleasant passage, though the weather was fine for the first few days. On the evening of the 22nd December the sky looked very stormy, and we double reefed the mainsail to avoid having to do so in the night. Just after dark the wind got up and we took in the mizzen and lowered the staysail. Rain started at 9 p.m., and lightning flashed at intervals during the night. At dawn next day it started to blow in earnest and the sea was rough. At 7 p.m. we hove to heading about S.E. and so remained until the following morning. It was an unpleasant time, and to make things worse the driving rain kept up and we could not see a quarter of a mile. A sharp look-out had to be kept as we were more or less in the steamer track. The motion became so violent that the lads could not remain seated in the fo'c'sle, and I found Stéphane sitting in the pantry alley-way with his back against the cupboards and his knees against the bulkhead eating his food, while Sam contrived to jamb himself in right in the eyes of the ship. Water for cooking would not remain in the saucepans, but Stéphane managed to fry some sausages and potatoes by holding the frying-pan on the stove, and we dined on these.

At dawn on the following morning the wind had eased and we took out the reefs; but at 11 p.m. that night we had to put them in again as the wind was again very strong. In the darkness and the driving rain, which kept steadily on, to say nothing of the heavy sea, reefing was a very awkward and slow affair, and took two hours, but in the end we got two reefs in and changed the jibs and then let the head sails draw and went on.

At 9 a.m. next day—Christmas Day—we hove to once more, as so much water was coming on board and the motion was so violent that I feared something would carry away. An additional reason was that I had not the heart to send the lads to the tiller. Steering had become pure torture. Spray was flying over the ship in sheets, and that, added to the incessant rain, meant that whoever was at the tiller became wet to the skin in a few minutes. At that stage of the trip neither of them had a dry stitch left to put on, and I decided that the game was not worth the candle and that we should be better hove to. It was not a Christmas Day to be remembered with pleasure. Everything below was damp, and the air was so full of moisture from the incessant rain that matches would not strike. However, we did succeed in lighting a stove and drying a few boxes and setting fire to one or two of them in the process. Beads of condensation formed on the beams and trickled down the panels, and in the spare cabin was a heap, about a foot high, of wet clothes which I had cast off. In due course Stéphane applied himself to the task of preparing the Christmas dinner, but the conditions were not favourable for a display of his talents as a chef, and I think he did very well to fry some potatoes. The menu consisted of:

> Bully beef au naturel
> Pommes de terre frites au beurre
> Pain moisi
> Fromage
> Fruits divers

As I partook of this frugal repast in solitary state I remembered with regret the pleasant Christmas Day I had spent in Grenada the previous year, and marvelled at my folly.

"Here I am," I reflected, "somewhere in the Tasman Sea, though exactly where I do not know, as I have not had any sights for the last few days, hove to in a strong wind and heavy sea, with driving rain thrown in, liable to be run down by a steamer at any moment, the deck practically untenable and conditions below not much better, my bunk wet with spray which has come in through the skylight, no chance of a decent meal even and no one to talk to. Why on earth do I do this sort of thing?" I do not know the answer to the question, unless it is that I like doing it, but why I should is the mystery.

In the afternoon the wind eased up somewhat and we started sailing again. The rain continued and we got wet to the skin each watch in spite of oilskins. The conditions remained about the same all that day, but after dark on the following day the wind eased still more and there were moments when it did not rain, but the sea kept up and the ship rolled heavily all night with the boom swinging about, in spite of tackles to hold it steady, and fetching up with a sickening jerk which made the ship quiver. A most uncomfortable night.

Dawn broke with the promise of better things. For one thing the rain stopped and at 10 a.m. the sun showed up. We took advantage of this to dry our wet clothes. I had seven pairs of trousers hanging up as a start, and the lads had out their entire wardrobes. But the first thing I did when the sun appeared was to get a sight for longitude. I knew that we were nearing the land and had been getting rather anxious about the position, as the incessant rain had prevented me from getting any sights for several days, and I did not know where we had been blown to during all the bad weather. At noon a thick fog came on for an hour and prevented me from taking the meridian altitude, but I got a doubtful sight at 1 p.m., which with the earlier one indicated approximately where the ship was.

The wind remained light all that day and all the next until the afternoon, when the Three Kings group of islands showed up indistinctly through the mist. The wind then died right away and left us rolling about in a slight swell. According to the Sailing Directions it is not advisable for sailing-ships, unless with a commanding breeze, to pass between the Three Kings and the mainland on account of the strong currents and tide rips. The proper thing is to pass about 6 miles outside them. That was what I was trying to do, but the total absence of wind rather defeated me. The afternoon drew on and night came and still no wind. I was up all night as I did not care to leave the ship drifting about in strong currents so near an unlighted group of islands and rocks. Why there is no light is not easy to understand, as they are very much in the track of vessels from the westward and there has been at least one disastrous wreck on them. It is true that the Authorities have got as far as putting a food depot on one of the islands, so that any shipwrecked survivors who may be lucky enough to reach that particular island will not starve, but a light which would probably save them from going ashore would be more to the point.

At midnight the sound as of surf on a beach could be heard and we were soon jumping about in that uncanny affair, a tide rip. After a time I could stand the racket no longer, and started the engine and got out with its help. It would have been better if I had started it before, but at that time I never used it at sea. Later on I became less scrupulous and used it whenever the ship lost steerage way in calms.

The calm, a flat calm with not an air stirring, persisted all the next day and I kept the engine running until the following morning, when a very light air came from the S.E. We were then passing along the east side of the North Island of New

Zealand. The land is hilly, and rather bare of trees, but looks very picturesque from the sea, while the coast line is broken up into a number of delightful little inlets and harbours.

At dark on the 31st December we had passed the Maro Tiri Islands and entered the wonderful Hauraki Gulf, which must be the finest cruising ground in the world, and next morning were off Tiri Tiri Matangi Island and heading for the Rangitoto Channel leading to Auckland Harbour. It was a lovely, sunny morning, and as we sailed along before a nice N.N.E. breeze several small yachts came by from time to time and asked us where we were from and wished us a Happy New Year, a graceful little courtesy which was very pleasing, and a foretaste of the welcome which was extended to us. As a matter of fact reaching Auckland was very much like getting home, partly because I met again a number of men whom I had known during the War—amongst them Messrs. T. Alexander, B. W. Beaumont, J. C. Hewson, C. H. T. Palmer, S. Reed—and partly because every one was so very kind. A high official, for instance, assured me that the resources of the harbour were at my disposal, and the Customs, by virtue of the Blue Ensign, excused me from all Customs formalities. Moreover, a berth was always found for me alongside the wharves, whenever I wanted to go there, which, as a matter of fact, was not often, as I found that the ship attracted an amount of attention which was embarrassing, and that it was more peaceful to lie anchored off. I also was delighted to meet again Mr. H. H. Hemus, whom I had first met at Tahiti, at whose house I was always welcome, while Mr. Ernest Davis and his family were kindness itself. I mention a few names at random, but the list could be extended considerably. I was also elected an honorary member of the Royal New Zealand Yacht Squadron and of the other Clubs in the town. In short, at Auckland, as at Sydney, all that could be done was done to make my stay pleasant.

The underlying motive of my visit, however, was the sale of the ship, and I let this be known, but as no results followed I advertised her in Christchurch, Dunedin, Nelson, and Wellington papers, without, however, getting as much as a nibble. It became clear that she was unsaleable, not being of the type that anyone wanted. Only two courses remained open, viz., to spend the rest of my days in New Zealand, using the ship as a house-boat: or to take her home again. It is a very much more simple matter to take a sailing-ship from England to the Antipodes than it is to reverse the process and take one from Australasia to England. In the first case fair winds across the Atlantic, the North East Trades, can be relied on once the latitude of about 25° N. is reached, and in the same way the South East Trades, though not quite so constant, will, broadly speaking, take one across the Pacific. But on the homeward passage things are very different, and whichever route is followed a fair amount of head wind will almost surely be met. Still, after studying all the information available, it seemed a possible though not an easy thing to do, and I decided to have a shot at it and started to make the necessary arrangements.

There were three possible routes, eastwards round Cape Horn; or westwards round the north of Australia and then by the Cape of Good Hope; or by the Islands to Java, Singapore, Malacca Strait, Indian Ocean, and so to the Mediterranean by way of the Red Sea. The first was not attractive. The second promised plenty of sailing, but very few places of interest or even harbours, and I decided in favour of the third, which took me along some extremely interesting coasts, but had the disadvantage of probable head winds in the Red and Mediterranean Seas. Head winds, and the sea which goes with wind, are, it is perhaps hardly necessary to remark, a great handicap to small vessels, and progress is always very slow. Working to windward for long distances is a heart-breaking, tiring business. However, I decided to go round by the Java route, and chance my luck as to winds. The next thing was to get the charts required. The ones I brought from England only went as far as Australia and New Zealand. I was amazed on going into the matter to find that several of the islands I proposed to visit around the New Hebrides had not been surveyed and that no charts of them exist, while others have only been partly surveyed. This was a bit of a jar, and the remark of a friend: "Why all this moan about charts? What charts had Cook?" did not greatly comfort me.

The next shock I got came from the Sailing Directions, which have the poorest possible opinion of the natives in the New Hebrides and Solomon groups, describe them as a blood-thirsty, treacherous crowd and recommend extreme caution in dealing with them, especially in the case of small ships' companies. I made enquiries, but could not get any definite information until I met Capt. Burgess of the Mission steamer *Southern Cross*. He laughed the description to scorn and said it was out of date and that the coast natives were all friendly in the islands I meant to visit, though perhaps the bushmen in some of them were not altogether reliable. He surprised me by saying that I should not be allowed to visit any parts of New Caledonia, nor the Loyalty Islands, without first going to Nouméa; none of the New Hebrides, Banks, or Reef Islands without entering at Vila; and none of the Torres, Santa Cruz, or Solomon groups without reporting at Tulagi. In my inno-cence I had imagined that a happy-go-lucky state of affairs existed in the islands of the Western Pacific, the least civilized part of the world to-day, and that I could blow in anywhere without asking anyone's leave; but not so, it appeared. Every vessel must first go to the Port of Entry before moving about in any group. The reason for this is that the various authorities fear the introduction of diseases which are fatal to the natives, and wish to satisfy themselves that ships have clean Bills of Health and are free from sickness before they visit the islands. It is really quite a wise regulation, though it upset my plans considerably.

I wrote to the High Commissioner for the Western Pacific at Fiji for permission to visit the New Hebrides, Banks, Torres, and Solomon groups, and to the French authorities in Nouméa for permission to visit New Caledonia and the Loyalties without first clearing at the entering ports. The former sent a refusal. The latter replied that I might visit New Caledonia and the Isle of Pines, if the French Consul at Auckland would certify that town as free from sickness. This was really a clever way of saying "No," as the Consul, from an admirable sense of self-preservation, flatly refused to do anything of the kind, which they knew he would do. These refusals cut out the Isle of

Pines and some of the Loyalties, Tucopia, the Santa Cruz and the Reef groups, and all islands east of Tulagi in the Solomons. It was disappointing, but there it was and I had to make the best of it.

The next thing was to fix up something for Sam. The simplest way out of the difficulty was to send him home, but he did not want to go there. He wanted to remain in New Zealand. Unluckily he came into the class of prohibited immigrants, and all sorts of difficulties arose. However, after a great deal of trouble I managed to get him admitted, though he very nearly came down over some of the questions asked. One of them was very blunt.

"Are you an anarchist?"

The simple-minded Sam had never heard of an anarchist, but he judged from the expression on my face that the answer was in the negative, and replied stoutly: "No."

The next question nearly undid him.

"Are you in favour of upsetting constitutional Government by force or violence?"

This time he made a bad shot. Of course he did not understand a single word and had no sort of idea of what was demanded.

He saw me smile, and replied: "Yes, I t'ink so."

After his papers had gone in and while his fate was in the balance, an event occurred which nearly ended his mortal career, and would have quite done so if his neck had been a bit longer, and his head not so solidly fixed on his shoulders. I had taken the ship over to Devonport Wharf to scrub the hull, and after this had been done, and while she lay secured alongside waiting for the water to rise, Sam went ashore for cigarettes. He came back filled up with beer by the mistaken kindness of a resident. It occurred to him that a bathe would be refreshing, and he dived from a height of 18 feet into 6 inches of water. His hands saved him to some extent, but he landed with a dreadful jar on his forehead. Stéphane came running to tell me, and I dashed round on to the beach expecting to find him dead. Not a bit of it, however. His forehead and nose were cut and bleeding freely, but he was conscious and able to walk back to the ship after a few minutes. For the rest of the day he was more or less dazed, but in the morning had recovered, except for the cuts.

A week or so later his papers came through and I paid him off. A friend took him into his employ, and when I last heard of him he was milking cows. I must say that I was glad to see the last of him. He had been rather a trial in one way and another, and was always a source of anxiety when in port. Stéphane was also very glad when he went. They had not hit it off very well together.

The next thing, once Sam was comfortably fixed up ashore, was to find someone to replace him. I made enquiries at the Shipping Office, but could not come across a suitable man who was used to sails, though any number of steamer men were available. Captain Burgess offered me a Reef Islander, Tommy, provided that I undertook to leave him at one of the islands where Captain Burgess could pick him up later on and return him to his own island. I saw Tommy, a likely looking Melanesian, who was very shy, but who said he would like to go. Next week, however, he changed his mind and said that he did not want to go. These natives like to be with their friends. The idea of being the only one of his tribe in a strange ship alarmed him, and he backed out. Then Captain Daniels of the Shipping Office found me a Niue Islander, Pinimaka, called Joe for short, a splendid specimen of a man, very much like a Maori in appearance. He was a fine seaman, as strong as a horse, and always willing and cheerful. He was also good at rope and canvas work and was a great acquisition. With Joe and Stéphane I had sufficient crew to handle the ship, though it was very hard work at times for three, and I turned my attention to trying to find a companion to bring the number on board up to four and make things comparatively easy. Various people applied, but I did not pursue the matter with any of them, as few, if any, were familiar with sails. As I did not intend to leave New Zealand before the end of April there was no special reason for hurry and I let things take their course and filled in the time very pleasantly by short cruises with friends in that magnificent stretch of water, the Hauraki Gulf, and up the east coast as far as Whangaroa. I also wandered about the harbour on one or two occasions in search of shelter. It is a fine harbour for big ships, but, at the moment, very inconvenient for small craft, as there are no little nooks or creeks in which to anchor. A small boat harbour is being built, but, as the ship draws 10 feet, we had to anchor out in the stream. Most of the time the anchorage was quite comfortable as the prevailing wind is from the south-west, but occasionally a strong easterly set in, and then we had to clear out and go across to the north shore for shelter.

New Zealand is a very pleasant place, and the only adverse remarks I have to make are that there are not enough trees on the land and not enough shelter in Auckland Harbour for small vessels. But for Hauraki Gulf there can be nothing but praise. As a cruising ground it must be unequalled in the world. It is of great extent, over 1,000 square miles, nearly all sheltered, deep water, teeming with fish and fringed with delightful little bays and coves giving sheltered anchorage. Thrice blessed are the Aucklanders to have such a sheet of water at their very doors, and they fully realize this and take advantage of the position. Every week-end the Gulf is dotted with small yachts of all sorts and sizes, dinghies, and launches.

There is a small extinct volcano just outside Auckland, Mount Eden, about 640 feet high, from which a splendid view of the surrounding country and of parts of the Gulf can be had. One can look right across the island to the sea on the west coast. It is the only point of view from which Auckland looks well. It is a fine city with good streets, parks, and excellent shops, but seen from anywhere except Mount Eden it is not beautiful. There are too many gaunt, square buildings. Of course I had to visit Rotorua, a flying visit which must have established a record for speed. Mr. E. Davis very kindly telegraphed to one of his managers there a programme which enabled me to see as much as was possible in the time. This programme was carried out to the letter, and on arrival in the afternoon about 5 p.m. Mr. Marsh met me, or rather us, as Mr. Montgomery went up with me, put us in a car and drove us round until dinner-time. In the course of the drive we saw some Maoris cooking over a geyser, and there is another place where it is possible to catch a trout in a stream and without moving from the spot cook it in a neighbouring pool of boiling water. After dinner we had a sulphur bath and then went to bed. Next morning we were dug out at an early hour and driven round to Woka, taken back for breakfast, and I returned in the 9 a.m. train to Auckland. It was rather a rush, but it is an interesting and impressive place, and I am very glad I went. For anyone who likes desolation, boiling geysers and mudholes, and the fumes of sulphur it is an ideal spot.

About this time Mr. C. R. Tadgell of Melbourne wrote for the second time to ask whether I proposed to sail back to England and if so whether I would take him. He was twenty-five years old and had done a good deal of racing in dinghies and metre boats, but had not cruised. He claimed to have an intense love of the sea—which possibly has waned a bit by now—and to have long cherished the ambition of taking a long cruise in a small vessel. I had not, of course, met him, but the fact that he had spent most of his leisure racing was in his favour, and I decided to risk it, stipulating, however, that if he were not comfortable on board he could leave at any port and that if I wished him to leave the ship I could land him at any spot from which it would be possible to return to Australia. It was a great risk, shipping a total stranger, but once again Fortune favoured me, and I could hardly have found a more suitable and agreeable companion. He came across on the 11th April, bringing with him about eighty charts supplied by the Navy Office in Melbourne. I was still, however, about twenty short, and in the end borrowed some of these from H.M.S. *Philomel* at Auckland. The others I had to do without.

Tadgell's arrival completed the ship's company, and we applied ourselves to getting in stores, overhauling the gear and making ready to start at the end of the month, when the hurricanes would be over in the Islands. I also had a steering-wheel fitted in place of the tiller. This was done for me by Mr. C. Bailey at cost price. As a matter of fact, at Auckland most of the work done was charged for at specially low rates and all the food stores at wholesale prices, so interested were people in the trip, and ready to show goodwill.

On the 30th April we left Auckland for Kawau, there to scrub the hull. Mr. Davis came with us part of the way, and then transferred to his yacht the *Viking*. He brought nuts, pies, and *crème de menthe*, while Mr. Hemus gave us a case of apples and some bananas, and a passing yacht threw a big watermelon on board; so we left laden with presents and amid a chorus of good wishes. My delightful stay in Auckland had ended, and though the thought that the ship was homeward bound was very stimulating and pleasant, yet I left with regret many good friends behind.

We reached Kawau after dark, and next day scrubbed the hull alongside the little wharf, and the following day reached Whangarei, again after dark. On the way in an incident happened which nearly had serious results. Tadgell was steering, and I was directing him from forward. The anchorage is round Home Point. As soon as I could make it out in the dark I told him to alter course two points. I noticed that the ship had swung several more points and was heading straight for the rocks, and on rushing aft found him struggling with the rudder lines which had got over the end of the drum and jambed round the axle. I lent a hand, but found it hopeless to put right in time and so cut the lines, and put the stump of the tiller hard down by hand. She just came round clear. We were right up to the rocks.

Next morning we were off again, after arranging the rudder lines so that they could not get off the drum, and proceeded up the coast towards Whangaroa, passing the beautiful Bay of Islands on the way. It is an historic bay, since it was there that the first European settler, a missionary, landed in 1814. Port Russell, the first capital, is also there, and Waitangi, where the native chiefs signed the Treaty of 1840 giving the sovereignty of the Islands to Great Britain. The inhabitants show with pride the spot where the first ship was built and launched, and where the first printing-press was erected. It is also a great place for big fish: kingfish, swordfish, and sharks, running into hundreds of pounds' weight. These are caught on the rod. They are all great fighters, and it usually takes hours to land them. People go all the way out there from home every year simply for the fishing.

Next morning we entered the excellent harbour of Whangaroa. The entrance is narrow—least width 200 yards—and lies between two high heads. It is sheltered from every wind and, with its bays and islands and surrounding hills, is very beautiful.

I meant to fill up with fresh stores there, but was only able to raise one loaf, no butter, cheese, or eggs. However, we filled up with water and left the next afternoon, though it was Friday. Whether this last was in any way connected with the bad weather we had on leaving is a matter of opinion, but Stéphane is firmly convinced that it was, and, moreover, attributes to it the breakage of two lamp chimneys that night. However that may be, we certainly did have an unpleasant passage. I meant to look in at Norfolk Island and get some fruit, but the wind came ahead at the very start, and we finally were set so far to the eastward that we had to give up the idea and go on to Nouméa. For the first few days the wind was light and variable, but usually somewhere ahead, and the sky overcast with a good deal of rain at times. On the evening of the sixth day out it began to breeze up and rain heavily, and no one got much sleep, as we were all out at intervals during the night getting first one and then another sail off. At dawn next day we double reefed the mainsail and changed to a smaller jib. Joe was very pleased with the ship and said he thought she was better than big schooners, which would have been hove to that day instead of sailing, as we were. I doubt whether he was right there. If we could sail, a schooner certainly could. At dark the wind eased up somewhat, but left a cruel sea behind in which we tumbled and pitched about in a very distressing way. At dawn we took out the reefs, but had to put them in again in the late afternoon, as the wind came harder than ever. At 6 p.m. we hove to and so remained all night. The wind was strong, the sea heavy, and it rained hard, while lightning was flashing all round; in fact everything was wrong. I remained up during Stéphane's watch, as he was rather too inexperienced to leave quite alone.

At intervals next day we had heavy rain squalls, but the wind fell right away soon after dawn and we rolled about without steerage way. This was bad, but much worse was the fact that it was not possible to get sights of anything to fix the ship. As we were near the reefs which extend off the south-east end of New Caledonia for upwards of 40 miles, it was most important to know where the ship was, but with a heavily overcast sky I could not get as much as a glimpse of the sun. All that day we lay stopped, and all the night. Of course it would have been possible to keep her moving along with the engine, but I disliked using it at sea. As a matter of fact I disliked having anything to do with it at all, although it was impossible to deny its extreme utility at times. When it was arranged that Tadgell should join I had hoped to be able to make him engineer and hand the thing over to him to look after. I argued that a young Australian would have ridden motor-bicycles and driven cars and would know a lot about internal-combustion engines, but when he arrived he disclaimed all knowledge of the subject. His forte was not mechanics. This was a great blow, as it meant that I should have to remain engineer. I tried to interest Joe in the matter, but he said, "No good, I no savvy this fella." No doubt if I had put the matter definitely to Tadgell he would have done his best, as he invariably threw himself heart and soul into anything I asked him to do. Even if he were turned out three or four times during his watch below it made no difference. Without a single exception he was always willing and cheerful. But he never offered to do anything. At first sight this seemed extraordinary, but it really was a very wise policy, and it is solely owing to the fact that he stuck to it throughout that we never had any friction. It seems simple, but is really profound. If I wanted anything done I had only to say so and he did it to the very best of his ability, but unless I asked him he held back, and did not thrust himself forward.

On the following morning a light air came from the N.N.W., a most unusual quarter, as the S.E. Trade should have been in full swing, and at 10 p.m. the sun showed through the clouds for a few minutes and I got a sight which, with another one I got later, seemed to put us ten miles from the edge of the reef. We headed in and soon afterwards sighted the wreck of a steamer standing up plain and distinct on the coral. This confirmed the position by observation, and we could work up to the westward with some confidence. Next morning Amédée Lighthouse showed up, and by 10 a.m. we had it on the right bearing and ran in through Bulari Pass, with a strong following wind from the N.W. which sent a heavy sea on to the coral. As the waves reached the shoal water they reared up, curled over, and broke on the reef with a roar in a welter of white foam, and with a suggestion of irresistible power. It was an awe-inspiring sight, and a beautiful one. The blue of the seas changed to a multitude of tints as they broke, while rainbows showed in the spindrift blown off the tops. In the gap through which we passed, with great seas thundering on either hand, there was no broken water, but a big swell ran in. As the waves overtook us, up would go the stern and the ship rushed forward, then down would sink the stern and the bows rose up. It was a most exhilarating time. We felt we really were alive.

CHAPTER V

THE WESTERN PACIFIC

In the early afternoon we anchored off the quay in Nouméa Harbour after an unpleasant trip of eleven days from Whangaroa, during which we had had every kind of weather from calms to strong winds, a great deal of rain, and all the time a heavy sea. It was quite a relief to be in and feel the ship lying quietly at anchor. Tadgell had never before made a long trip in a small ship. It would not have surprised me to see him sprinting up the street, making a bee-line for the hills; but as a matter of fact he claimed to have enjoyed the novelty of it all.

We remained at Nouméa for a week doing work on board, and trying to arrange for permission to visit Ile Maré and Lifu.

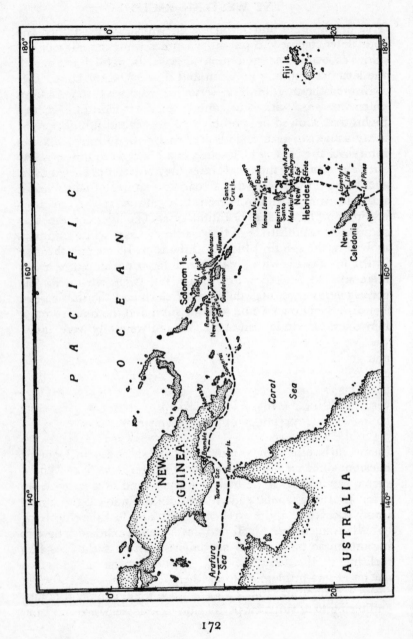

The former was quite out of the question it seemed, as it is a spot to which political prisoners are sent, and no ships are allowed to touch there, but the Governor gave permission for the latter island.

Nouméa struck me on this my second visit much as it had on the first, as a depressing, dirty, squalid, little out-at-elbows town, and I was glad to leave it. Joe was also glad to get away as he had gone ashore, had too much to drink, and got into trouble with the police, who had beaten him mercilessly with the whips they carry. He is an extremely powerful man, and it took quite a number of them to run him in. As he did not return that night, I went ashore next morning in search of him, and the first place I went to, naturally, was the police-station. I told them that one of my men was missing. As soon as I began to speak a frightful hammering and uproar arose in the back premises. It was Joe in his cell clamouring to be released. He heard my voice and judged the moment had come for a demonstration. They telephoned to the Chief of Police, and he agreed to release Joe if I undertook to bring him to the Parquet next day. The gendarmes at the Station were very philosophic over the affair, and said that to go ashore and get drunk was "un peu la vie de matelot," but the people at the Parquet referred to the incident as a "révolution." His trial was to come on two days after I intended to sail, but they very kindly agreed to let me take him away on depositing 50 frs, in order not to cause me any inconvenience.

On the 24th May we weighed and left the harbour after the usual police search for escaped convicts. The two gendarmes questioned me very closely as to my reasons for sailing about in such a small ship. They would hardly believe that I was doing it for amusement, and seemed to think that I had something up my sleeve.

"What an expense!" they said. "What an expense!" Spending money to be intensely uncomfortable struck them as very foolish.

The expanse of water outside Nouméa, but inside the great reefs, is a nightmare from the point of view of pilotage. The Sailing Directions describe it as "rock and reef strewn," and that is the fact. The greatest care and constant watchfulness are necessary to pass safely through, especially as the tidal streams are strong. In the Woodin Channel, between Uen Island and the mainland, they run at 5 knots, and as the flood was rushing through by the time we got there we had to make for Uie Bay just to the northward and anchor for the night. Next morning we got through on the ebb, passing Jack London's old ship, the *Snark*—now a trading-vessel—on the way. The water east of Uen is sprinkled with reefs, but the channel out through the Havannah Pass is fairly clear.

Joe, however, did not think much of it and said: "This bad place. This place no good at night."

To the south of the Pass in the midst of a mass of reef is the spot where Cook anchored in 1774. It is still called "Cook's Anchorage," but how he got his unhandy ships in there, and out again, is a mystery.

After passing Ioro Reef, on which the sea was breaking, we kept on the line of leading marks towards the Pass, leaving Kie Bank to starboard, and Toemo Island to port. The Sailing Directions take a gloomy view of the tide rips in the Pass and say that steamers can only be handled at high speeds, while small vessels must batten down. A note on the French chart was rather more cheerful, though it states that the ebb "y fait souvent briser la mer au milieu de l'entrée." However, "L'alignement indiqué sur Ndoua rassurera le navigateur sur cette fausse apparence de récifs." And I needed some re-assurance when we came to the line of breaking seas right across the channel.

Joe was steering and he stood up and shouted rapidly: "What this? What this?"

He thought he was about to be cast ashore on a reef. Steep, breaking seas rose up in all directions and rushed around, colliding with each other, and causing a fearful turmoil. The ship leaped about, the sails flapped, and the booms lifted and fell with sickening jars. A tide rip is a most uncanny, nerve-shattering business, and I was very glad when we finally tore ourselves clear.

Ahead of us, 60 miles away, lay Ile Maré, but that was out

of bounds, and we headed for Lifu to the north-west. During the night it fell calm, and heavy rain came on at intervals. It was an uncomfortable night, relieved by one amusing incident. At supper-time that night the two hands were both forward warming up some meat over a Primus stove. This type of stove shares the peculiarity with motor-engines that while those in the immediate neighbourhood can only hear each other with difficulty, others farther off can hear them quite plainly. The door into the saloon was open and I heard Stéphane say to Joe:

"Don't give them all the best pieces."

Thereupon I went in and warned them that if they had anything private to say to each other they must not shout it near a Primus in full blast, as people at a distance could hear. In the circumstances they thought it best to send all the food in without keeping out their portion as usual. We did not know this and ate most of it, and as a result they went very short, which was really a just punishment, though it was rather hard lines on them.

At dawn next morning Lifu was in sight, but the wind was very light, and as I wanted to get to the anchorage in Shepenehe Bay before dark I started the engine. Neither Lifu nor any of the Loyalty Islands have been properly surveyed and the Directions state that "their positions, forms and dimensions, as shown on the charts now in use, leave much to be desired." This is not very comforting to a navigator, as it means not only that he may bump an uncharted rock at any moment, but that he cannot make use of the bearings of objects on shore for fixing the position of the ship. However, we passed Cape Deflotte and Lefèvre Point safely and stood on into Sandal Bay. Nearly in the centre is Shelter Reef, and as we did not know its exact position, nor our own for that matter, Tadgell went up to the cross-trees to look for it. He could see discoloured water away to starboard, but nothing ahead, and we eventually got across the Bay without sighting any other reef, and anchored in the position recommended in the Directions. We were delighted with the beauty of the surroundings. A small yawl near us was dressed in flags, and had a

175

large number of natives on board, while more were being ferried off from the landing all the time. They were singing most tunefully, as were also the crowd on shore waiting to go on board. On a sloping bit of land a cricket match was in progress with quite forty men in the field. It was evidently a fête of some sort and it presented a gay and animated scene.

Next morning we landed, and the first man we met was Goa, the diver who had gone down to examine the copper at Nouméa after I had grounded on Tabu Reef the previous September. He wore only a lava-lava, or loin-cloth, which suited his splendid body a great deal better than the singlet and trousers he wore at Nouméa. He was all smiles, and shook hands, and then took us to the Administrateur with whom we left our *permis* to visit the island, and we afterwards went in search of a Mr. Chitty to whom we had a letter of intro-duction. He took us for a walk through the village, which, as a matter of fact, was invisible until one climbed the coral walls which bordered the street and walked through the cocoa-nut plantations. In amongst the trees were leaf huts here and there which formed the village. I changed a film in one of the huts, sitting on mats on the floor to do so. The entrance was very low and the interior dark. There was no furniture beyond cooking-pots and mats. The owner was smoking fish over a log fire in the centre. He smiled indulgently while I opened the camera and put in a new film as if I were a child with a toy.

The fine physique of the natives we met was very striking. The men wear lava-lavas, and the women a long gown. As they are of Polynesian descent they are a laughing, cheery lot and take life light-heartedly. After inspecting the village and photographing groups of natives we went with Mr. Chitty to his house, where he showed us a photo in a New Zealand paper of the *Amaryllis* leaving Auckland Harbour. As we had come from there with little delay, this seemed to argue a good postal service, but he said that they only received mails once a month. It just happened that the paper got there first. Mr. Chitty gave us a lot of fruit, cocoanuts, paw-paws, oranges, and custard apples, and the Administrateur and his little son paid us a visit and brought tomatoes and yams.

Next morning we started getting under way, but found the cable or anchor foul of the coral. We tugged and strained at the capstan without getting an inch. Two little boys came by in a catamaran canoe, and we asked them if they could dive and clear the cable. They said that the water was too deep for them, 42 feet, but that there were plenty of men ashore who could go down, and they went off to fetch some of them. While they were away we started the engine and succeeded in clearing the chain by slacking it up and going astern on the engine. We then hoisted sail and left for Efate Island in the New Hebrides, giving Iatio Point a wide berth, as Mr. Chitty had told us that there is an uncharted reef about two miles south of it. It was not a nice passage. Heavy rain came on soon after the start and blotted out the beautiful island, and the wind became so strong that we had to reduce sail. What with rain storms, grey skies, a strong wind and heavy sea, conditions on board were very uncomfortable, and we were not feeling particularly cheerful. My lamp had taken a header into my bunk, in spite of clips to hold it in position, and had emptied its paraffin all over the bedclothes, which still further depressed me. And then Stéphane came along all smiles and announced that the ship was half-full of water, which was showing over the boards in the cabin. He liked these little excitements and he liked things to break, but best of all he liked breaking them himself, while throwing things over the side was always a great joy to him. This peculiarity of his was only, I believe, a form of expression of his natural youthful spirits which could not find vent in any other way. As a matter of fact a small ship making long passages is not the right place for a boy, as he has no companion of his own age and can seldom get ashore to play games, while the exhibition of high spirits on board is usually sternly repressed. Anything out of the ordinary, any little excitement therefore pleased Stéphane immensely, especially if he could make a lot of noise in helping to put things right. The fact that we were fifty miles from land and that the ship was half-full of water did not alarm him in the least. On the contrary, he thought it a splendid and most amusing affair, and he was probably disappointed when I spotted the cause at once. The bilge pipe discharges under water and when she is heeled over on the starboard tack sea-water rushes up and would get into the pump chamber and back past the valve if a plug were not fitted to the inboard-end of the pipe. On the occasion in question this plug had washed out, and the water was pouring in and getting down into the bilges. We hove to and rigged the pump. It soon choked however, and we had to get up the boards and grovel about amongst the pigs of ballast in water up to the arm-pit to get at the suction end and clear it. The ship was soon freed of water and we went on once more, but an hour later had to heave to again and double reef the main-sail, as the wind was strong. Rain came driving along in sheets while the work was in progress and we all got wet to the skin. Once more we went on, but at midnight the sea was so heavy that sleep was impossible for everyone, and we hove to for the rest of the night. It is most important to let the crew have proper rest on a long trip, even if some progress is sacrificed. Anything may happen at sea with worn-out men.

In the morning we were able to sail once more, and next day sighted Efate Island ahead. We were rather too far to the westward. I had allowed 40 miles west-going current, but this was hardly enough, or else we had made more leeway than I expected owing to the heavy beam sea. Anyway we had to work up to windward for a few miles to make Meli Bay. By 7 p.m. we were off Pango Point, on which is one of the very few lighthouses in the Pacific Islands. It was erected as a War Memorial, an excellent idea on someone's part. In addition to the light on Pango Point there are two leading lights up the harbour to clear the reefs off Fila Island and Malapoa Point. The wind gradually tailed off, and inside Meli Bay fell flat calm. We lowered the sails and proceeded under what we called "power." But where were the leading lights? The lights in houses in the village were visible, but not a sign of the two red lights shown on the chart, which were stated to be visible for 9 miles. They certainly ought to have been in sight, as we could not possibly be more than 4 miles away. I got the village lights on to a bearing which led in between the reefs and made towards them with a good deal of misgiving. The proper and seaman-like thing to do would have been to go to sea again, but the sails were stowed, and, moreover, there was no wind and I decided to stand on a bit nearer. On and on we went, but no red lights showed up until we had long passed the reefs and were within a mile of the anchorage, and then a faint red glow appeared and later on a second one. For 9 mile-lights they could not be called good. We passed a small steamer at anchor loading copra, judging by the smell, and probably cockroaches as well, and anchored near another one closer inshore.

The dawn showed us lying in a scene of fairy-like beauty. Everything looked dainty and pretty. The main island reared itself up in irregular peaks covered with dense vegetation. Near the beach the roofs of houses appeared dotted about amongst the graceful cocoanut-trees, with the Condominion Court House and French Residency standing out boldly on higher ground. To the south were Iririki Island crowned by the British Residency surrounded by trees—the most beautiful spot in a beautiful picture—and Fila Island with its native village, while to the west lay the entrance channel showing blue in the rising sun. The water was so clear that the anchor and cable could be plainly seen 30 feet down, and we could also see the bottom for about 30 yards all round. A small white steam-yacht lay near, with the captain parading his quarter deck in pyjamas, and sipping at a cup of coffee. Later on, clad in an immaculate white uniform, he had himself rowed over and introduced himself as Commander L. R. Barrett, R.N.R., of H.M. Yacht *Euphrosyne*. He warned us not to go ashore until the doctor had been, as all the New Hebrides are under the Condominion, or dual control of England and France, leaving us to infer the reason for caution. Each country has its own Resident Commissioner and judge, while the Court is presided over by a Spanish referee. It is a most complicated and un-workable scheme, and the Condominion is known locally as the "Pandemonium." Enterprise languishes under its blighting influence, but the turbulent section of the natives, such as the bushmen of Malekula and Santo Islands, rejoice in the impotence of the alleged Government.

Presently Dr. Davis arrived full of apologies for the delay in his appearance. It seems that four different people had telephoned that there was a strange craft in the harbour demanding his presence, and he began to think he was in fault, but we reassured him. After his departure Commander Barrett came over, and we all went ashore together to call on the British Commissioner, Mr. M. King, who has been at his post for twelve years without leave.

We landed at a small stone pier, where splendid natives clad in lava-lavas were handling bags of copra, and on reaching the end stepped into the main street, which is actually a narrow path along the beach, with the Post Office, and a few stores, and houses dotted along it. The sound of galloping became audible, and presently a saddled but riderless horse dashed into view. The Commander stepped into the middle of the path and extended his arms. The horse recognized in him a formidable obstacle and turned off into a side-path up a slope, where he was ultimately captured by a native. His rider was farther back along the road, picking himself out of a bush into which he had been thrown.

Mr. King received us very kindly, as did the other Britishers in the settlement, and we were asked out to lunch and dinner several times. Commander Barrett was kindness itself, and we looked on the *Euphrosyne* as a home. On the 3rd June, the King's Birthday, all the vessels in the harbour got out their flags and "dressed ship," and we were invited up to the Residency to drink the King's health in excellent champagne. Quite unintentionally Tadgell and I threw the guard of honour of native police there into considerable confusion. We went up in company with the Commander, who was in full uniform and sword. On our approach bugles blew and the guard presented arms. We took this to be in honour of the Commander and hung back while he walked in. Everyone, however, it transpired, got a salute and officers a bugle as well, and as we did not go on the sergeant fell into great perplexity, and after keeping his men at the present for a space with no one in the neighbourhood he stood them at ease. We then felt it safe to advance, whereupon they presented arms again, much to the amusement of those already on the verandah. I usually do the wrong thing on these occasions and so was not embarrassed, but the sergeant was very worried.

There were canoe races for men and women, swimming races and sports on shore, in honour of the anniversary. In fact things were very gay for Vila.

One afternoon we went over to Fila Island in the dinghy to see the native village. One or two natives came to meet us and led us up. In front of a cluster of leaf huts was the village "green," of fine coral, on which were set up a number of croquet hoops. Several small boys, clad in very short shirts, were playing after a style of their own. The huts were one-roomed and the entrance was low. Some of them were packed with natives. The village covered a considerable area, as the huts were scattered about. We walked along a path among cocoanut-trees to inspect the house of the "boy" who had constituted himself our guide. It was built of wood and contained two or three rooms, and he was very proud of it. He then took us farther on to a hut where we bought some model canoes of the catamaran type. None of the men we saw seemed to be doing any work, but the women were cooking and busy around the huts. The men probably go over to Vila when they feel like work and load or discharge the trading-steamers, or do work at the stores.

A new British judge had just arrived at Vila, and we went up one morning with him and his wife to inspect the house which was being got ready for them, a large and comfortable wooden building on rising ground. He showed us over and then said:

"By the way, have you seen anyone in the garden? There should be three murderers cleaning it up."

But the murderers were not visible. They were probably sleeping happily under a tree somewhere, untroubled by any feeling of remorse, as murder is not a serious crime, if a crime at all, to the bushmen of Malekula and Santo.

The day before we sailed I called on the French Commissioner, Monsieur D'Arboussier, for permission to visit the other islands, and then to pass on without returning to Vila as is usual. He said that he had no objection if the British Commissioner had none. I then called on Mr. King, who gave permission provided that Monsieur D'Arboussier saw no reason for refusing. And that is the way everything is done in the New Hebrides. The natives would like England to have sole control.

As the Sailing Directions seem to think very little of the natives of some of these islands, especially of Makelula and Santo, and say of the former that they are "a wild, savage race, occasionally practising cannibalism," and of the latter that they have "the reputation of being treacherous, and as there have been many murders of white men in quite recent times, they should be treated with caution. Cannibalism is probably more prevalent than in Malekula Island," we made enquiries, and heard that this description is probably true of the bushmen, but that there was nothing to fear from the salt-watermen or coast natives. But a report which came in while we were at Vila that a trader named Filmer had been murdered in Ambrym seemed to show that the coast natives were not quite so friendly as stated. Later on, however, we met Filmer and found him very much alive, so the report that he had been murdered was not true, though he had been attacked.

More or less reassured by what we had heard, we prepared to leave for Mai Island, and on the 7th June weighed at dawn and went out with the decks full of cocoanuts, bananas, pawpaws, pine-apples, cucumbers, and lettuce, the two latter being a present from Mr. Wallace. Sisters Winter and Fraser at the Hospital also sent some eggs, which we had not been able to buy and which were a great treat. For some reason we never could get eggs, though there were plenty of fowls about. Commander Barrett turned out to wave us farewell, and before long we had passed out between the reefs, and the lovely harbour had faded from sight.

The wind remained very light all day, and in the afternoon it became clear that we should not be able to make Mai Island before dark. There is an anchorage at Na Ora Matua in Nguna Island and we headed in for it, but even that was too far in the circumstances. At dark I decided to miss out Mai Island and stand away north for Epi. The only known danger was Cook

Reef 5 miles west of Mai Island. The area has not been surveyed, but trading and recruiting vessels are always moving about in all directions and have been doing so for years, so that the chances of there being any unknown reef about were very small.

The night was perfect, clear and moonlight. The stars were magnificently bright. A gentle, warm, east wind fanned us quietly along over the smooth sea. It was delightful to sit at the wheel and float through a scene of such beauty in almost absolute silence. Beyond the soft ripple of water past the side, the slight creak of the jaws of the gaff, or the thud of a block on deck there was not a sound.

At dawn Mai Island was just in sight to starboard, with Epi on the bow, and Malekula away to port. Epi is a heap of mountains, densely wooded. The valleys are a mass of vegetation which comes right down to the water. Like almost all these islands it is very beautiful. The anchorage I was aiming at, Ringdove Bay, lies on the north-west side of the island, and in the early afternoon we were approaching it. All these anchorages are difficult to make, as it is very hard for a stranger to identify anything on the chart, and the best way is to have a hand aloft to look for submerged rocks, reefs, or shoals, though even this is not much use if the sun is ahead. For instance, on the way along the coast we had passed the Foreland anchorage the directions for which are:

"A conspicuous single cocoanut tree on the mountain, 1,025 feet high, in line with the south fall of the cliffs on the north side of the gorge at the head of the bay, bearing 112° true, leads southward of Miranda Rock, and up to the anchorage."

These directions were drawn up in 1893, and I utterly failed to identify the tree and was by no means sure which, out of the tangled mass of peaks, was the one 1,025 feet high. All sorts of things can happen to a cocoanut-tree in nearly thirty years, and very likely it has now gone, or is no longer solitary. No doubt these directions were the best that could be given at the time, and they show the great difficulty which exists in giving clear indications in that part of the world.

I managed to find Ringdove Bay, but could not pick out

either Bain or Facio Point. Reefs run along the shore with a few detached coral heads outside them, so that it was necessary to keep fairly well out. In the middle of the anchorage, half a mile off the beach, is Dick Reef. As we came up, Tadgell could see this plainly from aloft, and we skirted along outside it, and then stood in towards the shore and anchored about 200 yards out. A canoe put off from the beach with a native clad in shirt and trousers, and three others wearing loin-cloths only. The man in the shirt climbed on board, after warning the boys not to let the canoe "fight him ship," in other words bump it, and introduced himself as a native of Tahiti in charge of Hagan's repair shop. One would hardly expect to find a repair shop in Epi, but it appeared that the firm of Zeitler and Hagan have large interests in the group and find it handy to have somewhere where simple repairs can be made without having to go to Nouméa. Our Tahitian, who, unlike most of his fellow islanders, had a sour expression and seemed to have a grievance with life, left before dark just as *La Victoire* came in with M. D'Arboussier on board.

Next morning we landed and walked up to the trader's house. He is manager for Hagan's, who have a fairly large and well-stocked store. We enquired for bread. They run a bakery and could supply this. We also bought some lubricating oil and rope, and could have bought almost anything from an anchor and chain, by way of food, ironmongery, and clothes, to jewellery. Mr. Mitchell, the manager, took us round the buildings, and then for a walk about the plantation and up a lovely valley, escorted by a bull terrier and another dog. On the way we passed some children with eggs and asked if we could buy any. One little girl explained, however, that the eggs she was carrying "belong piccannini chuck-chuck," from which we gathered that they were to be hatched out.

The path lay at first through the cocoanut-trees, where natives were splitting nuts and extracting the kernel, which was then packed in bags and taken to the drying shed. It was there spread out on a platform over a fire and dried, and became copra, which is used for making soap, margarine, and articles requiring oil.

The soil is very fertile and, in the valley, cotton, maize, cocoa, taro, and paw-paws were growing luxuriantly. In fact anything will grow. After the walk we went back for lunch with Mr. Mitchell. It was served in a well-constructed leaf hut away from the main buildings. The floor was covered with mats, and the furniture consisted of a book-case, table, chairs, and settees. By way of an *apéritif* we had rum, and then came the lunch, mutton chops—a sheep had been killed on the other side of the island and some of it sent across—asparagus, green peas, yam, salad, with white wine to drink. An excellent lunch and a pleasant change from our meals on board. Two little boys, clad simply in lava-lavas, waited on us. They treated the matter very seriously, and their earnest little faces as they brought the various dishes in, or hovered anxiously round the table, were very striking. We invited Mr. Mitchell to dine with us on board, and then returned to the shore, walking through the cocoanut-plantation and over a ridge to the repair shop. As we passed along, ripe nuts would crash to earth from time to time. They weigh a fair amount and come down with a heavy thud; and neither of us felt very comfortable, though we had been assured repeatedly that accidents are almost unknown. Still if a nut did score a hit it would fracture the skull in all probability.

By way of supplementing the bill of fare for the evening Tadgell started fishing, and soon hooked and dragged on board a fish 3 feet long which had a family likeness to a shark. It had no dorsal fin, however, and the mouth was on the upper part of the snout. On the top of the head was an oblong ribbed plate of hard skin. We learned afterwards that it was a "sucker" which attaches itself to other large fish, or even ships, by means of the plate.

In the late afternoon a small trading-steamer came in, the *Saint Michel*, and discharged some cargo and took off some copra. Boats were passing to and fro until a late hour, and Mr. Mitchell found that he could not get away. He sent us a note to this effect, and a present of a number of young drinking-cocoanuts. Young nuts, of course, have very little "flesh" but are full of a slightly cloudy liquid, very pleasant to the taste. The native who brought the note wore a circlet of flowers round his head, with a hat perched on top. I gave him a pipe and some tobacco and also the two fish which Tadgell had caught. We did not know whether they were good to eat and thought that he would know. He accepted them, so probably they were all right.

That night Tadgell slept on deck. About midnight he was surprised to hear a canoe coming alongside. There were three natives in it who demanded calico and would hardly be persuaded that we were not traders with stuff to sell.

Next morning we sailed across to Port Sandwich in Malekula passing south of the heavily wooded Lamen Island said to be inhabited by a fine-looking race, quite different from the natives of Epi. The origin of many of the races living in these islands is wrapped in mystery. In some of the islands quite different languages are spoken in different parts. In Santo, for instance, there are seven, totally distinct from each other.

Malekula is densely wooded. The inhabitants, or some of them, are an unruly crowd, the Big Nambas at the north end being particularly troublesome. They are suspected of being cannibals on occasion, and probably are. The namba, by the way, is the sole article of clothing of some of the men of Malekula. It consists of a very inadequate plaited-leaf arrangement, slung on a string worn round the middle. Viewed from behind they appear to be clothed solely in a piece of string. The women wear a sort of petticoat.

The wind was blowing right out of the entrance, and we had to beat in, but had no difficulty with Tadgell, or "that fella" as Joe sometimes called him without meaning any offence, aloft, as the sun was behind him and he could see the reefs quite clearly. We could therefore stand on right up to them with confidence. He told me when to go about. As we came round Planter Point, we could see a schooner at anchor, flying the Tricolor. It was *La Victoire* once more. We anchored just outside them, after dipping the Ensign. The captain and the engineer rowed over. The former, a Frenchman named Broustail, has been in the Islands for forty years and is a tough old sea-dog of many strange experiences. When they went we landed at a dilapidated pier and, after passing a few deserted wooden houses, walked along a path leading to the east side of the island. We could not, however, find a living soul and after a time returned. In the evening we went over to *La Victoire*, on M. D'Arboussier's invitation, for a *vermouth*. He had only just been appointed it seemed and was making his first tour of the Islands to get to know the French settlers and hear what they had to say about island affairs.

Next morning *La Victoire* went out under power. As a matter of fact she never sailed, but always used the engine. We landed once more and walked along a beautiful path, through the woods towards the French Mission at Lamap Point on the east side. The trees, which were mostly big, and draped with climbers, met overhead and turned the path into a leafy tunnel. Small gold-coloured lizards with blue tails darted about the trunks, and innumerable winged insects droned along. It was a delightful walk, and not too hot, as the trees kept the sun off. After a time we heard dogs barking, and presently reached some small leaf huts around the first of which several natives, men and boys, were prowling. They all had curious elongated heads, caused by binding the skull during childhood, and were a truculent, haughty-looking crowd. We waved them into a group and photographed them. They submitted to this with a distinct air of condescension. We then went on towards the Mission. Other huts bordered the track at intervals. Finally we reached the Mission, a well-built cluster of houses standing in a large clearing, with a small church in the centre. Cattle roamed about, and the place struck one as being very well run and prosperous. There, surrounded by priests, nuns, and the Mission natives, were M. D'Arboussier and his engineer, and also a gendarme. We were invited into a house and sat there chatting for a space. We enquired whether any clubs and spears could be bought, but these it seemed were very scarce and hard to find. As a substitute pigs' tusks were offered, which were curious in that they formed complete circles, a result obtained by knocking out the upper tusk and allowing the lower one to grow unopposed. After a look round the buildings and sheds of the Mission we returned by the same path, and found Stéphane washing some of my clothes at a rain-water tank near the pier. I turned to and lent a hand. Presently a number of bearded natives stalked up and sat around watching.

One of them said to me: "This boy belong here you look him?" which meant, "Have you seen the man who lives here?" I waved my arm to the east and said "Mission" by way of answer.

After washing the clothes we hung them about on bushes and left them there all day. Several natives were wandering about all the time, but they never touched them nor paid any attention. In the afternoon a bunch of them came on board and seemed filled with admiration for the ship. Most of them wore nambas and a few feathers in their hair, and two of them wore necklaces in addition and seemed by comparison rather overdressed. They brought pigs' tusks and fruit which, after hours of bargaining, we bought for pipes and tobacco. They would sooner have had coins, English coins, as they will not take French ones, but I wanted to get rid of the trade stuff I had brought from Auckland. I was told there that in many of the islands money was not taken, only "trade," and in consequence bought calico, pipes, tobacco, needles, cotton, razors, scissors, fish-hooks and lines. Everywhere where there is a trader—and there are few islands where there are not more than one—the natives prefer coins, and my "trade" was rather a white elephant. It came in handy once or twice though. Then another native, named Tom, came off clad in shirt and trousers. He was caretaker of the deserted houses, and it was his business to go off and put a hurricane lamp on a buoy off Gedges Patches when a ship was expected. I do not know who paid him. He could speak fair English, and was in Sydney in 1914 when war was declared. He enquired whether it had ended and who had won and who would take over the New Hebrides. He noticed the fruit we had bought lying on deck and warned us not to leave the cocoanuts and oranges exposed to the sun as, when they are picked, it makes them "boil," i.e. ferment, and causes fever. He liked being on board and airing his English, and the other natives, real savages all of them, liked sitting on deck and examining the ship's fittings, and we liked seeing them there as evidence that we were really in the wilds and away from civilization. Very likely some of them were cannibals when occasion offered. Presently an open boat sailed into the bay with some pigs on board, whereupon our visitors crowded into their canoes and made for the beach. One of them offered to get us "One fella chuck-chuck," which we imagined was a fowl, but he did not return. The others proceeded to slay a pig. Judging by the uproar which arose the pig made a strong bid for life, but in the end it was overcome by numbers and despatched. The visitors then heated stones in a wood fire, and cooked the pig native fashion.

Just before dark Tadgell and the two hands went ashore for cocoanuts. Joe got these by walking up the trees and throwing the nuts down. We did not know who owned the trees. The settlement has been abandoned, and nothing seemed to belong to anyone.

Next morning we sailed across to Ambrym. There is an active volcano there, Mount Benbow, which was throwing out a good deal of smoke and steam. In December 1913 there was a violent volcanic eruption which destroyed the settlement at Dip Point and altered the whole coast line between Craig Cove and Krong Point. A good number of natives who would not leave the island were killed, but the whites got away. For days before the eruption the ground rumbled and quivered and the cocoanut-trees shook and the leaves rustled as if in a strong wind. The settlers and Mission people took the hint and left, taking as many natives as would go. The eruption formed a good harbour at Dip Point, but it has since silted up and is now a lagoon.

As we closed the island and got under the lee, we lost the wind and had to use the engine, with the help of which we finally crawled up to Rannon's anchorage on the north side. This has no distinguishing features beyond the trader's house, and when opposite to that, we stood in at right angles to our former course and anchored in 6 fathoms, with Tadgell aloft as usual, looking for submerged rocks. He was extremely good at this and never made a mistake, and, moreover, never reported things unnecessarily. There was no particular activity on shore.

A few natives appeared on the beach, and we could see some white children, but we did not land as night was coming on. Next morning we went ashore. The trader came to meet us and introduced himself as F. G. Filmer.

"We are very glad to meet you," I said. "We heard at Vila that you had been murdered."

"Oh, did you?" he replied. "As a matter of fact I was attacked by three boys armed with hammers and an axe. They knocked me down between them, but some of the other boys rushed up and pulled them off. I got up and soundly thrashed the one with the axe. Sprained my thumb. The others ran away. It was nothing. They were not really in earnest. Come and have some kai-kai."

We explained that we had had our kai-kai, or food, already.

"Well, come and have a cup of tea."

We went with him to his house, passing at the garden gate two very ancient roughly carved wooden images of a man and woman about 4 feet high. He introduced us to his wife, and to his five sturdy children. His assistant, Mr. Collins, then appeared, looking very thin and ill. He was suffering from an abscess in the arm, which would not heal. Filmer then took us round the plantation to where his boys were husking and cutting out cocoanuts. On the way back we visited a "heathen"— Filmer was once a missionary—village, lying at the back of his house. The villagers were apparently engaged in idling away the time, sitting in the shade. I never could make out how the natives, those not working on the plantations, passed the time. I never saw the men doing anything. Filmer introduced us to the chief, a wizened old man, with his great-grandchild in his arms. His hut was surrounded by a stone wall with one entrance. When he dies this opening is filled up and the hut abandoned. Here, as in Malekula, the men wore a namba and the women either a petticoat or a girdle of grass.

On our return to the store we photographed some natives who came in to buy various articles, paying for them in cocoanuts. One of them started a fire for our benefit, with two pieces of wood. One of the pieces was of hard wood, pointed. The other piece was soft. The hard piece was worked to and fro along the grain of the soft piece, gradually cutting a groove. Considerable pressure was applied, and after a time the soft piece blackened and then started smouldering, whereupon dry moss was placed along the groove and as soon as a spark appeared the operator blew on it gently, and ultimately the moss caught fire. They had almost forgotten how to make a fire in this way, and a lot of discussion took place before they could start. The first man failed to get any results and had to be relieved. The second man was successful. Filmer gave me a bow and some poisoned arrows, a club, a sacrificial spear for killing pigs, and some dancing sticks. He has made a sundial on the trunk of a tree, using a nail as shadow-pin. It did not work out quite well owing to the change of the sun's declination at different times of the year, but it was not a lot out. I could not tell him how to curve the hour lines, but I brought a compass ashore and gave him true north. He suggested that we should visit the Mount Benbow volcano next day, and this was arranged. The distance, he thought, was five miles, but he had never been there and was not sure. On the chart it looked much more, eleven or twelve miles, but the charts of those parts are not very accurate.

Next morning we were ashore before 7 a.m. ready for the walk. Mrs. Filmer had cut sandwiches, though we expected to be back for lunch, and a native, named Bong, carried these, our cameras, and a rope. Three dogs attached themselves joyously to the party, and off we went. The first part of the walk lay along the coast, and we then turned inland and followed a dry torrent bed for a bit, branched off, and eventually arrived at Bong's village. The huts were of the usual plaited-cocoanut-leaf type. A number of dogs and pigs wandered about. Naked little children gathered into groups to gaze at us. The chief came forward. He wore the namba, armlets, and pigs' tusks round his neck. He assured us in pidgin-English that the volcano was "close up," or near, and that the path was level. A man and a boy, both models of physical beauty, armed with bows and blunt-headed arrows for pigeons, joined our party. The object of having the heads blunt is to prevent the arrows sticking in the tree if the pigeon is missed. After a brief halt we went on, cheered by the thought that the volcano was "close up." The level path did not at once become evident, as we immediately began a fairly steep climb through dense vegetation. Up and up we went along an almost invisible path much overgrown with ferns, Climbers caught round our ankles or necks, and tripped us up, while branches knocked off our hats. At times we had to bend double and advance through leafy tunnels. Every now and then the path ran along the extreme edge of steep descents. So far it was a fairly strenuous walk.

Presently we came to a sharp descent, and lowered ourselves down by branches and tufts of grass and eventually emerged on to a perfectly flat torrent bed about 150 yards wide with a surface of black sand. Along this we went for miles. We had reached the "level path" all right, but the volcano was by no means "close up." It seemed as far off as ever. The walking was easy, but the sun was hot, and we soon became thirsty. The natives said that there was no water to be had anywhere ahead. This was a distinct jar, as it meant that we should not be able to drink for many hours, and we debated whether to go on or not. We decided to go on. Gradually the bed contracted and joined other beds, which we crossed, and finally, after plunging through dense scrub, climbed a steep cliff of crumbly soil, walked along a razor edge, down another cliff on to a different torrent bed. Here all vegetation ceased. On each side rose cliffs of black sand, cut into strange ravines by water action during the rains. On and on we went, rising all the time. Suddenly the boy, who was leading, sighted a man coming from the opposite direction. He retired in disorder on to the main body, and the man also leaped back two paces in alarm. Evidently at one time, not very far back, things were fairly lively in the island. The stranger recovered quickly from his shock and came to meet us. Filmer knew him and they discussed local affairs, while we took the opportunity of sitting down and resting. As far as I could follow the pidgin-English someone had killed someone else, though not intentionally.

After resting for ten minutes we went on, the party increased by one, as the new-comer, who was on his way from Port Vato across the island, volunteered to join. His business was not of a pressing nature apparently. The going got rapidly worse, and we were soon climbing on hands and knees up steep slopes of crumbly black sand, using footsteps cut by the Port Vato man with his long cane knife, and crawling, precariously, along razor edges of an unpleasantly yielding nature, inhabited by colonies of ants. What they lived on I cannot conceive. After advancing a certain distance we had to descend into a valley of sand, and cross it to the edge of the volcano. Lying at full length on the rim we could look right into the crater. The north corner was sending up a dense cloud of smoke and steam at intervals, always followed by a rain of black sand. The remaining part was steaming. Masses of sulphur lay about the bottom and sides. The crater was oblong, about three quarters of a mile long by half a mile, and 400 yards deep. The bottom seemed fairly level. I lay at the edge and took a photograph downwards, while Tadgell held my legs. Then I held his legs while he took another one. Filmer then took the sandwiches from Bong, and we munched them with mouths as dry as lime-kilns. It was then 1 p.m., and we had had nothing to drink since soon after 6 a.m., and had been walking all the time in a hot sun, or crawling through scrub.

After a rather hurried lunch we walked to the active end, but there was too much smoke coming up in spurts to look over the edge. Filmer threw a big stone in, much to the alarm of our followers, who declared that the volcano would reply by throwing out a shower of stones and pointed to several big lumps lying around on the surface as proof of what it would do. They retired in haste. They told us in all earnest that Mount Marum had been a volcano which had been put out of action by a witch doctor, who charmed a cocoanut and threw it in. On the way back Filmer conceived the idea of measuring the distance by counting his steps. He took long strides and counted up to one hundred and then started a fresh hundred, while Tadgell kept tally of the completed ones. We advanced at a rapid rate, retracing our steps, cheered on by the information that, near the point where we had to quit the torrent bed, was a pool of water; and sure enough there it was, lying back in the bush. The dogs were all for plunging in, but were restrained, while we drank, using a leaf which one of the boys twisted into a cup. The pool was more or less stagnant, and probably the water would not have passed muster if analysed, but it was as welcome as iced hock-cup, on the merits of which I had been meditating for several miles. A delightful drink. It was probably full of bacteria, but if so they were friendly, harmless little fellows, rather pleasant to the taste.

We rested at this pool for ten minutes and then scrambled up the bank to the path leading to Bong's village, Filmer well ahead and going at a great pace. I caught one boot in the branch of a tree, concealed by ferns, lying across the path and burst the stitches of the sole, so that it hung down. I was finally obliged to cut it off and walk on the upper. This delay put me some way behind the leaders, but all the retinue was farther back, luckily for me, as I missed the path twice and was retrieved by the next astern, the boy. On reaching the village Filmer clamoured for young cocoanuts. I do not think I have ever enjoyed a drink so much. Our followers eventually came straggling in, Bong, who was getting done up, a long way last. We paid them for their services, shook hands and bade them farewell, and then pushed on again, as it was getting late, and would soon be dark. Bong would have liked to remain in the village, but had to drag himself along. At sunset we got back to Filmer's house, only just in time, as very soon afterwards it was dark. The distance, by counted steps, worked out at 12½ miles, making 25 miles in all. Filmer urged us to stay to supper, but we were both covered with black sand, scratched and generally dilapidated, besides being tired, and we went straight on board, and had a bath. So ended a most interesting day.

Next morning we took some papers ashore, received two loaves in return, and heard that Bong had recovered sufficiently during the night to beat his wife, who made such an uproar that Filmer had to interfere. After bidding the hospitable Filmer family and Mr. and Mrs. Collins farewell, we returned on board, hoisted the boat and got under way for Aragh Aragh. It was a lovely day, but the wind was very light and the engine had to be brought into action. The distance to Aragh Aragh from Ambrym is not great, only 5 miles across Selwyn Strait, but as the east coast has not been surveyed at all and only part of the west coast over thirty years ago, the trip promised to make up in interest what it lacked in length. The Directions have a poor opinion of the natives, and amongst other disparaging remarks state that cannibalism was reported to be very prevalent in 1893.

We soon crossed the Strait, and the question then arose as to where we should anchor. We had been warned against Homo Bay, and so passed on. The next possible anchorage was Truchy Point, and we went in and had a look at it, but a swell was running in and it seemed an uneasy spot. On we went to Waterfall anchorage and brought up. A recruiting schooner was lying at anchor rolling heavily. Her boat was patrolling the beach waiting for recruits for the plantations on other islands to come down. The old "blackbirding" days have gone for ever, and now recruiting is very carefully supervised. Recruiters are not allowed to land on any island. The recruits have to wade out and be taken into the boat, to make it absolutely clear that it is a voluntary act on their part. Inspectors visit the various plantations and see that the "boys"—as they are always called no matter their age—are properly fed and housed and are not kept beyond the indentured period. The recruiters' boat did not seem to be doing much business; in fact, not a soul appeared in sight, nor could we see any signs anywhere of human habitations. We wanted to get hold of some natives if possible to buy some mats for which the island is noted, but there did not seem much chance at Waterfall anchorage. We did not care to go wandering about on shore in almost impenetrable bush searching for a village, as we were by no means sure what reception we should get. In fact, we kept an anchor watch that night, for the first and last time, in case of trouble and also because the swell had increased and was setting on shore, and I did not want to risk dragging the anchor without knowing about it.

Next morning, as there still seemed to be no one about, we weighed and went up the coast to the next anchorage, Steep

Cliff Bay, to try our luck there. The distance was short, and as there was no wind we went up under power and before long reached Grotto Point, which we were able to identify by a mushroom-shaped rock and a cave. As we opened up the Bay several recruiting vessels came successively into sight, until we could count seven, ketch, schooner, or yawl rigged, all lying at anchor with their boats patrolling the beach. We brought up on the outskirts of the little fleet in 7½ fathoms. The bottom was clearly visible. After lunch the boat was put over and we went ashore. A surf was breaking on the beach, and the boat could not go right in. Stéphane backed cautiously down, and when the water seemed sufficiently shallow we jumped in and waded ashore, while he lay off clear of the surf. Three or four natives sat moodily on the beach. They rose and shook hands. We enquired for mats, but they did not understand. Then we asked for cocoanuts. Cocoanuts? There were none. "One big fella wind," i.e. a hurricane, had blown the branches and nuts off the trees. It had also blown down the Mission house. They showed us the remains of this. We then tried to get inland along what they alleged was a path, but after wading for some distance through thick undergrowth we gave it up and returned to the beach. Stéphane brought the boat in, and we waded out and got into it. He had learned from the sailors in one of the recruiting vessels, while we had been away, that there was a path farther along the beach, and we rowed that way and presently saw it.

Once more we waded ashore. A native came to meet us and addressed us in good English. He said his name was Jimmy Tabbylip and that he had been born in Queensland. How he had managed to get born there I do not know, though I believe that at one time indentured Kanaka labour was admitted into Australia before the "White Australia" policy was adopted, and possibly that is how it came about. He took us up to his hut. The cooking-place was just inside the entrance, and farther in were his and his wife's sleeping-mats, both, strangely enough, protected by mosquito nets. His wife's hair was white with lime. Cooking-pots lay about, and gourds hung from the roof. We could only get one mat and that a poor one.

As we were walking down to the boat a native stopped us and enquired in pidgin-English if it were true that Filmer had been killed. On learning that we had seen him the previous day he said he was very glad, as Filmer was a good man.

Later on Jimmy paddled out with more mats, but not good ones, and also two spears, bow and arrows, and cocoanuts. I gave him a knife, pipe, tobacco, a razor, and some books. Off he went, but presently returned to say that he had lost most of the tobacco. I gave him a few more sticks, though I had already overpaid him.

A Monsieur Chaviade then came across from one of the other vessels. His English was nearly perfect, and he was an extremely alert person. He gave us much very valuable information about Aoba and Maewo, the next two uncharted islands; amongst other things he told us that there are now very few inhabitants in Maewo, which decided us to cut it out of the programme. During the War he had been flying, and if appearances go for anything he must have been pretty hot stuff as an airman. He added that his business in the bay was to obtain recruits, and that he had already been away for a fortnight but had only raised two. Some of the other vessels had none. Business in recruits seemed slack. As a matter of fact, labour is one of the great problems in the Islands, and the one which is holding them back. Most of them are extremely fertile and almost anything will grow, but a certain amount of labour is necessary to cultivate the land, and there is a distinct and increasing shortage of that. The natives are decreasing in number, and the present system of taking boys away to work on distant plantations for years is not helping to increase the population; moreover, quite a lot of them do not want to work, as they can get along quite easily without going on the plantations. Ultimately, no doubt, labour will be imported from India or elsewhere. The Chinese are already very numerous in the French islands, and one comes across Japanese in the most unexpected places. Rumour has it that they are alive to the possibilities of the position and have agents everywhere collecting information.

Next morning we left for Aoba. Most of the recruiters were

still rolling at anchor, with their boats patiently patrolling the beach. One or two of them, however, in sheer boredom, had weighed and gone farther down the coast. The recruiter's life nowadays is very dull in most places, but in the old days things were very different and the natives were often kidnapped, and retaliated by firing slugs at the boats of the recruiting vessels. Recruiting or "black-birding" was then full of excitement and interest, and even now things are occasionally lively in Malaita, where it is usual to have two boats off the beach, one close in and the other, with men armed with rifles, lying farther out to cover the first. Getting recruits is quite an art. One way is to make presents to the chief, who will then induce some of his tribe to volunteer. As a rule the recruit is not keen on going away to a plantation, and only does so as a result of pressure applied by his family or chief. Once he has gone and settled down, however, he nearly always improves noticeably in physique, as the result of regular hours and food, and of the care which is taken of his health. Many of them like the plantation life, and when their time is up sign on for a further term. Those that return to their homes with their pay, which they have usually converted into articles from the nearest trader's store, are as poor in a few days as when they started, as their relatives share out everything brought back.

Monsieur Chaviade had advised us to make for the south-west end of Aoba Island, round it and anchor off Duin Dui, which would be recognized by a large white A. painted on the cliff. Accordingly we headed that way at first, under power, as there was not a breath of wind. A swell on the beam made the ship roll considerably in the calm prevailing, and after a time I decided to make for the N.E. end of the land so as to bring the swell astern, and ease the rolling. About noon a light breeze came from aft and we were able to stop the engine. A couple of hours later we rounded the end of the land and opened up the north coast. A short distance to the west a reddish cliff jutted boldly out into the sea, "like the bow of a steamer" as Monsieur Chaviade had described it. This is the feature by which Lolowai Bay can be identified, in which there is an anchorage. We could not, however, head in at once, as there is a rock almost awash in the way, and we had to stand out until we were clear. Tadgell, as always, went aloft to look for dangers, and we cautiously worked our way in and anchored in 8 fathoms. The island has not been surveyed, and the Sailing Directions do not profess to know very much about it, but state that Lolowai Bay is "probably the anchorage reported as being the best in the island." This is distinctly non-committal, and I am tempted to go a step farther and say that, such as it is, it is the best in the island, though quite exposed to winds from east through north to west-north-west.

The island is clothed in dense vegetation up to the fine mountain, 4,000 feet high, which runs along the centre. No natives appeared on the shore, though a mission is reported to be there. We put the boat over with the intention of calling on the missionary. On the way in we crossed a reef over which there was very little water, but inside there were depths of about 6 or 7 fathoms. On landing we saw footprints in the sand. Someone had evidently been there recently, but he was not then visible. We found an opening in the bush which looked as if it had once been a path, and forced our way along it for some distance until it disappeared in a small clearing in which were the remains of some leaf huts. Charred logs lay in a heap in what had once been a kitchen. The place seemed to have been deserted for some time. But where was the Mission House? All round was impenetrable bush with no signs of a path or clearing anywhere. If a mission was anywhere near there would be a path to the beach, but except for the half-obliterated track up which we had scrambled, there was nothing re-sembling one. We gave it up and returned to the boat and had a swim, and then rowed round the point into the next bay, Vanihe, where it was said there was a trader. But he seemed to have disappeared too, and we could not find any signs of human life. Back to the ship we went, got under way, and proceeded along the coast under power with a hand aloft. This form of navigation was full of interest. We had got back to the times of the first navigators, who coasted along in exactly the same way, not knowing what they would come across from one minute to the next. Like them we had no charts, but the parallel ends there, as, though unsurveyed and uncharted, these waters have since been traversed by all sorts of craft and reported clear of dangers except for a reef farther along, noticed by the *Miranda* in 1884, and a pinnacle rock some miles beyond it to the westward. About 2 miles from Vanihe is an open anchorage, Bice Roads. It has no distinguishing marks, and is consequently difficult to find, but at about that distance a small wooden hut appeared amidst the trees, and when opposite to it we turned and anchored a cable from the shore.

When we landed, a few natives came out of the bush and watched us, but as soon as we advanced towards them they ran back towards the house and disappeared. We followed and found the building to be a small store in which a Frenchman was sitting at lunch, with his native assistant opposite to him. On the shelves were a few articles for sale, tins of salmon and meat and other oddments. In the farther corner was the bakery and a half-emptied sack of flour. The place looked miserable, poverty-stricken, and very filthy. Through the open door at the back several natives peeped shyly in. The Frenchman was polite, without, however, seeming very pleased to see us. He offered us some stewed pork, which we refused, but said nothing about a drink, though there were bottles on the table. The assistant seemed to have been applying himself to these to some effect and was incapable of speech, though still able to eat. We sat down and asked for information about the missionary at Lolowai.

"He has been murdered," said the Frenchman briefly, "and the Mission House was blown away in a hurricane."

He could give no reason for the crime. "A native shot him," and he shrugged his shoulders.

He sent out some of the boys for cucumbers and aubergines, and, in return, we gave him a tin of tobacco and then went on board and proceeded along the coast in search of an Englishman who, he said, lived a mile farther on.

Once more Tadgell climbed aloft and stood on the cross-trees looking ahead for shoals. A cutter soon appeared, anchored off the beach opposite to a small village almost lost in trees. We brought up near by and rowed over. A Frenchman, M. Caillard, was on board, and he told us that he was after recruits and had been there for several days without getting a single one. The "Englishman," Mr. W. M. Marshall, who is really an Australian, then appeared in a canoe and came on board. He was living all alone in his store until his house, which had been blown down, was rebuilt. He trades with the natives, selling them articles which they want for copra, which he sends away whenever an opportunity occurs. At the time we were there he had a hut filled with bags of copra to the very roof. Soon after his arrival several canoes rowed off and the natives came on board. They were delighted with the ship and wandered over it making clicking noises of approval. Several of them went ashore and brought back mats, arrows, stone axe-heads, and shells, most of which we bought, partly for cash and partly for "trade." They were very shy over offering things for sale, and drew Marshall to one side and told him in a low voice what they had and how much they wanted for it. We replied, through him, with a counter-offer, and finally the deal would be effected. Some of the mats were very beautiful. One of the natives was careful to explain that the stubby side of a sleeping-mat which he sold me "belong bed," while the smooth side "belong sleep."

At dark the canoes returned to the shore, but Marshall stayed to dinner and for some time afterwards. Indeed, in his craving for the society of his own kind, I believe he would have liked to sleep on board. At the time, however, this did not strike me, and in the end Tadgell and I rowed him ashore. It was not possible to land opposite where the ship was lying on account of the surf, and we had to row along in the inky darkness until we came across an outlying rock which marked the entrance to a sheltered cove. Next day we went ashore, in pouring rain, to visit him. The store consisted of a strongly built wooden shed which he had put up himself. These traders and planters are real pioneers, and must be able to turn their hands to anything. Alongside the store were the remains of his house, and until it was re-erected he was living in the store, and sleeping on the counter. As soon as I saw the conditions of intolerable discomfort under which he was living, I realized how "slow in the uptak' " we had been in not offering him a bed on board the previous night. Yet, living as he was, alone amongst natives without the society of his own kind, or any of the amenities of civilization, baking his own bread, and cooking his own meals, and generally having a very uncomfortable time with nothing much to look forward to, he told us that he liked the life well enough, and would just as soon be there as in civilization.

Lying just behind his store was the village of Tavolavola, a collection of leaf huts, most of them full of natives, idling away the time. Gourds and cocoanuts hung from the smoke-blackened roofs, and round the sides were sleeping-mats, wooden food dishes, and an assortment of articles, amongst which the inhabitants squatted. They seemed cheerful and happy enough; but it must be a dull existence.

Next day we weighed at dawn for Lonock Bay in Espiritu Santo Island, discovered by the Spaniard, Quiros, in 1606.

The track led us near the reef noticed by the *Miranda*, and we kept a sharp look-out for it, but saw nothing. I had not been able to get a chart of Santo, but I had a plan of Hog Harbour, in which is Lonock Bay. That was something to go on with if only we could find the harbour. It lies 2½ miles south of Elephant Island, which is 660 feet high and fairly easy to identify. Soon after noon it loomed up, and then the appearance of Sakau Island away to the north confirmed the position. We ran in between the mainland at Sugmar Point and Elephant Island before a smart breeze, and when the west end of the island was on the right bearing to clear Moror Reef we turned south for Lonock Bay, lowering the sails as we went on. In vain we looked for the white flagstaff mentioned in the Directions as near the Mission Station. It had been pulled down and put up on the other side of the harbour. However, we managed to pick an anchorage at the head of the Bay off the shore reefs.

Next morning we landed to call on Mr. T. O. Thomas, who owns a fine estate of 40,000 cocoanut-trees, besides cotton and cocoa. Some natives directed us and said that Mr. Thomas

was in, "belong house." On the way we passed five bush
natives stalking grimly along. Each of them carried a rifle.
With them was a bushwoman, whose sole article of attire was a
strip of leaf about ½ inch wide, which is all they ever wear.
The bushmen looked at us coldly and suspiciously, and did
not return our salutation. A few hundred yards farther on we
reached a path of fine coral leading to the house, a very comfortable one-storied wooden building. In front of it, under trees,
was the dining-room, a separate oblong bungalow with walls of
coral blocks about 3 feet high into which were inserted wooden
posts, supporting the thatched roof. At each end were wooden
gates to keep out the dogs and fowls. It was a most comfortable,
cool place, open all round.

Mr. Thomas has owned the plantation for seventeen years,
and has had some strange experiences. On one occasion it was
necessary to amputate a man's arm on account of gangrene.
No doctor was available, but Mr. Thomas had a medical work
and some chloroform. He studied the book, and then successfully performed the operation, and saved the man's life. The
resource and nerve of these pioneers is amazing.

During the afternoon Mr. J. R. Salisbury, the Condominion
officer, came in and a missionary, Mr. James. The former has a
very unpleasant job owing to the turbulence of the bushmen,
who are ever at loggerheads. Murders and vendettas are the
order of the day, and no bushman ever leaves his hut without
his rifle. It is strange how they get hold of these, but they all
have one, though many are very old, Sniders and similar
makes. Fighting rarely or never takes place on the plantations,
which are looked on as neutral ground, but once off these,
utter lawlessness reigns. Mr. Salisbury, supported by his two
native policemen and anyone else he can raise, has at times to
go inland in search of murderers who may be wanted. He is
sniped at all the way and usually has a rotten time. Less than
10 miles from where we were sitting is the village of Chief
Thingaroo, the local centre of disturbance. Punitive expeditions have at times been launched against him when he has
been more than usually troublesome, but they have never
been wholly successful. For one thing the bush is impenetrable,

and the only line of advance is along the native paths. At night Thingaroo has these strewn with dry twigs so that a body of men advancing makes a considerable noise. They are ambushed and fired at from the sides and cannot make any adequate reply, and when they do reach the village it is deserted, and all that can be done is to burn it down and destroy the crops, usually losing heavily in the process as they are under fire from cover all the time. Burning a village means very little, as it can be rebuilt in a few hours. In one of these expeditions Mr. Thomas was seriously wounded and had to be sent to Australia for treatment.

The conditions in Santo are very extraordinary, and are far from creditable to the Condominion Government. However, the whites are seldom involved in the disturbances, and the only precaution they seem to take is to make the bushmen put their rifles at half-cock when they visit the plantations. Mr. Anderson, the missionary, goes a step farther, however, and makes them withdraw the cartridge when they are on his ground. The bushmen probably consider him as very faddy.

We spent four pleasant days in Lonock Bay, delighted at the novelty of finding ourselves right on the very fringe of civilization. It was a stimulating thought that by walking a few hundred yards inland we should be in one of the most lawless spots on earth, amongst a very savage people, but Mr. Salisbury was strongly opposed to any such promenade, and assured us that we should certainly be ambushed before we had gone very far. We were at lunch at his bungalow when the suggestion of a visit to Thingaroo was mooted, but he scouted the idea as quite impossible, and on hearing what he had to say on the subject we both lost all interest in the proposed expedition. Neither of us had any desire to be shot from behind a tree.

At this lunch he gave us a "millionaire's salad," made from the heart of a young cocoanut-tree. As each salad means the destruction of a tree it is an expensive item in the menu. The one which furnished our salad, however, had been cut down to avoid overcrowding, and we enjoyed it without any feelings of compunction.

During the intervals of chasing elusive murderers in the bush

Mr. Salisbury devotes himself to gardening. His grounds are most admirably laid out, and contain a great variety of beautiful plants and ferns, besides some strangely carved stones collected from time to time from the interior. His garden is pleasantly situated on Moror Point, with Itheas Cove on one side and Lonock Bay on the other. Most of these islands are extremely beautiful, and Santo stands high on the list. Mr. Thomas took me for a ride up the hills behind his place, and the view from the top over the Bay was quite fascinating.

In one way and another the time passed quickly and pleasantly. We frequently dined with Mr. Thomas, and once had lunch with Mr. and Mrs. Anderson, when they gave us turkey, yam, bread-fruit, native cabbage, and French beans, followed by maize and arrowroot custard and chili wine to drink. A little boy named Bully waited at table. He was so occupied in staring at the guests that he hardly knew what he was doing, and had to be gently chided once or twice. Later he paid us a visit on board with Mr. and Mrs. Anderson, who have been missionaries in the Islands for twenty-five years. He was dressed in a sailor's suit and looked very smart. He had tried to part his hair, but his wool refused to lend itself to the operation, and he had got over the difficulty by cutting a parting with scissors.

One day Joe rowed us out to Moror Reef on which we landed to look for shells. We floundered about in water occasionally up to our waists, but did not find anything special. Some of the coral, however, was very beautiful in form and colour, and strange little fish, some bright blue, and others with unusual markings, darted about in the pools. Not meeting with much success on the reef we made for the beach. Presently Joe shouted to me from the boat, and on looking I saw a very hideous and formidable native standing near me with a hatchet in his hand. He said something which I did not understand, but I smiled and waved my hand and then made an abrupt retreat to the boat, which Joe had by then brought in. The native repeated his remark and pointed along the shore. Later on, I met him on Mr. Thomas's land when he offered me a pig's tusk curved in a circle, which I bought. He evidently had

had no hostile intentions when we first met, and my alarm was groundless, but he was not a nice-looking person at all, and his appearance did not inspire confidence.

On the last evening of our stay we dined with Mr. Thomas, and afterwards he lighted us down to the boat. On the way we passed some huts in which his boys lived and found them having a dance. There were two musicians, one of whom rapped two sticks on a log supported on uprights, and the other banged the earth with a stout bamboo. Both of them sang, and the others pranced round them waving sticks and stopping dead at the end of each verse. In the midst of the fun another boy wearing a mask appeared amongst the trees. To encourage him Mr. Thomas pretended great alarm, but the presence of so many strangers put the performer off his game, and he soon retired.

Next morning, 25th June, we weighed at dawn, as I wanted to reach our next port, Lakona Bay in Gaua Island, one of the Banks group, in daylight. We passed up inside Elephant Island, as the channel is reported clear, and then stood away for Gaua, leaving Sakau Island to port, with Cape Quiros, named after the explorer, away beyond it to the west. The wind was fresh from the east, and the sea was troublesome. At noon we were obliged to take the top-sail and mizzen off to ease the ship through the seas, and even then were doing between 7 and 8 knots. Heavy rain blotted out the island as we approached, and we did not see it until it was within a couple of miles. About 2 miles off the south-west end there is a reef awash, the exact position of which is not known, and we kept fairly close in to the land to avoid it. As we passed up the coast the sea fell, and we were soon sailing along in smooth water. Ahead of us were two schooners and a small trading-steamer, the *Saint Michel*, at anchor in the bay. We rounded up between the schooners and let go.

The Banks group was first discovered by Quiros and was not then again seen until Bligh touched there when making his wonderful boat trip to Timor in 1789. The Directions state "The inhabitants are of a type distinct from any of the New Hebrides group in manners, customs, habits, language and appearance. . . . They have a language of their own . . . quite distinct from any spoken in the New Hebrides or other islands." This is a most extraordinary thing, but the whole question of the origin and migrations of the South Sea Islanders is a mystery.

Next morning we landed and took the breakers with us for fresh water. Some very friendly natives met us and shook hands. They spoke pidgin-English and took us to a pool, but would not let us fill the casks there, "Belong swim" they said, and led us farther on to where a stream ran down the side of a cliff. "Belong drink." There we filled the breakers, which they helped us to carry back to the boat without any thought of a reward. A small party of them then conducted us along the beach to a hut from which a woman issued and let fall a mat over the entrance.

We stood outside wondering why we had been taken there. I think it was for inspection, as a minute or two later a Frenchman quietly stepped out from amongst the trees through which he had apparently been examining us. He wore a shirt and trousers, but no socks or shoes. We explained that we were sailing round for our own amusement, whereupon he thawed a bit, and, lifting the mat closing the entrance, invited us inside the hut. Just inside to the right was a heap of trocha shells. On the left was a collection of crockery and cooking utensils, beyond which his wife, a Frenchwoman, was sitting on a pile of mats. Farther on a baby a few months old was sleeping on a bed protected by a mosquito net. At the end were more beds and nets. He introduced us to his handsome wife, and told us that he was a dealer in trocha shells, which he collected from the natives and sold for export to Japan where they were made into buttons. He proposed to build a house and remain in the island. The hut he was then living in had been built for him by the natives out of pure friendliness. We went with him for a short walk to look at various vegetables which he had planted, all of which seemed to be doing well. The soil, he said, is very fertile, and practically anything of a tropical nature will grow. On parting he gave us some "native biscuit," dried bread-fruit —wrapped up in leaves.

These traders lead strange lives, cut right off from civilized society, and it must be worse for their wives.

After we got back to the ship, several natives came off with carved sticks, which we bought for tobacco and calico. The half-caste skipper of one of the schooners also had himself rowed over with poisoned arrows and mats for sale. He wanted whisky, but I refused to give him any and bought his articles for trade goods. He complained that his motor was "broke" and that his ship could only do 1 mile per hour under sail. During the afternoon he left, and that certainly seemed to be about his speed.

Next morning we left Gaua and its friendly, courteous natives, and proceeded up the west coast with the idea of making Port Patteson in Vanua Lava Island. A few soundings are marked on the chart around Lakona Bay, but the area lying to the north is blank and has not been surveyed at all. Mr. Barclay and Mr. Stephens, who called from the second schooner in Lakona Bay, had told us, however, that it was all deep water, and we sailed along and admired the bold, well-wooded coast without any feeling of anxiety. As soon as we had cleared the north end of the island we met a strong S.E. breeze and heavy sea. As Port Patteson, named after Bishop Patteson who discovered it and who was afterwards murdered by the natives of Nukapu in 1871, lies on the east side of Vanua Lava, it looked as if it would be an uneasy anchorage with so much swell running in, and at 10 a.m. we decided to make for Avreas Bay on the lee side of the island, and altered course accordingly. This brought the wind aft and we got along fast, and soon had Paut Point, a lofty promontory 2,650 feet high, abeam. From there we coasted along at a distance of 5 miles from the shore towards Avreas, but on reaching it decided once more to change our plans and go on to Ureparapara, as there was rather too much swell in the anchorage for comfort. As a matter of fact, there are only two harbours in the whole group, Port Patteson and Ureparapara, and the former is exposed to easterly and north-easterly winds. Everywhere else there are only open anchorages. Our new port lay 30 miles north, but we felt confident that we could get there easily before dark considering the fresh breeze blowing.

A high, heavily wooded ridge runs all along the west coast, and there are three fine waterfalls on the north-west side, one of them with a drop of well over 100 feet. As soon as we got away from under the lee of the island we picked up the good breeze again and made short miles of it across to Ureparapara. It was fine sailing, sunny and warm, a slashing wind and the ship going like a train. Just off the island we hooked a big fish. What it was I do not know, but it snapped the stout tackle as if it were packthread.

The entrance to Dives Bay lies between two bold headlands. The harbour extends inland for 2 miles, and is really the crater of a volcano the north-east side of which has been blown out.

Off the harbour mouth the sea was very confused, and as in addition the wind was fresh we stayed round instead of gybing, and then ran in between the heads. Eddy winds and gusts off the steep mountain-sides rushed at us from all directions, and we staggered down the centre in a series of spurts. At the head of the bay is a small village on the port hand, off which we brought up. No sooner had we anchored, however, than we found ourselves close to a reef, and were obliged to weigh again and get farther out. Two natives paddled off and came on board. One of them was dumb, "no savvy speak" as his companion put it. They were very much impressed by the ship, and when we took them below they gazed round quite awe-struck. Both of them had bark spiral wristlets on their left wrists to protect the skin from the string when using bow and arrows. We bought these for tobacco, and also gave them the "native biscuits," which we had experimented with but had found uneatable.

Next morning four men, a woman, and a child came off with yams, oranges, bananas, cocoanuts, paw-paws, and limes, as well as clubs, shells, kava bowls, native forks, and a food bowl, most of which we bought for trade. Later on we went ashore and were met by a very pleasant and dignified head-man, who took us round the village, which consisted of perhaps twenty leaf huts. A considerable proportion of the population followed us about. In the centre was a large hut in which the bachelors lived. The sleeping-mats were ranged round the sides, and gourds, cocoanuts, and other articles hung from the roof. At one end was the cooking-place, and four natives were eating the "native biscuits" which we had given to our visitor of the previous day. They had boiled them up, and so had made them eatable. The headman then took us to his house and presented us to his womenfolk. On a sleeping-mat a boy was lying sick, but we could not find out what was the matter with him.

We told the headman that we should like to buy some food bowls, forks, and such articles, and he passed the word on. For a time things were quiet, but by degrees they livened up, and we ultimately secured most of the surplus stock of the village. One enterprising native after he had apparently sold us all he possessed came up with a handful of cocks' feathers, which he thought might attract us. When the time for payment came a good deal of confusion arose, as we could not remember which articles we had bought from whom, nor how much we had agreed to pay. The headman, however, came to the rescue and cross-examined each claimant, and then told us how many sticks of tobacco to give them, and in the end we discharged all our liabilities, and every one was satisfied. It was a most amusing day for us, and a great day for the villagers. They are not often visited by ships of any kind, and almost certainly they had never seen a yacht before, while the lavish way in which we gave them trade stuff for articles which to them had little value must have been a revelation. I think the women swindled us most horribly, even the headman seemed shocked at some of their claims, but when all was said and done the whole thing cost less than £1.

Next day we got under way at dawn. Strong gusts were blowing off the sides, and we made rather a scrambling departure, with the sails full one minute and everything aback the next. The harbour has not been surveyed, but the centre is known to be deep. How far out the shore reef extends is uncertain, however, and, to be on the safe side, I kept the ship dodging along down the centre as best I could with the help of the engine. Finally we reached the entrance and sailed out into the open sea, bound for Tulagi in the Solomons, via the Torres group. A fresh S.E. wind drove us along at a good pace, and by 3 p.m. we were in the Grande Channel between Tegua and Lo Islands. There are five islands in the group, all of them covered with trees, but only 100 inhabitants altogether in the lot. Moreover, the anchorages are not very good, and as we had a smart, fair breeze we decided to go on to the Solomons without stopping. Away nearly 100 miles to the north are the Santa Cruz Islands, discovered by Mendana in 1595, and Vanikoro Island, where La Pérouse was wrecked in 1788. We were anxious to visit them, as they are full of interest, but they were out of bounds for us until we had first reported at Tulagi, hundreds of miles to leeward. It had been suggested by a high official at one of the islands we had visited that if we found ourselves short of water or supplies when off Santa Cruz and went in to replenish probably nothing would be said, but I did not want to leave a bad impression behind with the Authorities, and so we missed them and went on.

On the evening of 1st July we were nearing the Solomons, and at midnight when we were within 20 miles of Olu Malau we hove to until dawn in deference to a Caution printed on the chart, "as these islands [Solomons] have been only partially examined, and the larger portion of them being quite unknown, great caution is necessary while navigating in this vicinity." That being so, it seemed advisable to move about as far as possible only in daylight. The wind eased after dark, and a series of heavy rain squalls blew up at intervals all night.

At dawn we went on once more, and at 9 a.m. sighted Ulawa ahead, our first sight of the great group of the Solomon Islands which extend over an area 600 miles in length. They were discovered in 1567 by Mendana, the Spanish explorer, but both he and Quiros were unable to find them again in sub-sequent expeditions, and they were not visited for two hundred years. Indeed, their very existence was doubted until Captain Cateret, of the *Swallow*, sighted them in 1767. They are now coming rapidly to the fore, as they are extraordinarily fertile. The chief product at present is copra, which does not require a great deal of labour. Cotton has been temporarily given up until more hands are available. Here, as in the New Hebrides, the labour question is delaying the development of the islands.

There are plenty of natives in some of them—Malaita, for instance—but they do not want to work on plantations. As a matter of fact, Malaita and one or two other islands in the group are fairly savage still, and a certain amount of cannibalism still goes on. Mr. John Ellis in his interesting *Manners and Customs of the Solomon Islanders*, surmised in 1919 that probably there are very few natives over thirty years of age who have not tasted man.

At noon Ulawa, which is said to be 5 miles out of position on the chart, was abeam to starboard with Aliiti away to port, and soon afterwards Malaita loomed up through the mist. Bauro also showed up at intervals indistinctly. There was a good deal of mist about, and none of the islands was clear; not that it would have been much help, as far as fixing the ship was concerned, if they had been, as most of them are out of position and "neither Latitude nor Longitude of the off-lying islands or prominent points can be considered as more than approximate," as the Hydrographer sadly notes on the chart. He adds that the whole island of Malaita is probably 5 miles farther east than charted.

During the afternoon, as we ran before the fine, fresh wind I brooded over the position, and considered which of three things I should do at dark, heave to, run on during the night with islands all round, or seek an anchorage until dawn. The first I ruled out, as the strength and direction of the current are unknown, and we might have been set anywhere during the twelve hours of darkness. In the end I ruled out the third also, as the only available anchorage was in Maru Bay, at the north-west end of Bauro, and to reach it we should have had to go 20 miles out of our way. Moreover, the chances of finding it were remote, as all the assistance the Directions can give to that end is that it is "about 3 miles south-westward of Cape Recherche" and that there is a "steep, dark beach" there. To coast along a reef-strewn shore looking for a steep, dark beach did not appeal to me, and I decided to run on during the night up Indispensable Strait between Malaita and Guadalcanal. The Strait is about 27 miles wide, and "apparently very deep," and it is a thoroughfare to and from Tulagi from the

east, so there did not seem to be much risk in using it. Soon
after sunset we altered course to enter it and took in the topsail
and mizzen, as we did not want to go fast, since the island of
Nura lies only 30 miles along, and right in the centre of the
channel. I did not altogether like sailing along in the dark in
unsurveyed water, surrounded by islands and reefs, most, if not
all, of which are out of position, and at midnight when we
were by calculation 10 miles from Nura I had the ship hove to
and waited for light before going on.

At morning twilight we let draw and proceeded. The area
south of Florida Island, in which Tulagi lies, is sprinkled with
reefs and low islets, but we managed to pick our way through
these without misadventure, and even got safely across the
piece of water between Guadalcanal and Florida which the
chart briefly describes as containing "numerous shoal patches."
At sunset we were close up to the harbour, and soon after dark
were at anchor off the little pier.

Tulagi, the chief Port of Entry for the Solomons, is an island
about 2 miles long. A central ridge runs for nearly the whole
length, and the view from the top is very lovely. To the south
is a wide expanse of blue water dotted with islands crowned
with cocoanut-palm-trees with the mountainous Guadalcanal
in the distance, while to the north, across the harbour, lies
Florida with its jagged peaks and well-wooded spurs.

Next morning we called on the Resident Commissioner,
Mr. K. K. Kane, and then went to the Post Office for letters.
We asked the Postmaster for news of the world, but he said
there was nothing special.

"No new wars or revolutions?"

"Not that I know of," he replied. "None round here anyway. The others do not trouble us." A happy spot.

Tulagi is a semi-military post with some smart, well-drilled
native troops. In fact, it is extraordinary what progress the
natives have made. For instance, we went over to Makambo
in a launch which was run single-handed by a native clad in a
loin-cloth and a necklace, with a comb in his mop of woolly
hair. His muscular bronze body was a joy to see. He ran the
engine, steered, and made fast or cast off all by himself, yet

quite a few years ago he must have been a pure savage, who had never seen or imagined such a devilish thing as an engine, or had any idea of mechanics. Yet there he was running the show as one to the manner born. He seemed to understand his engine a great deal better than I do mine, but that is not perhaps saying very much.

The wind kept very high during our stay, and as we were very badly placed in the outer anchorage we weighed and went round a point of land into the real harbour, which lies a mile north-west of the settlement. There we were quite sheltered in a good anchorage. No ships, however, go there, as it is too far from the centre of things. The walk from the inner harbour to the settlement was very pleasant except when it rained, which it did at short intervals. The path climbs up and down along the beach and passes through Chinatown, where John Chinaman lives in leaf huts. Five or six very crazy piers jut out into the water. John seems to like to have plenty of rickety piers about. Their construction is extremely simple and consists of branches stuck vertically into the mud, with tie pieces lashed at a suitable height on which other branches are laid. Anything may happen with piers like that. The whole thing may collapse, or fall over sideways, or you may put your foot through between two branches. Bare-footed John strode confidently along them, but Tadgell and I walked delicately. John washed our clothes, and a tailor made me some white suits. He was very interested in my ship and asked many questions. When he had extracted the information that we carried no cargo, he said:

"Ah, allee same gentleman ship."

A Japanese shipwright who did some repairs was also pleased with her.

"Good fella ship belong you. Good fella too much."

One of the things I wanted this shipwright to do was to repair a block. Block making is a special art, and I expressed doubt as to whether he could do it, whereupon his mate, who was not a craftsman and who may have been one of those sent out to collect information, replied with scorn:

"He not make block? You want he make ship!" meaning

"Of course he can make a trivial thing like a block, why if necessary he could build a ship."

The presence of these Japs is rather a mystery. Five of them were living in a leaf hut, in the midst of an amazing collection of miscellaneous rubbish, with nothing whatever to do, as far as I could see, except develop an occasional photographic film.

We dined several times with Mr. Phillips. His house was delightfully placed on the crest of the hill, with magnificent views all round. Two little boys waited at table. They wore scarlet loin-cloths, which contrasted pleasantly with the beautiful bronze of their skins.

Phillips told us that one day he heard a smash in the kitchen followed by much subdued talk, and then all his five boys came in. One of them held the handle of what had been a cup.

"All together we break this fella cup," he announced. By shouldering the responsibility in a body they hoped to dilute Phillips's wrath—and succeeded, as their tactics amused him.

In spite of the magic beauty of the scenery the residents do not like Tulagi, which they state is the worst spot in the group, with a rainfall of over 120 inches and a lot of malaria. The harbour round the point where we were lying certainly seemed a fever-stricken spot, but it cannot have been too bad, as we met in Mr. John Ellis's house several old timers, men who had been twenty, thirty, or forty years in the Islands and who looked quite fit and as tough as leather. One of them, Jock Cromar, came on board. He is seventy years old, and when war broke out enlisted as forty-three. He got as far as Salisbury Plain and was then bowled out, but succeeded in getting to France as "batman." He told us some fascinating yarns of the old days. At one time he became manager of an estate for a firm of soap-makers who now have immense interests in these islands. While in their employ he was burned out by the natives five times, and his successor was murdered. These old timers have all led the most amazing lives, those of them who have survived. One and all declare that the old wild native was honest and truthful and a finer fellow than his modern descendant.

On 13th July we weighed and left for the Pavuvu Islands, 80 miles to the westward. The wind was fresh at first and we got along well, passing Savo Island at noon. For some reason the sea round this island is infested with sharks. The natives there bury their dead chiefs at sea, but this can hardly be the explanation, as the supply of chiefs is not sufficient to attract sharks.

In the afternoon the wind tailed off, and it was dark before we reached the group. There are fifty islands and islets in a space 20 miles by 12 miles and, as the survey is very imperfect and "caution is necessary when navigating in this neighbour-hood," we did not attempt to find an anchorage in the dark, and hove to for the night. At dawn, to my surprise, we were not many miles from Ysabel Island, a large and mountainous island north of the Pavuvu group. Either we had had a strong set that way or else the ship had been forereaching much faster than anticipated. The wind increased as the sun rose, and we had a fine sail back in a big sea. Ships sailing fast in rough water often cause the waves to break alongside in a roar, and that is what happened on that occasion. It was very exhilarating to rush along with foaming seas on each side, but it made steering rather difficult, and I had to take the wheel from Stéphane, who seemed a bit tired and unable to keep the ship steady. As soon as we got into smoother water he took the wheel again while I tried to fix the ship and find our exact position. This proved to be a difficult business at first, as I could not be sure which was which in that collection of small islands. One mark was distinct, however, a 1,600-foot hill in Pavuvu, and this fixed Bycee Island.

Our track into West Bay lay between the latter and Leru Island, and in due course we opened up the passage and passed in. Money Island nearly put me off my game at the last minute by appearing open of Leru, which it should not have been according to the chart, but another bearing taken of the 1,600-foot hill convinced me that we were all right, and on we went. Even in West Bay the wind was fairly strong, and we crossed in at a good pace and came round for Macquitti Bay, at the head of which is Anonyma Cove where we intended to anchor. As we sailed along we saw several well-built houses in Hooper Bay, and some more amongst the trees on the shores of Macquitti Bay, but in beautiful Anonyma Cove there were only two deserted huts standing on the fringe of virgin forest. We landed and examined these and saw that they had long been abandoned, and then rowed and drifted along over the shore reef. The many-coloured branches of coral were beautiful to the eye, and little fish of strange hues darted about. It resembled a submarine garden, with fish instead of birds, and Tadgell and I were quite fascinated by the beauty of it all. Stéphane, however, was not interested and devoted his attention to trying to transfix fish with a small fish-spear which he had made, but he had no success. Neither he nor Joe liked these beautiful islands. I used to send them ashore for walks, but they always returned very soon and reported: "This place no good. Only trees, and rocks and bush." Towns, on the other hand, they liked, no matter how dirty and uninteresting they might be. In fact, Stéphane gauged the merits of a place by the number of places of amusement, especially cinemas, which it contained.

Next morning we rowed down to the houses on the shores of Macquitti Bay and landed at a small wharf. There was a row of neatly built sheds standing a few yards back, labelled "Tools," "Pharmacy," "Stores," etc., and a Japanese carpenter was engaged in erecting another one. He told us that "Marsta stop along house," so we made for a large bungalow painted white with a red roof, standing a few hundred yards back in a large clearing. On our arrival a boy appeared and announced that "Marsta go paddock." After an unsuccessful search for the paddock we returned and sat in the verandah to await "Marsta's" return, listening to the ripe cocoanuts thudding to earth. The bungalow was raised about 6 feet from the ground. On the right of the steps leading up to the verandah were the kitchen, pantry, and bathroom. The verandah ran from back to front and divided these rooms from the living rooms, all of which were mosquito-proof. After a time Mr. Widdy, the "Marsta," a keen-faced, alert-looking young Australian appeared, and bade us welcome.

When war broke out he was mining in the Northern Territory of Australia, but he left everything and enlisted. On his return he took the position of manager of that estate, under Messrs. Lever who own the islands and much land in the rest of the group. After lunch we walked down with him to the stores to see the issue of food and tobacco to the boys. These were all drawn up in a line, and Widdy walked down and looked at each boy for signs of skin disease. Any so afflicted were sent to the Pharmacy, where the sores were treated with a preparation of tar. The daily rations were then issued, two big biscuits, fish, and 1½ lb. of rice to each, also tobacco and pipes. In addition, each boy gets around £1 per month. Suitable accommodation has to be provided, and inspectors come round and see that there is no overcrowding. I believe that once a year each boy gets a mosquito-net, which, however, they usually use for catching fish. In a separate hut was a lad suffering from a horrible Solomon Island ulcer in his shin. It was 2 or 3 inches in diameter, but Mr. Widdy said that it was improving rapidly. He asked us to go with him to shoot alligators, so the next day we got out the rifles and rowed down. Horses were waiting to take us across the peninsula to the next bay. My steed took life very quietly and seemed to doze off once or twice on the way, but he collected sufficient energy to wind up in a clumsy canter. A boy was waiting on the shore to take the horses back. We embarked in a boat and were rowed across to a small steamer, the *Hawk*, belonging to Messrs. Lever, which had just come in.

Monsieur Hillien, a Frenchman, is the Captain, and his business is to collect from Tulagi the stores brought there from Sydney and to distribute them among the various estates, taking back copra and produce. He made me a present of some beautifully carved arrows and a war club from the Santa Cruz Islands. I hardly liked to accept them, but he insisted.

Mr. Munson, the manager of the Hooper Bay estate, was on board the *Hawk*, in which he had travelled from Tulagi where he had been in hospital with a wound in his neck. He had been knocked down and gored by a bull. Mr. Widdy had sewn up the wound with horsehair, and had sent him to Tulagi in a launch. Planter one day, surgeon the next, these pioneers have to be able to turn their hands to anything, and they never seem to fail. Though we did not know it, Mr. Munson was there while we were at Tulagi, and had seen us come in from his bed in the hospital. He told us that the ship looked very well as she came up before the fresh breeze, with everything set and drawing well.

While the introductions were taking place, and Captain Hillien was insisting on my accepting the club and arrows, Tadgell was losing interest in mundane affairs and beginning to find himself very unwell.

We rowed ashore and were introduced to Mrs. Munson and five children, and to Mrs. Thomson, and then Tadgell collapsed, and had finally to be put to bed. He was alternately hot and cold and seemed to be suffering from a form of ptomaine poisoning. Mrs. Munson and Mrs. Thomson cross-examined me closely as to how we lived on board, and what we ate. As soon as they heard that we had breakfasted that morning on rissoles made the previous day, and that these contained onions, they declared that there lay the cause of Tadgell's sickness. No food, it appears, containing onions should ever be left over and eaten the next day, in the tropics. Tadgell's condition caused me a good deal of anxiety, he seemed to be absolutely down and out, but Mr. and Mrs. Munson were sure he would soon recover. The alligator hunt, of course, fell through, and while Tadgell lay in bed, I wandered about the estate. Near the landing-wharf was a huge clam shell, over 2 feet long, big enough for a bath for a small child. Some boys had dived for it, and succeeded in bringing it to the surface. In the evening Mr. Widdy lent me two boys to row me round to Anonyma Cove. It was quite out of the question to move Tadgell, and he had to be left behind, in very good hands.

On reaching the ship I found Joe also in a state of collapse. He declared that he was dying, a statement which alarmed me very much, since once these natives get it into their heads that they are dying nothing will keep them alive. I gave him a big dose of castor-oil topped with twice as much whisky, clapped him on the shoulder and told him he would be all right in five minutes. By that time the whisky began to take effect and he felt better and sat up. I then got him into his cot, and he promptly went to sleep. Stéphane had also been troubled by vomiting and diarrhœa, but had not suffered greatly. Taking it all round, it had been a most unpleasant day for the ship's company, except myself. For some reason I escaped.

Next day Joe and Stéphane had recovered. Mr. Widdy sent up some boys during the morning with papers, limes, oranges, a cake, and news that Tadgell was convalescent, which relieved my mind greatly. While waiting for him to appear I took a shotgun, on the off chance of getting a pigeon, and got Stéphane to row me up Brewis Inlet at the head of the cove, which has never been explored. The inlet soon narrowed down to a stream much encumbered with fallen trees. The banks were covered with primeval forest, quite impenetrable. We proceeded for a long way up the stream, which finally divided into two arms, and then returned in case Tadgell had arrived and needed nursing. Mr. Widdy appeared soon after we got back, and next came Mr. Munson and his family, with Tadgell, in a whaleboat rowed by five boys. Tadgell reported himself as recovered. Mr. Munson then took the whaleboat a short way up the inlet to try and get some fish. These do not take the hook very readily in these parts, as they find plenty of food in the ordinary way, and as large quantities of fish are required to feed the boys it is usual to use sticks of dynamite with five-second fuses. The boat is rowed up to a likely looking spot, the fuse lighted, and the dynamite thrown into the water. The boys are ready and when, after the explosion, the stunned fish begin to show, they dive in and collect as many as they can before the sharks arrive. The latter have, it seems, learned that an explosion means fish, and they now make for the spot in haste to get their share. They must have reasoning powers, or they would not be able to make the inference. We were told that a case had been known of a shark snatching a fish out of a native's hand.

On this occasion the yield of fish was small, and another trial farther along was not more successful. Altogether the bag was about forty fish, most of them small. Of these Mr. Munson gave us nearly half, and we ate them for supper.

Stéphane brought in five for us, and he and Joe polished off thirteen!

Next morning Mr. Widdy came off with two boys to help us heave in and make sail. He brought off a duck and a copy of *Omar Khayyam* as a parting gift. I gave his boys a few small presents, at which they were highly delighted and told Mr. Widdy that I was "good fella too much."

There was very little wind at the start, and we had to use the motor to get out of the Cove and through Macquitti Bay. Off the entrance to Hooper Bay Mr. Widdy left us, and we worked out through the channel between Leru and Money Islands.

The wind outside was also very light; and we rolled about in a troublesome swell until the afternoon, when a breeze came from the N.E. with rain.

At 4 p.m. the uninhabited island of Buraku, 1,000 feet high, and heavily wooded, was abeam, and we ran on towards Gatuki, which I planned to leave 5 miles to starboard.

Between it and Tetipari is a break in the reefs into Blanche Channel, a wide expanse of deep water leading to the north end of Rendova; but in the dark it was not possible to make use of it, and we had to pass south of Tetipari and keep in the open sea. The wind increased in the afternoon, and at intervals heavy rain squalls blew up, during which it usually shifted. The sea was rough, and steering demanded a great deal of attention. As a matter of fact, everyone who went to the wheel seemed to have kept the ship a bit to windward of her course to avoid the risk of a gybe, as at dawn we were a long way off the land. To recover our position we had to gybe and run in towards Tetipari. This brought the sea on the quarter, and we reeled and swerved about in a most unpleasant way. In fact, it was a very uncomfortable sail, and the almost incessant rain made things worse, and, moreover, obscured the land to such an extent that we could not see the Balfour Channel between Tetipari and Rendova, which I meant to take in order to get smooth water, until too late. In consequence we had to pass round Banyetta Point at the south-west end of Rendova and enter Blanche Channel from the southward.

At 3 p.m. we were off the Point, and soon afterwards lost the wind under the lee of the land, and had to start the engine. We also lost the sea and got into smooth water, which was a great relief. The engine chugged manfully on, but progress along the land was slow, and it was clear that we had a strong current against us. It became doubtful whether we could get into the harbour before dark. For the first 7 miles past the Point the water is deep right up to the beach, but after that reefs extend off the shore to a maximum width of 3 miles. As we neared them Tadgell went aloft, but was unable to spot them. On and on we went, but nothing appeared. Then he reported reefs on the other, the port side.

"There cannot be any reefs there," I replied. "You must be mistaken."

"Not a bit," came back. "I can see them clearly, and not far away either."

"Then what I have been taking for Bau Island must be Rubiana Island, and we are on the wrong side of the channel. That absolutely tears it, and we cannot get in to-night. However, we will have a shot at it."

But at dark we were still a few miles from Kuru Kuru Island, which lies at the entrance to the harbour, and as the water all around was everywhere too deep for anchoring there was no choice but to go to sea again for the night. Very reluctantly we brought the ship round and headed out. Another night at sea! It was a hateful thought. Still there was no cause for great anxiety, as, once we were clear of the land, we had all deep water ahead. By 10 p.m. Banyetta Point was abeam once more. For hours lightning flashed continuously, and heavy, black clouds hung around. At intervals rain fell in torrents, but the wind kept light. It was a disturbed night for me, as I was called out repeatedly; but it gradually wore away, and at 4 a.m. Joe reported a breeze, and we stood in again N. by E. for Banyetta. This time we kept well to starboard, skirting the line of the shore reefs which were plainly seen from aloft, until we had passed Kuru Kuru Island, and could lay through the West Pass between it and Lumbari, and so round to the anchorage off the small jetty in front of the manager's house.

Rendova Harbour is an extremely beautiful spot. It is well protected by several small tree-covered islands with lanes of blue water between, and the general effect is delightful.

We spent five very pleasant days there and were most hospitably received by the manager, Mr. Sprod, and his beautiful Danish wife. At the time of our visit the latter's sister, Miss Larsen, was staying with them, and, I rather fancy, found life at Rendova very dull. As a matter of fact, life in these islands cut off from all civilization is dull for white women unless there are children. All the housework and cooking is done by boys, and there is very little to occupy the ladies, who usually find the time hanging heavily on their hands.

The day after our arrival Mr. Sprod arranged with five of his boys to scrub the hull with cocoanut husks. They did not care to do this where we lay at anchor, on account of the sharks and alligators, and we took the ship alongside the little jetty. In two hours they had finished the work, and I offered them the choice of tobacco, knives, or calico by way of payment. They all chose calico, of which I gave them 2 yards each.

After lunch we went back to the anchorage, and then Mr. Sprod and the ladies came off in the launch to pick us up and proceed to the native village of Ugeli along the coast, with the idea of hiring canoes for a trip across to New Georgia. At the moment of starting, however, excited shouts from the boys on the beach announced the arrival of a ship, and the little *Hawk* was soon seen coming in through the West Pass. This cancelled the arrangement, but we were able to make the excursion next day. The party had meanwhile been increased by two planters from Kenlo in the Banyetta district, Messrs. V. C. Dixon and R. H. Carrick, who were at a loose end. It seemed that the boys on their estate were from Malaita, and that their time had run out. A schooner had left some time previously to collect another gang in Malaita, but she had not yet returned to disembark the new hands, and take back the time-expired ones. Until she put in an appearance things were at a standstill and no work could be done. Dixon and Carrick therefore came over to the Uweli estate to fill in the time, and to see who we were. They were both typical Australians, keen and full of energy, and delightful companions. Both had been at the war, and the tales they told were of absorbing interest.

Before we started they took the launch and went off to get some fish. They only used one stick of dynamite, but got a good bag, and the boys picked up 200 fish before the sharks arrived, losing about 100. After lunch we started for Ugeli, through the reefs south of Kokorana Island. The channel is very narrow and complicated. At times there were "nigger heads"—isolated masses of coral—within a few feet on each side, but the one-eyed coxswain steered confidently on, guided at the sharper turns by stakes on the reefs. After a time we emerged into Blanche Channel, and proceeded 6 miles down the coast to the village. The shores all the way along were littered with the remains of large trees which had been destroyed when clearing the ground for cocoanut-trees. It seems a sinful waste of good timber. Possibly the difficulties of transport leave little choice in the matter.

It rained at intervals on the way, and we arrived off the village in a perfect deluge. Indeed, it rained daily during our stay, heavy downpours each time. Mr. Sprod said that the rainfall is over 200 inches in Rendova, and as a result it is impossible to sun-dry the copra, and kilns have to be used.

As soon as the shower was over we landed, and were met by Mr. Wrigley, the Seventh Day Adventist missionary, who took us to his bungalow, and also showed us the chapel and school, and then led us to the village on the other side of a stream. A cocoanut-tree had been thrown across to serve as a bridge. The bare-footed natives walked across without difficulty, but for those wearing boots it was rather slippery, and we had to use great caution in crossing. We all hoped that the others would slip in, but no casualties occurred. The ladies, however, refused to attempt the crossing and remained with Mrs. Wrigley at the bungalow. The village lay a few hundred yards beyond the stream, and consisted of about twenty huts, most of them very dirty, and crowded with natives and miscellaneous gear. Many of the inhabitants were suffering from some frightful skin disease, and the squalor, dirt, and obvious sickness produced an unpleasant impression.

Some of the women cracked narli nuts and offered them to us. These are triangular in shape, and resemble Brazil nuts in size and flavour.

Mr. Wrigley tried to arrange for the hire of three large canoes to take us all over on the morrow to Rubiana on the large island of New Georgia, a distance of about 6 miles from our anchorage, but the matter seemed to hang fire. The natives dislike women in their canoes, and this may have been the reason for their lack of interest in the matter. The chief, however, showed us some small canoes, which are very neatly built up of narrow planks sewn together and calked with the resin from a nut. Wooden knees are lashed in at intervals. These canoes are not fitted with outriggers, as in the case of those in the New Hebrides, and in the islands to the east. From the Marquesas right across to the New Hebrides the canoes are all hollowed out of tree-trunks, and are fitted with outriggers to give them stability. The hollowing out is now done with an adze, but originally it was done by means of red-hot stones and stone implements. The Papuan canoes also have outriggers, but, strangely enough, we did not see any such in the Solomons. Another form of canoe, though it is really a raft, was in use in Rendova. It is of very simple construction and consists of three long straight branches which are lashed close together at one end and spread out, fan-shape, at the other by means of cross pieces. A box for the paddler to sit on is placed about one third of the way from the bow. They did not seem to have much stability, but the natives managed them quite easily.

With great difficulty we succeeded in buying a few curios. Mr. Wrigley laboured manfully on our behalf, but the owners seemed indifferent and listless, and we secured only a few baskets, combs, gourds, and a rush candle. There was a beautifully made wicker shield in one of the huts, but the owner could not be found. In another hut was a carved alligator, about 3 feet long, a fine bit of work. This, however, had been specially made for a Government official, and was not for sale.

Next morning we were out at dawn to receive the three large canoes which we hoped were coming, but nothing arrived until after 10 a.m., when one small canoe appeared, propelled by five paddlers. In the centre was a large heap of copra. We gathered that no more canoes were available. It was, however, impossible to get seven more people into that one, and in the end only Tadgell and I embarked. The crew paddled, or "washed," out of the harbour and then set a small spritsail. The canoe travelled fast, but seemed to have very little stability. A slight swell on the beam caused it to rock to a rather disconcerting extent, and I was very glad when we had crossed the channel to the opposite reef. There we all had to get out and unload the canoe and then carry it across to the lagoon inside. Some of the sprays of coral on the reef were very beautiful, purple branches with green tips, or pink and white. We also saw some bêche-dé-mer, or sea-slugs, fat fellows about 6 inches long. A big trade is done in these with China. On the way across the lagoon to Rubiana heavy rain came on, and we arrived absolutely soaked.

We landed and started towards the house of Mr. Norman Wheatley, who is well known all over the Solomons and whom we were very anxious to meet. On the way another downpour began, and we took shelter in an apparently unoccupied store. It was filled with blocks, ropes, and boat gear of all sorts. Outside lay a Sydney harbour 18-foot racing boat and other craft. The shore was littered with launches of all sorts and sizes, one of them a high-speed vessel, and sailing-boats in every stage of decay, while one or two bigger vessels were moored off the beach. Altogether there were probably twenty-five ships and boats hauled out or at anchor, all the property of Mr. Wheatley, and all more or less derelict and abandoned. The total amount of money which that fleet had cost must be considerable. Presently Mr. Griffith's, Mr. Wheatley's assistant, appeared, negligently clad in socks, pyjama trousers, and a torn shirt. He told us that Mr. Wheatley was away and asked us to walk up to the first floor of the store, where he was living under conditions of extraordinary discomfort. We sat and chatted for a time, and then as he could not offer us any food and we were both by that time very hungry, we started off in the rain to walk to the Methodist Mission about a mile farther on. As our clothes were already saturated, the rain could not make us any wetter and we stepped briskly out followed by one of our canoe boys. In due course we reached the missionary's house, a large wooden building in a clearing on rising ground, the view from which over the many small islands in the lagoon with Blanche Channel beyond, and densely wooded Rendova in the background, was magnificent. There the Rev. Mr. Goldie very kindly received us and had some tea, bread and butter, and cake brought on to the verandah. We sat at the table with water dripping from our clothes and finished off everything in sight. He then conducted us round the Mission. The place is lit by electricity, generated on the spot. The Mission teaches the natives various trades, such as carpentry, boat-building, etc., and, moreover, runs cocoanut estates and makes copra. At the time the Rubiana Mission was, in fact, a self-supporting affair, even capable of paying a dividend. Mr. Goldie was also in negotiation to have wireless telegraphy installed, partly with the idea of following the markets and making advantageous contracts.

Before we left he presented us with a very rare Bougainville spear covered from end to end with very finely made plaited work, and armed at the business end with nasty looking bone barbs; a shield: some well-made baskets; and clam-shell brace-lets. He then walked down to the shore and took us for a trip in the big war canoe in which he visits his district. There were thirty paddlers, and he made them show us the cruising stroke, which is the one employed when making long trips; the Malaita stroke, a variation of the first; and the silent stroke, formerly used when nearing a hostile village for the purpose of attack.

On the way back rain fell continuously, and we both took a "washee," or paddle, and worked our passage home in order to keep our circulation going. With seven paddles at work the canoe shot along at a fine pace, and we were soon in the harbour, and alongside the ship. We paid ten sticks of tobacco for the use of the canoe, and two of the boys also chose tobacco for their pay, a third chose a knife, and the others all voted for biscuits and meat.

Next morning Mr. Goldie paid us a visit on his way to an out-station. The canoe was rather bigger than the one we had seen on the previous day, and contained thirty-eight people, of whom thirty were paddlers. The stem and sternpost were continued vertically upwards for perhaps 10 or 12 feet, and both were ornamented with large cowrie shells. At the stem, a foot above water, was the carved head of the water-god gazing downwards on the look-out for reefs. The natives consider this figurehead as a most important part of the equipment.

The crew asked and obtained permission, through the missionary, to come on board, and the ship was soon swarming with about thirty of them, all laughing and talking at once, a jolly crowd. After a good look round the ship they all scrambled back on board the canoe, the missionary took his seat in the centre under a canopy, and off they went at a great speed, to crush by a display of pomp and circumstance the rival Seventh Day Adventist Mission at Ugeli.

After their departure we went ashore and said good-bye to Mr. Sprod and the ladies. They gave us a parting gift of bread, eggs, onions, and paw-paws, and after we had hoisted the boat and landed it on deck we weighed and left by the western entrance for Samarai, one of the entering ports of Papua. There are two routes which would take us there, the one south of the Louisiade Archipelago, and the other rather more northerly and between Misima and Deboyne Islands and the Conflict group. Which of these two we should follow had been the subject of much discussion between Tadgell and myself. The latter had the disadvantage that it was practically unsurveyed, though in 1872 H.M.S. *Blanche* had run a line of soundings from Narovo Island in the Solomons to the Archipelago and had found deep water all the way. On the other hand, it was nearly 100 miles shorter, and for the last 200 miles the water should be fairly smooth. The former is, perhaps, less risky, but it is longer and we should be skirting the edges of a series of reefs in a heavy sea for nearly 250 miles, and should, moreover, have a rather complicated approach to Samarai. The prospect of smooth water and the more interesting sailing by the Conflict group were the deciding factors, and we finally chose that route.

Things, however, began to go wrong from the start. Instead

of the fine, hearty S.E. breeze which had been blowing when we arrived at Rendova, and which by all the rules of the game should have been going as merrily as ever, we found a light and variable air on the first day, which improved on the morning of the second day to a fair breeze, but from N.W., and then during the afternoon fell right away to a stark calm. Heavy black clouds hung about the horizon, but the air remained stagnant. This was most unusual, and I could think of no explanation except a general upset in the weather. The calm persisted all that night and all the following day and night. The sea was oily-smooth and looked like molten metal, and the swell was hardly perceptible. Three sharks followed astern for several hours. I got a rifle and fired a number of shots at them, but they were too deep down to be in the least upset by the bullets which touched them. They signalled hits by a flick of their tails, but continued to follow. At length one came to the surface, and Tadgell shot it in the back, apparently in the backbone, as it seemed to lose control of its movements and was last seen swimming in circles upside down with the other two following it round. After that they all disappeared, and we presumed that the two unwounded sharks ultimately kai-kaied their mate.

On the evening of the third day a rapid change took place in the weather. At sunset the sky was covered with heavy black clouds and a light breeze had started, which by 8 p.m. had hardened to a fresh wind from the south. The topsail had to be taken in, and later on during the night we had also to stow the mizzen and the staysail. A nasty short, steep sea got up, and sleep became almost impossible owing to the violent motion. Things were no better at dawn, and I found great difficulty in getting good sights owing to the extreme liveliness of the ship. Those which I did take showed that we were being set to the northward by the current, and I had the sheets hauled in and went on, close hauled, on a S.W. course. Misima Island appeared at 4 p.m., and soon after dark we hove to for the night, as it was inadvisable to go plunging on in the dark in unsurveyed waters with so many islands and reefs about.

As a matter of fact, I was far from easy in my mind. I had

confidently relied on the wind being S.E., or at the worst east of south, instead of which it was, if anything, west of south, and all my carefully laid plans had gone wrong. Unless the wind changed to its proper quarter, it seemed probable that we should be very awkwardly placed on the following night, when we should be amongst a perfect maze of reefs and small islands. There was, however, just a chance that we should be able to reach Panniet and anchor for the night in Deboyne Lagoon, but this pleasing prospect gradually faded away when we found the wind as hearty as ever in the morning, and still from the south.

All day we toiled on, close hauled in a heavy sea, and gradually worked up to East Island and towards the Conflict group. In the afternoon we were as close to them as it was wise to go and came round on to the other tack and stood over towards Torlesse Island. I was very anxious to sight Lunn Island before dark, and spent a lot of time aloft and eventually could make out the tops of trees. In spite of the fact that the engine had been running since soon after dawn to help the ship through the short seas, progress had been slow and it was clear that the current had been making north all day. The tidal streams and currents in that part of the world are very imperfectly understood, but they are known to be strong and irregular and to run for days at a time in one direction without apparent reason. This adverse current had been holding us back all day, and I had long given up hope of reaching Deboyne Lagoon before dark.

I could not avoid feeling some anxiety and, now that it was too late, regretted that I had chosen this route in preference to the one south of the archipelago. Had it been possible to anchor anywhere things would not have been so bad, but the water was much too deep. Again, had the wind been blowing from its usual quarter, all would have been well, as we could then easily have got to Deboyne, or even right through the Conflict Channel. However, there we were, and we had to make the best of it. At any rate we could see Lunn Island, ignored on the Papua charts, but shown on that of the Coral Sea, which was on a very small scale—30 miles to the inch—

and, assuming it to be approximately correct, we ought to be able to get safely into the Conflict Channel, which is reported to be clear. It is, however, not as wide as it seems, as the whole of the Conflict group of islands is several miles out of position.

Taking it all round, there was a good deal too much uncertainty about where everything was in the neighbourhood, added to the chance of striking a submerged reef, to make sailing about on a dark night really pleasant, while the fact that we were in a strong stream, but did not know whether it was setting north, south, east, or west, in no way improved the position. By 7 p.m. we had Lunn Island abeam and stood on into the Conflict Channel until we were, as far as could be judged, in the centre. To the south lay Duperré, Kosmann, and Imbert Reefs studded with a few low, wooded islets; ahead there were several islands scattered about; while to the north the islands and rocks of the Conflict group were strung along for twenty miles. At midnight the moon set and it became much too dark to see either reefs or low islands in time to avoid them. I could not harden my heart sufficiently to give the order to continue sailing west into that wall of blackness which covered a series of scattered islands and decided to sail back east for a few hours, and then to turn once more. In this way I hoped to keep out of trouble and avoid getting ashore.

The night was fine but overcast and dark, and the south breeze held. I fully intended to alter course to west once more at 4 a.m., when Stéphane would relieve me at the wheel, but at 3.30 a.m. I quite suddenly changed my mind and decided to make the alteration at once. A strong feeling that now was the time to turn had arisen in my mind, and I acted on it and put the helm down and then went forward to pass the head sails over and to call Stéphane. He turned out at once. As the ship came round I saw what looked like a small steamer, without lights, on the bow and unshipped our stern-light and turned it towards the other vessel. No reply was made, and on examining her through the binoculars I saw that it was a large rock and not a steamer. We had been heading straight for it when I decided to turn round, and in a few more minutes should have gone crashing ashore if I had kept to the original plan. The fact that I did not do so saved the ship, but why such a strong feeling that I must alter course at once should have arisen so suddenly in my mind is what I cannot understand.

The ship had hardly settled on to the new course, and I was still meditating over the strangeness of the incident, when Stéphane reported another island on the starboard bow, and there it was sure enough about half a mile distant. I immediately had the course altered four points away and shouted to Tadgell and Joe to turn out, as we were amongst a lot of islands. A moment's reflection convinced me that these were some of the Conflict group, probably much farther out of position than was supposed, and that we were therefore on the north side of the channel. Had we been on the south side we should probably not have seen any islands at all, but should have struck the reefs instead. No further islands appeared, and after a time Tadgell and Joe were able to turn in again. At dawn some of the Conflict group were still in sight away to starboard, with Moresby Island on the bow, and by 4 p.m. we had passed in between Doini and Sideia Islands, rounded the south end of Samarai and anchored off the settlement.

It is an amazing little place. Imagine a small island dotted with cocoanut-trees, half a mile long, a quarter of a mile wide, rising into three hillocks, the highest of which is 155 feet, and set in the centre of a strait about a mile and a half wide. Houses and bungalows are scattered about all over it, but on the western side, in the business quarter, they cluster thickly. A number of schooners are usually at anchor off the beach, for Samarai, though so diminutive as to suggest a doll's house, is a Port of Entry and, after Port Moresby, is the most important settlement in Papua. The stranger is surprised to find a Port of Entry on a tiny island which has nothing to offer in the way of sheltered anchorage, and which is in the centre of a strait where the tides are strong, while all around on the mainland and on neighbouring islands are good well-protected anchorages. Perhaps the explanation may be that in this island the malaria mosquito is absent, though numerous on the mainland, or else that in the days when the settlement was first made the natives were troublesome and uncontrolled, so that an island was safer than the mainland as a place of abode. Even now the centre of Papua is unknown, and the natives are savage and fierce.

The usual kind welcome was extended to us, and we were invited out to lunches and dinners, and met a number of extremely nice people, amongst others the Resident Magistrate, Mr. C. B. Higginson, Dr. Giblin, the Rev. Mr. Warren, Mr. E. Solomon, and Mr. Bert Ellis. The view from Dr. Giblin's house on the hill is extremely fine, and one looks over the tops of waving cocoanut-trees across a stretch of beautiful blue water to the lofty and densely wooded mainland and the islands of Rogeia, Doini, Sariba, and their smaller neighbours. An enchanting scene of delicate colours. But it is not always so, and we heard of a man who came from Australia to seize and paint the shades and who remained several weeks, during the whole of which rain fell and overcast skies prevailed, so that in the end he had to retire unsatisfied.

During our stay Mr. Solomon asked us to visit his rubber and copra plantation on the mainland. He included the R.M., the Matron from the Hospital, and two other ladies in the party, and off we started in his launch for the 3-mile run across, towing my dinghy. On arrival it was found that the tide was quite unusually low, and the launch had to anchor a good way out. The dinghy then came into action, and we all piled into it, together with about six boys. Very soon the dinghy grounded in the mud, and the boys got out to lighten it.

This enabled us to proceed for a further short distance, and then it grounded again. All the men then got out, leaving the three ladies only in the boat. With ten men pulling and pushing more progress was made, and then the dinghy absolutely stuck and could not be moved forward. We were still 200 yards from the beach, and the mud was unpleasantly soft. Two of the ladies seated themselves on the crossed hands of two boys, and the Matron, who was no light weight, seated herself on an oar carried by two other boys, steadying herself by seizing their great mops of hair; the procession started, but trouble was in store. One of the ladies, slightly built, was carried ashore in safety, but the second one, of more generous proportions, had only got half-way when her boys weakened and had to deposit her in the mud. She waded ashore in slush nearly up to her knees. This was bad enough, but the Matron was in a worse case. In view of what one of the boys described as "plenty too much grease" she was seated on an oar, as stated, carried by two boys. They had great difficulty in advancing at all, and had not gone far before they collapsed, and down came the Matron into the soft mud in which she made a considerable impression. We splashed and dragged ourselves to her rescue, and supported her to the best of our ability until another oar and two more boys arrived. With great difficulty she was extricated from the mud and hoisted on to these, and then her four bearers started off once more. They swayed about and staggered painfully along, and it seemed likely that the whole lot might come down at any moment.

It was a most ludicrous scene, and I laughed so heartily that I could hardly stand. Near the beach were the slight lady and her two bearers; behind her came her more solid friend plunging pluckily along through the mud; while the R.M. splashed cheerfully on as a sort of convoy with his trousers black to the knees with mud. Farther back the Matron contingent tottered uncertainly on, with mud flying in lumps all round. Mr. Solomon, Tadgell, and I brought up the rear. Mr. Solomon was rather chagrined that affairs should have taken this turn, though as a matter of fact all were enjoying themselves immensely. The ladies at first grieved somewhat over their dirtied finery, but the Matron's good humour was infectious, and they soon saw the humour of it all. On reaching the beach we washed off the worst of the mud in a stream, and then climbed up a steep path, running through luxurious vegetation to the house. The ladies retired in turn to the plaited-cocoanut bathroom and tidied themselves up, and the men followed. Mr. Solomon then produced drinks and a gramophone, and those who knew how danced on the verandah while the lunch was being got ready. Afterwards we all walked to the plantation and were shown how the rubber-trees are tapped. A strip of bark cut at an angle of $45°$, about $\frac{1}{4}$ inch wide is removed from one third of the circumference, and a cup is placed in a wire holder at the lower end of the cut. The milk-white latex runs down and is collected in the cup. In about fifteen minutes it stops running, and the cup is then emptied into a bucket which is taken to the shed, where the contents are filtered and run into a pan containing a weak solution of acetic acid. There the latex coagulates and is then taken out, pressed into slabs, and hung up to smoke.

While the inspection was going on, rain started to fall heavily, and the boys came running down with raincoats and umbrellas. On the way back the Matron slipped and fell in the mud, and also succeeded in bringing down the R.M., who tried to save her. Both were plastered with dirt, and the Matron finally arrived at the Hospital minus her skirt and stockings, which she had discarded. Altogether it was a most amusing time.

Next day we went ashore to pay bills, get a clearance, and say good-bye to the R.M. and Mr. Solomon. The former gave us some pearl shells and a book, and the latter some grass petticoats, which is all the native women wear, and carved sticks, while the Rev. Mr. Warren brought off cocoanuts, limes, and paw-paws, and the Matron sent a cake and a small carved image. Everywhere we went it was the same. People received us with the greatest kindness, gave us the best time they could, and when we left loaded us with presents. It was very pleasant, and the welcome we received everywhere was quite the feature of the trip.

Before leaving we went on board one of Burns Philip's steamers, the *Morinda*, which had come in during the night, to get G.M.T. As the area through which the steamer had passed outside is dotted with reefs and islands, I asked the captain how he managed to get through in the darkness. He replied that there is a peak on the mainland which they can usually make out, and which leads through if kept on a certain bearing. It is a matter of practice and knowing the locality, he said. Certainly no stranger would be able to identify one peak out of a score, but even for men "locally acquent" navigation round these parts at night is a great strain, and is really desperate work. Wrecks are frequent, and I believe the *Morinda* has recently been lost. The surprising part is that there are not more wrecks, especially as the charts are very imperfect. As an instance of this, the mate showed me a reef on the way to Port Moresby which is miles out of position; indeed, the whole coastline is wrong.

At noon we weighed and left for Port Moresby. The wind was fresh once we were clear of Rogeia Island, and right ahead. A nasty short sea rolled in, and it took us all day to reach the Brumer Islands, which we rounded at dark. Three miles farther south is the Sunken Barrier Reef, which extends for over 100 miles along the coast. In one or two places where the depths are about 30 feet the waves break, but small ships can cross anywhere else. As soon as we had passed it, we altered course along the coast keeping a good 10 miles out. With the wind on the beam she got along very nicely and quietly, but for some reason I could not sleep when Stéphane relieved met at 2 a.m. As soon as he thought I was asleep I heard him remove the sail-locker hatch, slip down and get a cocoanut. I waited a few minutes, quietly got the electric torch, and suddenly appeared on deck with it trained on him and alight. He was brilliantly illuminated, sitting at the wheel and enjoying the nut, while I was invisible behind the light. It was a very awkward position for him, and he did not know what to say or do. A sickly smile appeared on his face, and then faded. I switched off the light and then disappeared without having said a word, leaving him covered with confusion. It was rather a malicious thing on my part, but I wanted to check him from consuming so much fruit during his watch. He had told Tadgell that he had once eaten fifteen bananas in fifteen minutes. I should have thought that impossible. Still he had a wonderful appetite, and it was almost his only vice.

On the following day the wind came E.S.E. and blew fresh, and we got along at a good pace in a heavy sea on the quarter. Next morning we were nearing our port and stood in towards the coast, and in due course the beacon on Nateara Reef, marking Basilisk Passage, appeared and we passed in. We rounded Bogirohodobi Point and anchored off the little town. Tadgell found an old friend in the doctor, and also an old school-fellow in Mr. V. W. Maxwell, who is managing an estate in the neighbourhood. We stayed four days at Port Moresby and were very hospitably entertained, and lunched with several people and also at Government House with the Governor. We also went for a spin in probably the only car in the place, which ran very badly and was driven by a man who seemed afraid of it. In the course of the drive we visited the native villages of Hanuabada, Elavara, and Tanubada, which are all thickly populated. The natives are a fine race with pleasing features. The men wear loin-cloths, the women a large number of grass petticoats, and the little boys nothing at all. The women are all much tattooed.

The villages of leaf huts are built out over the water on stakes, and are very picturesque and rather rickety. We went into one or two, climbing up a roughly made, wide ladder, in the company of Mr. Maxwell and the Crown Solicitor. One of the huts belonged to the village constable, who showed us a native pipe. It consisted of a length of bamboo about 3 inches in diameter with a hole at one end in which the tobacco is placed in a leaf. The smoke is drawn into the bamboo, and the tobacco and leaf removed. The bamboo is then handed round, and each in turn draws the smoke from the hole. In the second hut the women were cooking the evening meal, vegetables and fish. At the village of Elavara, lying on each side of a small neck of land, the women were baking some earthenware pots, which towards the end of the season of the S.E. trade wind are loaded into the large canoes called lakatoys. Two or three of these are lashed together, and will sail along the coast to the westward under their very curious spinach-leaf-shaped sails. When the wind comes from N.W. they return loaded with sago obtained in exchange for their pottery.

There is very little vegetation round Port Moresby, which lies in a dry belt. Thirty miles on either side, however, there is dense vegetation with a rainfall of 100 inches.

One morning I walked out along a very stony road to the W/T station to get a time signal. Groups of natives going into the town passed from time to time, the women swinging along in their swaying grass petticoats. They all wished me good day, and the little naked boys, out of devilment, ranged themselves in line and gave me a military salute as I passed.

While I was waiting on the verandah of the station for the operators to tune up their instruments, a most formidable-looking armour-plated centipede about 9 inches long, and $\frac{1}{2}$ inch across, crawled out of a corner. I called the attention of one of the men to this loathsome insect. He uttered an exclamation of annoyance, sprang into the air landed on it with both feet, and flattened it out. That is the worst of the tropics. They teem with every form of insect life. We had the greatest difficulty in keeping the ship clear of cockroaches, but by freely sprinkling powdered borax about held them in check. From time to time a few flew on board, or came off in the fruit and vegetables, but they never succeeded in establishing themselves, and for weeks and months at a time we never saw one.

On 12th August we double reefed the mainsail as the Trade Wind was blowing fresh, set the second jib, and left for Thursday Island in Torres Straits. Mr. L. Murray, the secretary to the Governor, had given me a typed copy of directions which he had drawn up himself for passing inside the reefs up to Caution Bay. He is a very able navigator, and the directions gave leading marks and all the necessary details, but I preferred to get into the open sea, as working along inside reefs in narrow waters is always very anxious work for a stranger, owing to the difficulty of identifying with certainty the various headlands, villages, and islands. As we ran out through the Basilisk opening, we passed on the starboard hand the wreck of the Government yacht *Merrie England*. Another yacht of the same name was destroyed by fire, and yet a third one wrecked.

On the afternoon of the following day we sighted Bramble Cay, a sand heap, 10 feet high, under the lee of which we intended to anchor for the night. As the Cay is so low, we did not see it until we were close up. In theory it is marked by a beacon 45 feet high; this fell down in 1919 and has not been replaced. Indeed, the Australian Government has treated the Great North-east Channel with scanty respect, and has not troubled to replace the beacon, nor has it cared to go to the expense of setting up a single light through its entire length, in spite of the fact that it is a perfect maze of reefs and low islands. As a result no vessel can use it at night. They are all obliged to anchor at dark. I was not at all anxious to anchor at Bramble Cay, as the fresh wind had raised a nasty sea, and that small sand heap gave very little protection. However, as we could not reach Stephens Island, the next possible anchorage, in daylight there was no choice, and with a hand aloft to look for submerged rocks, we skirted the south-west corner, and anchored between two arms of the fringing reef in 18 fathoms.

The Cay is a noted place for turtle and birds, and also for sharks, which come after the young turtle. As we were on the spot, it occurred to us that we might as well go and try to find some eggs. Accordingly, the dinghy was launched, and Tadgell, Joe, and I went ashore. We pulled the dinghy partly out of the water and secured the painter to an oar thrust as far as it would go into the sand. The beacon lay where it had fallen, and the beach was strewn with driftwood. In the centre of the little island was a depression covered with coarse grass. Thousands of birds were sitting about, and scores of their carcasses lay around. The birds were extraordinarily tame and quite unconcerned by our presence, and would hardly move sufficiently to save themselves from being trodden on. Turtle eggs, however, were the chief objects of our coming ashore, and we returned to the beach to look for them. There were numerous turtle tracks up the beach ending in small circular hollows. Not being expert turtle-egg finders we dug in these with our hands without coming across any eggs.

Later on, we learned that the eggs are not in the hollows at all but on the edges, and that the correct method is to thrust a thin stick in along the edge until it comes out marked with yolk. Not knowing this at the time we exhausted ourselves with scraping away the sand in the hollows, and then, giving it up, Tadgell and I went for a stroll across the island, a distance of about 400 yards. Presently we saw Joe running towards us. He announced that the dinghy had broken adrift, and was well away to sea, and when we reached the beach there it was driving quietly past the ship before the fresh wind.

Stéphane had seen it coming and was making feverish preparations for salving it. The simple expedient of jumping into the
sea and swimming to it may have occurred to him, but if it did
the thought of sharks must have deterred him, and he decided
on other measures. He dashed below and presently appeared
with the hip-bath. This he launched successfully, but as soon as
he lowered himself into it, it naturally sank, and was retrieved
with difficulty by his prehensile toes. Evidently the bath was
no use. The spinnaker boom next caught his eye and he started
to drag it out, but abandoned it in favour of the gratings,
which he seized and lashed together. He was trying hard to
rise to the occasion, and thoughts were evidently chasing each
other through his little brain with great speed, but as he did
not carry anything through, and dropped each thing in favour
of something else, it became clear to us on the beach that it
was our turn to move. The position was only too simple. The
dinghy was out of reach, and as there was neither food nor
water on the island we must sooner or later swim off to the
ship. We all thought of sharks, but none of us mentioned them.
There was plenty of driftwood on the shore and Tadgell and
I rolled a log into the sea. He hid his camera, under another
log and we embarked, each with one arm over the log, and
swimming with the other one and our legs. Joe also got a log,
and the flotilla put to sea. Luckily the distance was short,
about 300 yards. Joe went ahead at great speed and soon got on
board. Tadgell and I wallowed heavily along, slow but sure.
On the way my pipe floated out of my pocket, and Tadgell
seized it as it bobbed past. Eventually we arrived and climbed
up the bobstay, right glad to have reached the ship safely.
Every moment we had been expecting to be grabbed by a
shark. In addition, I feared that we might be swept past by
the current, in which case the position would have been very
serious, hopeless in fact. I am an indifferent swimmer, and was
fairly well pumped by the time we arrived, and the others
were none too fresh, but we got to work at once on the capstan,
and hove up the anchor. Very heavy work it was too, in that
depth. Finally we got it on deck, hoisted the mizzen and headsails, started the engine and sailed off after the dinghy long

since lost to sight. Stéphane soon spotted it from the mast head, and before dark we had it in tow and were beating back for the anchorage. It became dark before we sighted it, and after working for a time to windward we anchored where we were, using a kedge and 60 fathoms of wire rope. I should have liked to get back under the lee of the Cay to get what shelter was going, but as reefs fringe it for about half a mile, and as there are other reefs and rocks in the neighbourhood, it would have been unwise to sail about trying to find it. The stream swung the ship into the trough, and she rolled heavily, gunwales under.

As Tadgell and I sat at supper in the cabin, swaying to the roll, we discussed the question of how the dinghy could have got adrift, but could find no solution. When we reached her the painter was still fast to the oar, which she must have dragged out. Two days later on our arrival at Thursday Island Mr. May suggested that, as the sand on the Cay is largely drift sand, the strong wind had probably whirled away the heap into which we had thrust the oar, and that it had fallen down, and the same gust had blown the dinghy off the beach. That is, in my opinion, the correct explanation.

At 9 p.m. a heavy jar ran through the ship, and I heard Tadgell running aft along the deck. "More trouble," I thought.

"The wire has parted," he said.

"All right. Call the boys. We must get under way."

We hauled the remaining length of wire on board, and then set the mainsail and headsails, and after sailing N.E. for a time, to clear Nautilus Reef, hove to heading about east. At dawn we let draw and ran down towards the Cay to recover Tadgell's camera. It took us most of the morning to find the Cay again. The sky was overcast, and we could not fix the position by sights until nearly noon, but the sun came out, and then we got an idea where the ship was, and soon afterwards Tadgell sighted the sand heap from aloft. It took some time to beat up to it, as the sea was rough, but we got there in the end and anchored once more. Tadgell and Joe then went ashore in the dinghy and fetched the camera.

We remained at anchor for that night, and next day entered

the Great North-east Channel and, with a strong beam wind, made good progress all day, passing a number of small, low islands covered with cocoanut-trees. Just before dark we passed Arden Island, and then made for another small island lying a short distance out of the channel, and anchored under its lee. This island has not been named, and all the *Australia Pilot* says about it is that it is small, low, and wooded, and is situated on a reef 2¼ miles long. However, as it adds that "a native village was seen on the island" it is clear that though the authorities are obviously not sufficiently interested in it even to name it they did go so far as to send someone once to look at it.

It is a mystery to me why the Australian Government takes so little interest in the Torres Straits. Except along the steamer track farther south, leading to the east coast of Australia, there are no aids to navigation, in spite of the fact that it is one of the most rock-and-reef-strewn areas in the world, and is gaining daily in importance. It is not even properly surveyed. Large portions of the chart are marked "several reefs seen in this direction," "reefs reported," "reefs doubtful," "not surveyed," while we were warned at Port Moresby that an unnamed reef east of Long Island, and close to the steamer track, extends very much farther south-east than shown on the chart.

At 4 a.m. next morning we weighed and started off to complete the run to Thursday Island. It was a very pleasant sail, plenty of sun, a strong breeze, and, as we were under the lee of innumerable reefs, a smooth sea, while the intricacy of the navigation added interest to the passage. By the early afternoon we were nearing Flinders Passage, and looking out for the buoy which marks Scott Rock lying 5 feet under water in the centre of the channel. On and on we went, but no buoy hove in sight, and we concluded that it had broken adrift. As soon as we had passed the rock, according to bearings of the surrounding islands and points of land, we altered course for Hovell Bar. Taking accurate bearings in a small sailing-ship is no easy matter. The compass is necessarily low and swinging about, the ship is usually heeled over more or less, while the masts, sails, and gear often get in the way.

After crossing the bar we ran down the narrow Ellis Channel, and brought up near some pearling-ketches off Port Kennedy. Thursday Island, like most of its neighbours, is of moderate height, sandy, and scantily wooded. It is the centre of the pearl-shell fishery, and at one time was a gay, devil-may-care, dissipated, and rather lawless spot, but civilization has laid its blighting hand on it, and it is now dull and comparatively respectable. The pearling has fallen almost entirely into the hands of the Japanese, who also do much of the shipbuilding, while the stores and market-gardens are largely run by Chinese with a sprinkling of Indians. A fair number of Australian "black fellows" are to be found among the crews of the pearling "luggers," as they are called, though really ketches, so that it is rather a cosmopolitan community. The streets are sandy and wide, and the houses are mostly built of corrugated iron. Sand and corrugated iron, added to the scarcity of vegetation, do not strike a picturesque note, and Port Kennedy is frankly not beautiful. The white inhabitants, however, welcomed us with the usual kindness, and we received many invitations, and incidentally played golf on what they claimed to be the worst golf course in the world, bar one.

As we had again entered Australian waters, I had to enter the ship at the Customs, and supply a list of all stores on board with a view to the assessment of the duty to be paid on any of my own stores which were used while in port. The Customs officer telegraphed to headquarters for permission to excuse me from this formality in virtue of the Blue Ensign. The reply was a refusal, whereupon the clerk in one of the shipping firms volunteered to make out all the lists and fill in the various forms, and all I had to do was to sign them and pay the duty. Australians, as far as my experience goes, are always ready to take any amount of trouble, and put themselves to unlimited inconvenience to help anyone who seems in need of assistance, and they do it so much as a matter of course and with such good will that one cannot help being impressed. It is a delightful characteristic.

While at Port Kennedy I tried to arrange to have the ship put on a slip, of which there are five or six, to clean the hull and examine the copper, but she was too deep to get on any of them, and it was finally arranged to take her to a jetty, where she would partly dry out. In going alongside this the topmast forestay caught in a projecting beam which I had not seen, and the sudden jerk snapped the topmast and brought it crashing down. To see one's topmast suddenly break in two and fall to the deck without apparent cause is rather startling, and I was filled with amazement until the explanation was forthcoming. Joe was forward at the time and claimed to have warned me, as soon as he saw the beam, by shouting "here stick," but I had not grasped his meaning, and proceeded, with results disastrous to the topmast.

This, however, was only the beginning of our troubles, as the rush of the tides through the piers was so great that we found it almost impossible, even with the help of a Japanese shipwright and a gang of his men, to drag her alongside the jetty. The shipwright was a very excitable man, and the amount of frenzied shouting that went on, and the confusion which resulted from the way he and his men rushed about the deck, all screaming at once, and hauled on this and that, was both deafening and maddening. The only momentary relief from the uproar was when he fell bodily into the sail locker, disappearing from view like a flash of lightning. For a few minutes there was peace, but he reappeared almost at once more energetic and noisy than ever. On his advice, we did not haul the ship up to the beach until she grounded, as he feared we should not be able to get her off again. This was a mistake, and caused us much trouble and anxiety. By midnight, after a most exhausting struggle, we got her alongside, but when the tide turned we found that she was in a very dangerous position, as the rush of water was then forcing the keel and hull towards the jetty so that she had a tendency to lean outwards and fall over. To remedy this we got the broken topmast over the side and rigged it as a shore-leg to hold her up.

By the time this was done the work of scrubbing was started by the light of a hurricane lamp. The tides round these islands are very strong and irregular, but there are usually two unequal tides each day, of which the early one was, at the time of our visit, the lower. For this reason we had to start scrubbing in the dark, and, incidentally, did not get a wink of sleep all night in consequence. The next high water was what is known as the "lower high water," and was not sufficient to float us off, and we had to wait for the "higher high water" at midnight. By that time the wind had freshened up, and, as my small, weak engine would certainly not drive the ship against the rushing tide and so much wind, I went ashore to borrow a motor-boat. The Customs Officer arranged the matter, and in due time the motor-boat appeared out of the black night, and the Customs Officer also arrived, as did the shipwright and his gang of desperadoes.

If there had been sound, fury, and confusion in getting alongside, the getting away was ten times worse, and defies description. The shipwright, the Customs Officer, and the motor-boat man all had different plans, and all proceeded to carry out their individual plans quite irrespective of anyone else. The result was deplorable. However, in spite of the divided counsels, and the deafening uproar, we did get the ship afloat in the end, and with the help of the launch and our own engine crawled back to the anchorage.

One day while we were waiting for the shipwright to turn the squaresail yard into a topmast, Joe went ashore and came back rather mellow. He brought with him a bagful of eggs. I had given up buying these as they cost $4\frac{1}{2}d.$ each, and Joe thought he would give us a treat, but was rather diffident about breaking the news. However, he was at peace with the world and ventured:

"Some skipper no like crew to pay for food," he said, "but we good friend. That is best way."

Having thus introduced the subject he retired to allow the idea to sink in. Then he came along again.

"Skipper, I have egg. I cook you egg and bacon. That good?"

Of course I accepted and thanked him, and we feasted on eggs and bacon that night, he stood the eggs and I provided the bacon.

Stéphane was suddenly seized with the desire to become a pearl diver, and I made enquiries from Mr. May, who thought it could be arranged, but as soon as Stéphane heard that he would have to be "indented" for three years he lost interest in the matter.

"I like more to be my own master," he decided.

The Japs have recently invented a new diving-apparatus by means of which a diver can go to 45 fathoms, twice the usual depth, without inconvenience, and the strange feature about it is that he does not wear a diving-dress, but merely a water-tight mask over the upper part of the head including eyes and nose, leaving the mouth free. Compressed air is pumped down from the boat. A tube leads from the mask to the diver's mouth terminating in a valve, which the diver opens with his tongue when he wants air. We were told that trials had been quite successful. Though the diver does not need a dress he wears a boiler-suit to cover his white body which might otherwise attract sharks.

CHAPTER VI

THE EAST INDIES AND MALAYA

ON 27th August we left Port Kennedy for Timor. The original intention had been to go to Port Darwin first, to give Tadgell a chance of once more treading his native soil before leaving for the other side of the earth, but the fact that we were getting short of whisky when we reached Port Kennedy prevented us from following this plan. The connection between the two is not very obvious, yet it exists. I went round to the store to arrange for a case in bond. Sea-going ships are allowed to have wines and spirits duty free, and the store people said they could supply the whisky, but on learning that my next port was to be Port Darwin they assured me that with duty-free spirits on board I should have to comply with so many irritating Customs regulations that it would be better to forego the whisky. The alternative was to forego Port Darwin, described

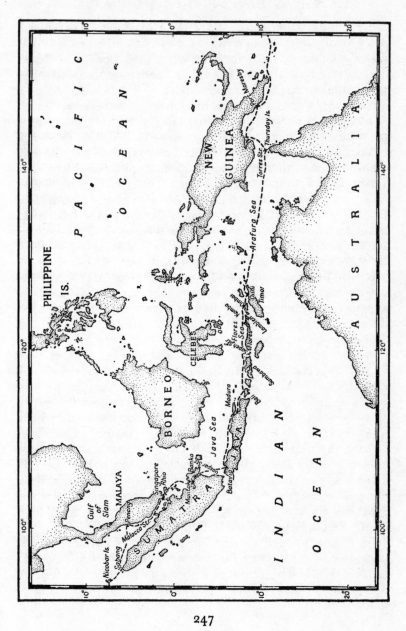

247

as an uninteresting town and a hot-bed of Bolshevism, and proceed direct to Timor, where there would be no trouble with the Customs. In the end, we or rather I, decided to "take the cash and let the credit go," in other words, to take the whisky and leave out Port Darwin. Tadgell, who does not care for whisky, would probably have decided otherwise, but I do not like tank water undiluted, and as he did not make a point of seeing Port Darwin we cleared for Dilhi in Timor.

The wind was light at first, but before dark Booby Island, the last link with the great Australian continent, had disappeared astern, and we had fairly entered the seas of the Eastern Archipelago. Behind us lay the lovely South Sea Islands with their doomed, uncivilized, primitive peoples, while ahead were some of the oldest known civilizations, together with some fierce, savage tribes, sunk, as the Sailing Directions say, "in a state of utter barbarism."

It was on the whole, a very pleasant run, and day after day we had a nice S.E. breeze, and bright sun. The sea was a good deal heavier than I had expected, though the Directions had warned us that it would be "considerable."

On the way we passed through several patches of discoloured water, which had every appearance of being shoal water over a sandbank. Tadgell drew up a few bucketsful and we found that this peculiar effect was caused by small, thin marine weeds, or confervæ, about $\frac{1}{8}$ inch long, and of about the thickness of thread. It is sometimes known as "sea-sawdust," which well describes its appearance when seen floating in patches. We also saw some flying fish with dark wings marked in yellow circles. They looked rather like misshapen butterflies.

Far away to the north lay the Aru group of islands, and to the west of them the Tenimbers, the inhabitants of which are "without civilization, savage and touchy," while in Timor Laut, one of the group, the natives are cannibals.

At 2 a.m. on 2nd September the light of Brisbane Rock appeared, and the same evening we entered Wetta Channel, between Wetta and Timor. On Wetta Island head-hunting is still practised, and it is not safe to go inland without a strong military escort.

As soon as we entered the Channel we lost the wind and rolled heavily about in a short swell, and made a very slow passage to Dilhi, where we arrived on the 4th.

The island of Timor presents a very volcanic appearance. Lofty, rugged peaks are massed together, with well-wooded ridges but bare slopes. In the rainy season the slopes are covered with vegetation. The eastern part of the island belongs to the Portuguese, while the western portion is Dutch. The chief Portuguese port is Dilhi. The harbour there is sheltered by extensive reefs, and there are also an inconvenient number of small, detached reefs spread over the enclosed portion, which reduce the space available for anchorage to relatively small dimensions. Indeed, after we had run down S. by W. for the lighthouse until we made the entrance buoys and passed in, I had to rearrange all my plans for anchoring, as I saw that we should not have room to round up in the position I had fixed on in my mind. The *Amaryllis*, like most heavy displacement ships, carries her way for a long time even with no wind in the sails, and this has to be allowed for when bringing up. A glance at the chart showed me that we should have to pass inside a reef lying a hundred yards from the shore, and then round up. The bowsprit did not actually knock off anyone's hat on the beach, but we had to go very close in, and I could see the crew forward shifting uneasily about and casting anxious looks aft.

The little town looks charming from the water. It is stretched out along the front and the white houses peeping through the big banyan trees which fringe the sea produce a most pleasing effect. In fact, we were delighted with our first glimpse of the East. The streets are planted with trees for the sake of shade, and the houses are widely spaced and buried in more trees. The population consists of a few Portuguese, many Chinese and Arabs, and the natives proper, the latter rather small and slight, wearing sarongs and vests. After a walk round under the hot sun we proceeded to cater. Unluckily we could not find anyone who could speak English, but we managed to buy some fruit at a Chinaman's. The next thing was bread, and our efforts to get that created quite a stir in the Chinese quarter.

We marched into a shop and demanded bread. The Chinaman looked at us, diagnosed us as British, and produced two bottles of beer. We waved them aside. He then offered an egg, and finally one small roll. We explained by signs that we wanted several of those, whereupon he went outside his shop and directed us in fluent, high-pitched Chinese to another store farther along. His fervent harangue attracted the attention of all the little Chinese boys and loafers within hearing, and it was quite a formidable body that descended on the bread shop. Our escort filled it to overflowing and loudly explained our needs. The proprietor brought out a basket of rather dirty-looking rolls, and then the question of price arose, and a great argument ensued. All within reach pawed over the rolls to ascertain the number, and then announced the result of their calculations. There seemed to be a good deal of difference of opinion, but in the end the matter was adjusted, and we bore off the bread at the head of a small procession which saw us down to the wharf.

While waiting for our boat to come off we called on the captain of a small Government steamer lying alongside. He could speak English and received us very kindly, and paid us a visit on board. He told us that his steamer is sent by the Government to develop the settlements along the coast by taking them stores and collecting their produce. He is the only officer on board, and when he gets to sea spends his whole time on the bridge. He eats and sleeps there, and never leaves it until he returns. He mentioned that the charts of the island are so inaccurate that he has had to make one of his own. For instance, a headland at the east end is 5 miles farther north than shown, and Lamsana Bay, charted as a narrow inlet several miles long, is really only a slight indentation on the coast. He told us that he had often to make an anchorage at night when his only guides were the chance sight of some peak or tree inland which he could recognize, and the sound of the sea breaking on the reefs! He invited us for lunch on board his ship next day, when he gave us a great spread. The Harbour Master and his wife were present, also the Captain's wife. The latter had brought her two little children on board in charge of their nurse, a little boy of about twelve! Girls, it seems, are never used as nurses, as "they are not sweet to children," Mrs. Captain said. Neither are they used as servants in the houses, where all housework is done by boys or men. Luckily, all at the table could speak English, though Mrs. Harbour Master had a tendency to relapse into French. The lunch consisted of vegetable soup; fish mayonnaise; meat and omelette together and also vegetables; asparagus; a sweet; fruit; coffee; with red and white wine to drink, followed by champagne and port. In our honour a tin of bully beef was also opened, as it was supposed that Englishmen could not possibly live without it, and that it appeared at all their meals. It was a most enjoyable lunch, and some considerable change from our usual meals on board.

At about 4 p.m. the steamer went to sea taking with her a number of native soldiers, most of whom had a game-cock tied up in a cloth on their backs. Cock-fighting is almost a national sport.

Once or twice we dined ashore at the little hotel. Most of the guests sat in a large room, but our table was always set on a verandah. On the first occasion I ordered a bottle of "vinho tinto" which I imagined was Portuguese for red wine, but the waiter thought I must mean beer, and brought a bottle, and when I sent him away he just retired out of sight and then returned with the same bottle. He could not bring himself to think that we could possibly drink anything else, but in the end we got the wine. Perhaps "vinho tinto" does not mean red wine, but at any rate I am sure it does not mean beer.

I asked the Harbour Master if there was an engineer in the place who would come and try to find out what was the matter with the clutch and gears of the engine. He brought off a Chinaman, a remarkably alert young man—a quality very unusual amongst his race. All day he toiled over the engine, but could not get the gears out, and in the end had to give the matter up.

[*At this point Lieut. Muhlhauser's narrative comes to an end. The rest of the story of the cruise is told in extracts chosen from his diary and from letters which have been kindly lent by friends.*]

6 Sep. On this day in 1920 I sailed from England.

7 Sep. While I was waiting for the Bill of Health I went out through the Chinese and Arab quarters to look at three old and very large banyan trees, one of which was twenty paces in circumference. The trunk is made up of roots, to use a bull. I passed a number of reed houses belonging to the natives proper. The sun is very hot here, but there do not seem to be any flies or mosquitoes.

We hoisted the boat and got ready for sea, and were under way just after noon. Farewell to Timor and to Dilhi, the quaint! Dilhi reminds me of Tahiti in some ways. Both are spread along the beach, with the houses buried in trees. But in Dilhi the water is so deep close in that steamers anchor with their sterns made fast to trees on the shore.

My original plan was to pass south of Ombai, through the Lamakwera Channel to Leba Leba, but the captain of the Government steamer said the tides were much too strong, and the ship would be ungovernable. So I decided to pass north of Ombai to Bali. A light breeze held all night, but I got no sleep until after 2 a.m., as, the weather being very hot, I tried sleeping on deck. The plan has its disadvantages, as I am too near the helmsman and am often called without reason. Once however I did hear an ominous sound as of surf breaking on a beach, but that could not be, so the sound must be caused by another tide rip, and sure enough we were soon in the midst of a very rough and irregular sea. As there was very little wind, the boom jumped about in a terrifying way. Great seas reared up all round and rushed about in all directions. The ship had no steerage way and drove about anyhow. I ran the engine until we were out of the race and had put some distance between it and us. The wind was then on the beam, but she was quieter with the boom in and we let her go along N.W. all night. We are keeping well off the shore, as the *Pilot* says it is not safe to pass within twelve miles of the straits on account of the tremendous tides.

The sunset last night was wonderful. The sun sank amidst scarlet clouds behind the mountains of Ombai, which were all shades from purple to a sort of green. A marvellous sunset, the most striking I have seen. The sunrise this morning was also fine.

8 Sep. The wind kept light all day, but as there was no sea we found this a pleasant change, though we did not get along very fast, and only made good 71 miles in 24 hours. The sunset was again very fine, the sun setting blood-red. Perhaps volcanic dust accounts for these grand sunsets. This whole region is a mass of old volcanoes, with a few active ones spread about.

9 Sep. Fine day. I took a sight for practice to see how it worked out by land bearings, since we were nearing Komba Island and could see Lomblen. The result was good, the position line running right through the estimated position by the land. This is the Flores Sea, about which very little seems to be known. The sun is very hot and the spokes of the wheel get almost too hot to touch, while metal work burns the hands. A fish, presumably a shark, has bitten one of the vanes off the log rotator.

10 Sep. Sukur Island is in sight ahead and Flores can just be seen to port. I am keeping about 25 miles out, hoping to get a better wind. At the moment I have abandoned the course and am keeping her right before the N.E. swell, as she rocks about with the sea on her quarter, since there is not enough wind to keep the sails quiet. This is a windless part of the world. At noon there was no wind at all, a complete calm, which lasted until 9 p.m., when a breeze came off the land. For a time we got along well, and then the wind fell completely away. Sukur Island was abeam at midnight; it was still in sight next morning. We are not getting along at all; I do not want to run the engine, as it is not in good condition, and I am keeping it for an emergency and for entering Soerabaya.

11 Sep. At noon a light E.N.E. breeze worked round to north of east, and as we could not come off any further on account of Paloë Island, I gybed and had to start the engine. Slowly we crawled along with all sail set, including the spinnaker set as a balloon jib, and finally got past Paloë before dark. All night we lay becalmed, not a breath. It would seem to be best to anchor off the coast at night, but the water is too deep for that. These islands rise steeply from the sea.

12 Sep. Last of the eggs for breakfast. I told Stéphane to put the eggs one by one into a cup of fresh water; if they floated they were bad. Presently I saw him getting a bucket of sea water.

"What is that for?"

"To try the eggs; they all sink in fresh water."

He was quite disappointed not to be able to announce some bad ones.

An absolute calm. If this goes on we shall have to miss Bali and go right on to Soerabaya. We are taking too much time. It was a lovely night but a heart-breaking time, as the ship rolled incessantly to a slight swell, and the jars and the wear and tear of gear were frightful.

13 Sep. At 6 a.m. a very light wind came from E.S.E. and gradually got stronger, causing us to gybe.

Joe is suffering from some ear trouble and seems depressed. I tried Coué on him, but he was not very enthusiastic.

We are now off Sapeh and Linta Straits between Flores and Sumbawa, 25 miles out to avoid tide rips, and are getting along fairly well, probably at 4½ knots. The daily runs so far have been very small, and we are six days out for 328 miles. We have been becalmed for hours at a time, not moving ahead at all.

14 Sep. At 11 a.m. a light air came from N.E., but it did not last and the intolerable calm set in once more. Roll, roll, roll, with the sails swaying to and fro. We may have a breeze to-night, the sky is cloudy. . . . Sure enough a breeze came along, a strong one. The sky looked bad, heavy clouds all over it and low down. Under ordinary conditions I should have reduced sail, but as things were I was very loath to take anything off and chanced it.

15 Sep. She was going fast in the early morning, about 7 knots. At the morning sight we had run by log 60 miles since half-past four yesterday afternoon, but the position worked out at 48 miles, so either the log is over-registering or we had a stream against us. We are now nearing Tambora Mountain, which causes errors in compasses. There is a good deal of traffic about; three ships are in sight now. This is a change for us who did not see a ship at sea since leaving Auckland until we got into the Torres Straits.

Nearly all our biscuits are bad, mouldy. Just now we are making no progress and are running short of stores. We have enough for six days and must try to get to Buleleng by then. . . . A light breeze has come N.E. and we are moving.

16 Sep. At 2 a.m. the boom was crashing about and I turned out and had it got in. There was a horrible short, confused sea and the poor old ship had a bad time; it is a wonder she stands it so well. A breeze came at 6 a.m. and I turned every one out and got sail on, light stuff. At dawn we could see Tambora bearing south-west, and we were about where I had placed her. The compass does not seem to have been affected by the mountain. Hurrah, we are moving along! We have to go on to a short allowance of meat, and we are quite out of breakfast dishes, except three tins of sardines.

All day long we have had our wings spread and have been moving slowly along. The morning sight was very disappointing and put us five miles back. We logged thirteen miles and only made good eight of them. It seems there is an easterly current along the north shores east of Java.

At eleven p.m. there was a strong south breeze, which was a great help. It lasted for about twelve hours and then fell right away, leaving us rolling in a confused swell, which came all ways.

Joe has made a wonderful fish pancake; three sardines each is the allowance, but the pancake was as big as a plate.

18 Sep. We have 80 miles to Buleleng. The wind is now south, light, but enough to keep the sails quiet. That is the main thing.

19 Sep. At dawn we were nearing Sangsit, and the lighthouse of Buleleng appeared soon afterwards. The swell kept up; it is a mystery whence it comes, as there has been no wind for at least a fortnight. We anchored in $9\frac{1}{2}$ fathoms, but when she swung round the stern was in less than 2 fathoms, and we had to heave in during dinner and get farther out. This time we dropped the anchor in 12 fathoms, and behold, the stern was in 3 fathoms. The bottom must be an extremely steep slope.

Seen from the sea Buleleng is a charming spot. The beach is littered with all types of boats, and the town lies hidden in groves of cocoanut trees. A quaint trading vessel is anchored near us. Her foremast is a tripod; the bow is very low and open, forward of a bulkhead; the rudder or rudders are not fixed, but are worked from the side, one on each side. There is no boom to either sail, but only a standing gaff. The Harbour Master told me that there was no wind here but at midday, except in the N.W. monsoon. We noticed a number of schooners out at sea with all sail down except a mizzen. When the breeze came at midday they hoisted sail and went on. Perhaps that is the way to do things here.

This is a bit of the East, Malays, Arabs, Chinese. A fascinating place. We saw a meat vendor squatting on his heels in the street. He had meat on a bamboo and was cooking it over a charcoal fire, which he kept going with a fan. He then made a sauce in a leaf, added the meat and skewered it all together. The police have so far imbibed the spirit of the place as to sit about anywhere, nursing their truncheons. One never sees them standing.

There is a Temple to the Sea on the beach, and, we gathered, Temples to the Land and to the Mountains. But the Harbour Master was very difficult to understand.

20 Sep. As there is no Bank in Buleleng, an Englishman, Edgar, advanced me 300 guilders to be paid in at Soerabaya. He drove us in the afternoon to Singaraja, and on the way we stopped at a temple. The entrance gate was of fantastically carved figures in soft soapstone. Inside was a courtyard, with on the further side three shrines, approached by steps. The whole was beautifully carved. From there we drove to the Rest House at Singaraja and had our introduction to a "rice-table." First comes rice, then follow a soup sauce, meat, salad, chicken, salads again and small condiments, all piled one on the other. A bowl is placed by each guest, in case the plate will not hold enough. We then drove to a place along the coast where Edgar keeps a sailing sampan, in which he has fitted a Watermota. The road was good and lay between fields of rice and groves of cocoanuts and bananas. Along the roadside were small stalls of fruit, meat and drink, presided over by very demure little Balinese girls. Everywhere we passed groups of Balinese, smooth-faced and healthy, the women moving most gracefully. The men wore coloured sarongs, the women a sarong and at times a bodice. An interesting day.

21 Sep. Eclipse, partial, of the sun, starting about 11 a.m. and lasting for about two hours. A religious procession to the Temple passed. The music was monotonous but pleasing, a gong and drums. They went out to sea, still playing, in a large sampan and then came back to the Temple to the Sea.

At noon we left. Wind very light and then calm; not so much swell.

22 Sep. At 2 a.m. Meinderts Light was sighted to port. We were then in Madura Strait, between Madura and Java, the latter said to be the most populous large island in the world. It is very mountainous and some of the mountains are of fantastic shape. Mount Tenger has the largest active crater in the world. We kept along the coast about 8 miles out. After sunrise the wind had died away for a time and then came E.N.E., light, until 10 p.m., when it shifted very quickly to S.S.W. and hardened to a nice breeze. This change puzzled me, and as it seemed my turn to move I had the topsail taken off, but nothing special happened, except that there was a great display of lightning over Madura.

It is very hot, 87° F. in the cabin.

23 Sep. At 2 a.m. we were off Koko Lighthouse. The wind was light and dead ahead so I started the engine and we worked slowly up the East Gat. A great many native craft were fishing with nets. In one case a net was out supported by floats, both ends in the boat and two men swimming around tending it. The sails are lateen with the base or widest part upwards. At 2 p.m. we were through the Gat and in the Soerabaya Roads. I could not pick out a snug anchorage anywhere. Anchored out in the stream were many large ships, but that was no place for us. While I was dodging about a pilot came off and said there was no snug anchorage for small ships, and that we were then in as good a spot as any, so we promptly let go. The tidal streams run very hard in the Roads, and we found the dinghy too heavy to make way against them, except at slack water, so we usually hired a sampan.

24 Sep. Went to the Harbour Master, to the Port Doctor and to a ship-chandler. We had tiffin at the *Hellendoorn* and then imagined that we were being driven to a band, that was what I told the waiter I wanted, but instead found ourselves at the harbour once more. At dark the wind against the tide raised a steep sea, and the old ship sat heavily on a wave time after time. The blows shook her and suggested that the counter might come off, an example of the evils of a counter.

25 Sep. Saw the British and the Chinese Consuls. Bought clothes. Our way to the Chinese Consul led us through the native and the Chinese quarters. The shops were crowded together and full of strange wares. Barbers operated in the streets. The mixture of colour was wonderful. We passed a Chinese girls' school coming out, all dressed in neat white jackets and trousers. The streets were crowded. Little traps driven by Malays, with the passenger sitting aft in great state, were mixed up with push and motor-bicycles motor-lorries, and cars. The Malay Police are most unsuitably dressed, in blue serge and gaiters, and armed with swords and truncheons. A puny looking lot. The Malay is not very robust.

26 Sep. A fair amount of traffic was moving about as we started off for the Droogdok. First came a dredger from the Naval Basin, crossing our bows; then several launches whizzed past; sampans and praus were also moving along and lighters in tow of tugs. When the dock people were ready we pulled away on to a buoy, and they submerged the dock. As soon as it was low enough we entered, and a crowd of pirates boarded us, an evil-looking lot, and dragged off dog-shores, which after a great deal of shouting and confusion were adjusted, two on each side. The dock was raised at a great speed and was right up in ten minutes. The ship was well placed. She was clean and the copper was in very fair condition on the whole; but the keel was foul and encrusted with barnacles and oysters. Then came the turn of the motor and another gang of ruffians was put on under a young engineer of mixed pedigree. They wrestled with it all day, but made very little progress. The ship

258

was full of natives, and the decks were in a state of great confusion.

In the evening we drove in to the *Hellendoorn*. We sat in front of the restaurant, and kris sellers came round and going on to one knee offered their wares, krisses and brasses from Madura. One man offered me a 'beautifully worked kris for 25 guilders, but at once accepted my counter offer of 5 guilders. We tried to find a native theatre but failed.

27 Sep. Work going on all day on the hull and aloft. Van West and the engineer, Styn, said that the engine had better go ashore to be overhauled. The former also offered to put us up for the Club, Simpan Vergunning. A gang was let loose on the engine and started taking it down. It was a terrible business and took most of the day, while the ship suffered in her fittings. Finally they got it off its bed and hoisted it up by the chain purchase. A crane was brought along the dock and lowered into the cabin and finally the engine was hoisted out and sent away to the shop in a tug. A sailmaker ruffian and his attendant thief put a pair of my pliers into their bag to take away. However I spotted the act and demanded restitution. They were not at all abashed, but much amused.

The disadvantage of Soerabaya lies in the fact that it is spread about so much; the distances are too great. The heat prevents one from walking and the taxis are very expensive. It is an interesting place and the costumes are great. As regards hats alone one could write pages. There are turbans of all sorts, forms and colours, fezes of felt or velveteen, felt hats, ordinary straw hats, mushroom hats and others such as Robinson Crusoe wore. A tram conductor wore his official cap on top of a turban. The bulk of the population sleep out of doors. Coolies seem to lie down anywhere and go to sleep.

28 Sep. At 9 a.m. the dock was submerged and we floated out and tied up to wait for the engine. I saw this in the very fine engineers' shop of the Company. The engine in general is all right, but the thrust was a bit worn and allowed the gears to fall back out of position. Ordered stores; the prices are awful, simply frightful.

29 Sep. We sleep on deck under mosquito nets; it is too hot below. Went ashore for a sandwich and a glass of beer at a small restaurant near the quay. The usual panic of waiters occurred; they all buzzed round, but none of them could speak English and we could not order a sandwich but had to have a full meal.

30 Sep. Arranged to have the ship disinfected in the afternoon. All ships are disinfected before leaving Soerabaya, or at their next port. If we are done here we need not be done at Batavia. Went round to get fresh water, but the supply had failed and all we could get was from a tap in the dispensary. Filled two tanks. Meanwhile the engineers wrestled with the engine. After a good deal of trouble it was induced to start and then ran well, and we anchored off the west dockhead. The doctor then came along and put three pots of sulphur on board —they never use cyanide. We had taken out the metal fittings, chronometers, sextants, etc., and put them on deck. After starting up the sulphur and closing up we went ashore with the doctor, leaving Joe and Stéphane camped out on deck. A map of the world hung in the Harbour Master's office, and I showed him and the doctor my track. The doctor kept on exclaiming "Good God" in tones of almost pained surprise. We drove back along the Kali Maas, which runs through the town. The water is dirty, but the natives were bathing in it. On clearing the Kali our sampanmen set sail. The sampan mast is about five feet high and the sail is shaped like a jackyard topsail. A strop round the bamboo yard keeps it to the top of the mast, and the heel is put in a snotter round the mast at the deck. The yard is fitted with a vang and the boom with a sheet. On arriving on board we opened up. Clouds of sulphur poured out. I went below and got out the pans and had also to remain below while the various articles were passed back.

The weather is very hot and one gets wet through at the least exertion, while the quantity of liquid taken is enormous.

2 Oct. At 8.30 a sampan came along with stores. The prices are awful, 8 lb. of mutton, nearly all bone, cost 19s. 6d., and other things in proportion. Going to an agent has been an expensive lesson; we must manage better in future and leave these agents alone. We hoisted the boat, covered the inside with bags, put a few buckets of water into her and were ready to weigh. As soon as the cable was on board, we hoisted sail, going into the wind for the purpose, and bore away for the West Gat. The stream was fair and strong, but, as luck would have it, the wind came right ahead and we had to beat through. At 3 p.m. we were through and went off W.N.W. over the Bank. I had to run the engine at the end of the Narrows, as the wind fell light and a nasty little sea got up.

3 Oct. The meat which cost so much is uneatable, it is so hard. We must try mincing it and making some sort of stew with a tin of peas.

The wind fell by degrees during the day. At noon it was calm, but an air came at 2 p.m. from E.N.E. At dark Manda-like Island showed up. The sky is heavy with leaden clouds and there has been thunder during the day. A depressing evening. The night may pass quietly, but quite likely not. An extraordinary game, this.

4 Oct. The day was fine but calm, and I started the engine, as I want to get on. We are late and the monsoon is almost done. As I write this, perspiration is pouring off me. I spent most of the afternoon trying to stop oil and water leaking from the engine; and then read up winds and weather for Banka Strait and Gaspar Strait. We are in for a lot of bother there, I think, from currents and gales, and I cannot decide which way to go.

A breathless night. There was, however, little swell, and what there was came from aft, so that I could keep the ship before it. I set up one topping-lift to take the weight of the boom, brought amidships, off the sail. I have practically decided to take the Banka Strait, in preference to the Gaspar or the Stolze Strait. There are too many "stones," as the Harbour Master at Soerabaya called the rocks and reefs, in the two latter. I must now concentrate on getting the ship along towards home. Time is getting on but we are not, or very slowly, owing to an entire absence of wind. The sea is flat except for a slight easterly swell. Swimming snakes are fairly numerous, and just now porpoises are lazily rolling by.

5 Oct. In the afternoon a dark line showed to windward, a

light breeze coming over the water. Slowly it advanced and at last reached us. The sunset looked stormy; the sun set in a dense bank of purple clouds. Thunder rumbled inland.

6 Oct. At noon there were 95 miles to go. I shall be glad to get to Batavia and away again, as we are now at the change of monsoon and anything may happen. The breeze held all day and we got along well.

7 Oct. Wind light. These gentle breezes are little good to *Amaryllis*. She likes a good breeze and is too heavy to respond to light winds. The praus here sail away from her with ease; they carry a lot of sail for their size. Three passed in the small hours. I could hear their wash a long way off while we were hardly moving.

At the time of writing we are round Krawang Point, ten miles from Batavia. The wind hardened during the afternoon and came slowly round to west and we were romping along. We saw first the tops of trees and buildings, then the masts and funnels of ships, and then the harbour. The spot I had chosen for an anchorage, to the west of the breakwater, did not attract with a fresh westerly wind, so I decided to anchor to the eastward, which we did under sail. A pilot came off at dark; I told him we should go in next day.

8 Oct. The ship-chandler got us a sampan, which remains alongside all day for 2.50 f. This place, Tanjong Priok, is the harbour for Batavia, which lies seven miles away. It is formed by two breakwaters running out for a mile.

9 Oct. Our sampan, flying "C" flag to distinguish it, came off soon after noon, and brought an engineer to look at the motor. He found it wrongly adjusted but soon had it right.

10 Oct. Went ashore early with the water breakers. Paid Light Dues at the Customs. Called on Balderston, who asked us to lunch. Tadgell and I had a "rice table." There were ten waiters all bearing dishes standing round our table in single file. Balderston then drove us to his house where we had tea and saw some good tennis. Then he dined with me.

11 Oct. Weighed at 10 a.m. and left the harbour under power. The wind remained variable all the afternoon and fell away at dark. At noon next day a very heavy bank of clouds formed in the N.E., in the heart of which lightning appeared and thunder rumbled. We stowed the topsail, luckily as it happened, as a stiff gust came along with a torrent of rain which lasted half an hour and was followed by a flat calm. At dark it was still calm and the sky looked wicked. Thunder and lightning were going on all round. We lowered the mainsail to save chafe, as she was rolling heavily in a nasty easterly swell, and also to be on the safe side in case there was a lot of wind in the disturbance going on. One smart squall with heavy rain blew up and after that it was again calm.

13 Oct. The sun bore south at noon to-day for the first time since early in 1921. It was a delight to sit at the wheel and feel the ship sailing, and sailing fast too at times. The light winds we had been having were no use to her; they hardly filled the heavy canvas, and she was very bored. The sun shone most of the day and the sea sparkled. Here and there a wave broke in a white crest, white on blue, and our bow thrust aside foaming waves as the ship pushed on. In the afternoon a school of porpoises came to visit us, a dozen of them gambolled quite close to us; in fact, one was nearly cut down. At midnight Dapur Light suddenly appeared; it had been hidden by rain-clouds. At 6 a.m. I got a rough bearing on Lucipara Island and the Lighthouse, and that was the last we saw of anything for a time, as the rain blotted all out. The wind was then west. The sky soon became black with a yellowish patch in the centre, and a waterspout appeared, which, by bearings, seemed to be advancing straight for us. As we could not get out of the way we prepared to receive a quantity of water by battening down completely and fitting the skylight boards; we also lowered the mainsail. The wind shifted from west to east and blew fairly hard, with heavy rain, and we lost sight of the waterspout and never saw it again. The position of the ship was very uncertain, as I could not see any marks on account of the rain. Conditions could hardly have been worse for making the south entrance to Banka Strait, never easy at any time. For a while we lay hove to. It was lucky we hove to when we did or we might have run on to the Melville Bank, though I think we should have cleared it. The tides round here are very difficult to make out. In the Banka Strait for instance they run for twelve hours in one direction. After lunch we went on, but as the stream was clearly against us we brought up off off Pulo Besar Lighthouse.

15 Oct. There was no wind, but we ran the engine, and when in the afternoon the stream turned against us we brought up off Second Bight. At sunset the sky looked very wicked, heavy purple clouds all round, with glimpses of blue, green and yellow sky, and squalls everywhere. We seem to be anchored in the middle of the ocean, as the nearest bank is just visible seven miles away. The Strait here is twenty miles across. At 6 p.m. a very heavy rainstorm came on; we could hear the hiss of the approaching rain while it was still a long way off. Very little wind came with it. I got out the hip-bath and a breaker and collected rain-water; then we stripped for a fresh water bath.

Joe came along and told me that there were no more potatoes or onions. They never tell me that anything is getting short until it is actually finished. Altogether we are very short of stores and of lubricating oil for the engine. Muntok at the north end of the Strait is a possible place to replenish at, and we have decided to use up what little oil there is in getting there, if possible. The barometer is lower than it has been for days.

16 Oct. We weighed at dawn. The morning was calm, except for squalls, which were blowing about in half a dozen places. Usually there was not a great weight of wind in them, but one never knows, and I had to be watching them all day. While we were at dinner, Stéphane managed to gybe. He has no luck in that way; as soon as he goes to the wheel something usually happens. About 5 p.m. we let go our anchor off Muntok Pier.

The difficulty about buying stores was that we had only a few guilders and no way of getting more. The Harbour Master, who was very courteous, as were all the Dutch officials we met, was amused at the idea of our coming for stores without money to pay for them, but referred us to a Chinaman, who agreed to buy a few odds and ends of "trade" left over from the trip through the islands—knives, razors, needles, pipes, cotton, etc. The amount they realized was not enough to square the account, whereupon he made a show of reducing the quantities, but actually reduced his prices to make things balance. A real gentleman is Mr. Lim A. Pat. He failed to understand why, since a passage in a steamer would not cost more and would be more comfortable, we did not take a steamer. The whole thing struck him as very amusing and quite incomprehensible; but he was interested and helped us all he could.

We weighed the same afternoon and went out. We had a nice gentle breeze and a smooth sea all night and kept moving. The breeze died away at 10 a.m. the next day, and I got the engine going, my plan now being to keep the ship going ahead all the time, at any rate during daylight. At last we are clear of the Banka Strait; we have had to fight our way through it. I could make nothing of the tides there. The *Pilot* devotes two pages to them, and after careful study I could not make out which way they would be running at any time. The information seems contradictory. In the evening thunder-clouds appeared and lightning was flashing all night. All this thunder and lightning and shifting winds made things very uncomfortable; one never knew what to expect. I am very fogged as to our exact position and cannot identify anything. There are islands galore and the tops of trees showing over the horizon, but I cannot fix them. This is an awkward place to be in at night, as the tides run thwartwise; moreover, the rain clouds obscure things.

19 Oct. At 10.30 a.m. we crossed the line and are now once more in north latitude. No ceremonies marked the occasion.

20 Oct. At 2 a.m. Joe called me. I sent him aloft to look for Karas Light, in the hopes he might see it from there and we might learn which way we were being set. The streams are strong round these Straits, and we might have been set a long way during the night. He saw a dark line to starboard which might be land, though this seemed impossible. At dawn islands appeared all along the N.E. side, which I inferred were Pulo Gin and Pulo Telang, and a sight at 7 a.m. confirmed

this. We had been set 15 miles N.E. during the night. . . .
Now we are airing along and advancing slowly against the ebb
from Rhio Strait. On account of this ebb I had intended to
bring up off Pulo Pankel, but a light air drove us along and we
went on to Chemara Bay.

21 Oct. We weighed and passed out through the north end
of the strait, along the line of beacons, under power, as it was
calm. At 11 a.m. Pan Reef Lighthouse was abeam to port,
and we were then within sight of Singapore. Rhio Strait is
full of islands and makes a fine picture. The water was like a
mirror, quite smooth and polished. I saw a fish hopping over
the water on his tail. The sails of the junks round here are
shaped like the wings of a butterfly, and are spread on bamboo
battens. . . . The stream was foul and strong, and we were
swept back and had to anchor in Bulang Bay, a charming little
spot on the south shore. We are down to our last tin of soup,
and have no jam and only two tins of vegetables, so it is time
we got in. . . .

22 Oct. Reached Singapore itself. It is an open anchorage, no
harbour, but a breakwater three-quarters of a mile long
opposite the wharves.

(*From a letter*) This is a big port and the Roads are crowded
with ships. As we approached we could see forests of masts,
and the inner harbour was crammed. However I found a
place, but was told that all that part was required for merchant
ships, so had to shift. We are now half a mile from a landing.
At the moment a fisherman and a sampanman are quarrelling
alongside over the price to go ashore, the fisherman being for
us. You write about "luscious tropical fruit." Would you
believe that we have had the greatest difficulty in getting
anything but bananas and cocoanuts? Occasionally paw-paws,
very fine, and a few odd things. We got oranges at Dilhi, pine-
apples at Java and mangoes here, but in the main a scarcity.

Both the Boarding Officer and Stevens, the ship-chandler,
had heard of us from Sydney. The latter is a member of
the Royal Singapore Sailing Club and is putting us up for
it.

24 Oct. When I returned from my visit ashore, I found two

coolies on board and the deck strewn with krisses, spears and pearl shells, there was even a turtle. I chided Joe for allowing them on board, and then found it was Mahomed Hussein and his brother. I had promised Hussein that I would go to his house and look at his stuff, but as it came on to rain, he and his brother had brought it off to save me.

25 Oct. A sailmaker and a painter came off, also a laundry-man and a tailor. I made Joe go ashore in the afternoon and have a walk round; he is too much on board; so is Stéphane, who by rights should be playing football with lads of his own age.

1 Nov. The Vice-Commodore and the Sailing Secretary called, coming alongside very skilfully in their rater. We went ashore at dark to dine at the Chinese restaurant. The streets of the Chinese quarter were thronged and bright with lights. Chinese notices hung on strips of canvas or were painted on the corners and over the shops. Along the kerb was an end-less line of stalls. All was movement, and yellow skins shone wherever one looked, as the Chinaman is fairly indifferent to clothes. The women however always wear black trousers and a loose jacket. The restaurant refused to receive us at first, but after a time an English-speaking Chinaman came and we ordered a dinner at 2.50 dollars each. The room was plainly furnished and not very clean. Cheap prints of "The Coast of Sweden" and "A Mill in Holstein" hung on the walls, together with notices in Chinese. The dinner appeared, pots of tea and three small plates of jam, chillies and sauce. The waiter then brought hot, damp towels for us to wipe our faces with. He next produced chopsticks and a dish of mixed food, followed by another dish of small squares of something, and yet another of fish and vegetables, and then a bowl of soup with meat and vegetables in it, all of which we tackled and found good, but had difficulty with the chopsticks. Other hot, damp towels appeared and the meal was over. The scene from the window was very animated and I could have spent a long time watching it.

7 Nov. Finished the log for the Royal Cruising Club, and inked in the track. I shall have to send twelve charts.

11 Nov. Armistice Day. Found that many ships had dressed, so we did likewise. Went to the Yacht Club. Just outside are the Tamil Lines, a colony of long-haired Indians. They look like women with their long hair. Arabs, Indians and Chinese keep the shops and do the retail trading. The rickshawmen are all Chinese, and Stevens says they can do enormous distances. He was once taken 26 miles in an afternoon and evening by one man, who averaged 7 miles to the hour when going. These rickshaws are very convenient, but one has a feeling of repugnance at being run round by a human being. The Malays will only drive cars and act as policemen and postmen; they will not do any manual work.

13 Nov. Joe came on board very drunk and said he wanted to go back to New Zealand.

17 Nov. Still searching for a crew, having rejected an Irishman and a Chinese. One suggestion was to take a Chinese cook, who would contract to feed us at so much a day, but he would be useless on deck. Another to take two Malays, but they require special feeding. I am coming to the conclusion that we must take a white man if we can find one. I met Captain Humphreys, who brought off the Belgian he had mentioned, Enden, who has never sailed but has always been in steam. The Captain said he was a real good man, so I decided to take him, though he is not really a sailor. Then I saw Captain Morris of the Sailors' Home about Joe. In the afternoon Joe left and right sorry was I to see him go.

21 Nov. Dr. Hoops, his two daughters, and Mr. Vickers came to tea. After they left we said good-bye to Mr. and Mrs. Morse. Mr. Morse was a film man who wanted to interest me in moving pictures. We then dined at the Sailors' Home with Captain Morris and others. Very jolly dinner.

(*From a letter.*) How is business? It sounds absurd for me to write about business, but I have a lingering feeling that I ought not to be here, but hard at work in Essex. However I am here, and yesterday had my first ride in a rickshaw to the famous Raffles Hotel. This sounds as if I were living a life of luxury, but the actual facts are different, and I am usually working hard. It amazes me that anyone should be such a fool as to do a trip like this. At sea I have always to be on the alert, always watching. Worry and expense sum it up, but I suppose I like it or I would not do it. It has really been a great trip and very enjoyable. *Amaryllis* has had a tough time, but comes through all easily and sedately.

22 Nov. Weighed at 6 a.m. en route for Penang. Very little wind and some mist. Used engine until well past Raffles Lighthouse. At noon heavy black clouds worked up and we had squalls and rain. We are now in the Malacca Strait, a place celebrated for "Sumatras," or heavy squalls. This is not the worst time however, as the N.E. monsoon is starting; the S.W. monsoon is the season for them. On our port hand is Sumatra, and at noon we were off the south point of Asia. At dark the sky was full of black, evil-looking clouds. The wind remained light and variable for a time and then came N.N.W. A very confused jobble got up and the poor old ship could make no headway. I started the engine and even then she could hardly go ahead, but rose and fell without advancing. Thereupon I headed in N.E. by N. for the shore in search of smoother water. She got on better on that tack. At noon we had what was probably a gentle "Sumatra." The sky became black in the west and rain and wind came up.

25 Nov. At midnight stowed the mizzen. A nice breeze finally turned up, but from dead ahead, raising a horrible sea. We crashed and bumped along, and at 2 p.m. had Cape Rachado abeam to starboard, 1 mile. At dark we were in a rotten position; a heavy sea and a dropping headwind; between two shoals, both unmarked, Bambek and Pyramid. The problem was what to do. Cape Rachado Light was a guide, as we could keep it on safe bearings, but both Enden and Stéphane are poor helmsmen. At last the wind came off the land and enabled us to steer our course. All night we ambled along, but I had very little sleep, being continually called. Soon after midnight I was called, as the north shore was in sight. I kept her away one point. It is impossible, or rather, difficult to fix the position by shore marks, as the coast is low and nothing can be identified for certain. However some steamers passed which seemed to show that we were about right. At noon a wind sprang up dead ahead, and at 1 p.m. we saw One Fathom Lighthouse. The sky looked vile. Again navigation gave cause for thought. We had the Arva Islands and detached rocks on one side and the Blenheim and other shoals to starboard, while the sea was short and steep and the stream against us. And we had to beat, standing towards the Arvas on one tack, and towards the shoals on the other. In addition Enden is not accustomed to steering "by the wind." Soon the wind went dead ahead. She would not pay off either way, until I gave her reverse helm, when she came round. Rain began falling fast. We had just time to set up the weather runner when a heavy squall drove up.

(*From a letter.*) By great good fortune I had stowed the top-sail and mizzen at dark, not liking the look of things, and so was more or less in trim for it. A perfect deluge of rain came with it, a curtain, a blanket, of rain. The ship behaved magnificently, as she always does when the air is full of trouble, but she as good as said, "This is a bit thick. What about reefing and changing the jib?" "My dear girl, it cannot be done. There are rocks on one side and shoals on the other. We must get clear. Get on with the job and don't talk so much." She saw the point at once and went off like a scalded cat. A perfect seaboat! When the rain cleared off we were fairly close to a large steamer lying stopped, or steaming dead slow, waiting for a sight of the lighthouse. We had not seen them nor they us on account of the rain and general turmoil. In the midst of the uproar, when I wanted something done on deck, it was found that Stéphane had turned in. The confidence of youth is a wonderful thing.

(*From the diary.*) I kept west for a bit until the gusts eased, and then went W.N.W. The lightning became very vivid and thunder rolled and crashed around; the flashes were blinding and gave the illusion that we were right in them. We were dripping wet, but there was no further cause for anxiety, as we had driven well to the W.N.W. and were clear.

27 *Nov.* Usual evil-looking dawn. No sun and wicked clouds. After tea we double reefed the mainsail and set it with the topsail over it. Sembilan Islands appeared to starboard, but

they did not agree in any way with the chart. There were too many of them for one thing, important rocks were not visible and the shapes were wrong. Tadgell and I puzzled over the matter and examined it in every way, but without result. We looked at all the surrounding coasts on the charts, but the Sembilans seemed the only possible spot. We imagined abnormal tides and everything else. At dark a light should have lit up, but nothing appeared. Then Tadgell went aloft and sighted a light which did not agree with anything within hundreds of miles. The only thing to do was to go to sea and heave to, which we did. At dawn we made sail again and went off N. by W. No wind and a rotten swell. Doubtful sight at 10 a.m. It proved correct however, and the noon sight showed that we really were off the Sembilans last night. They are quite different from the chart and the lights seem to have been changed. Of course I do not get the "Notices to Mariners" regularly. At dark heavy clouds hung about and I got the topsail down for one which looked like swooping down on us, but it passed away and presently the wind fell after coming ahead. The motion was horrible, and it is a marvel that things are not torn out, the mainsheet buffer, for instance.

29 Nov. The wind came N.E. strong with heavy rain. I meant to go in by the South Channel, but as we nearly got involved in fishing stakes, of which the channel is full, and as, moreover, it is narrow with the wind strong right down it, and as visibility was practically nil on account of rain, I decided to go round by the North Channel, much farther but fairly simple. On we staggered and at 1 p.m. were off Saddle Island. At 6 p.m. we were off Muka Head Lighthouse. Enden had been at the wheel, practising steering a sailing ship close-hauled. He has not got the hang of it yet. Finally Fort Cornwallis Lighthouse showed red, then farther on white. I got the mainsail down, stood over to the north shore and anchored in 7 fathoms.

30 Nov. Next day we entered Penang Harbour under power. We are lying a fair way out, which, though a disadvantage in some ways, has the great advantage that we are outside the flying range of mosquitoes.

(*From a letter.*) So Stéphane has been promoted to deckhand and Enden cooks. The latter cannot steer by the wind and Stéphane is not very good at it, so that I do not expect much sleep on the way across the Bay of Bengal and the Indian Ocean. Still, we shall manage somehow. We toil on and on for thousands of miles. It is a hard life, a hard life. You gentlemen of England who live at home at ease, how little you know of the trials and tribulations of a poor shipmaster in foreign parts. Still there are compensations. Our welcome here is one. We arrived without knowing a soul. The Boarding Officer had heard of the *Amaryllis* somewhere and placed a launch at our disposal. Then two reporters came off and an account appeared in the local papers, and from then invitations poured in, and I have had to start an engagement book. This is a bright, cheery place, and my only quarrel with it is that I am never allowed to pay for anything. That is the way they do things here. Life rolls pleasantly along. There is no comparison between the life of a business man at home and that of a man in a similar position here. Here all have an airy house and generally a car, with several very efficient servants, all male of course except the amahs or nurses, and tennis, bathing, golf, boating, cricket and football, all at their very doors, to say nothing of good clubs. . . .

(*From another letter.*) On Sunday we were taken to the bathing-place and then to tiffin. Then the representatives of the Press turned up in a car and took us to the Chinese Snake Temple and the vast Kek Lok See Temple.

(*From the diary.*) The Snake Temple is a small place approached by broad steps. There is an open space at the top with a large bell in one corner. The porch is ornamented with tiles and brass dragons on top. This leads to the Temple where we were met by a Chinaman. Joss sticks burned in pots. Round the walls were images of gods and everywhere were green snakes, resting on any ledge or flat spot. From there, after subscribing a dollar, we drove to the Kek Lok See Temple, an immense place on rising ground. Beggars lined the approach. The first chamber was full of images of gods and goddesses and sacred animals. Joss sticks again. Then we passed on to where the sacred turtles were kept, and thence to the sacred fish. A further court brought us to the gold fish and still mounting we passed carved rocks and so to another court where huge gilded figures were shown with their feet on various sins represented by carved men. More chambers, more images, and finally out on to a roof from which we had a fine view.

2 Dec. Went to the lighter repair yard to see if it would be possible to beach the *Amaryllis*, but it was not. It will cost 60 dollars to dock her to repair the copper put on at Soerabaya, Japanese rubbish which is simply falling off. This is a perfect whirl of entertainment. We are ashore for tiffin and dinner daily.

16 Dec. We went into dock to be scraped and scrubbed. The hull was covered with barnacles and slime, very difficult to get off.

17 Dec. Caught the 6.30 boat from the Dock to Penang, where Dr. and Mrs. Tull met us. Four chairs slung on poles, with four coolies to each, six in my case, were awaiting for us, and we were carted up the Crag. The road wound along the side of steep ravines and round endless bends. The banks were covered with beautiful ferns. On the way we passed an army of black ants on the move. They were crossing the road about eight deep or more in very good formation, with scouting parties out on both sides. The line went right across the path and up into the bush. From the top of the hill we had a moderate view of the island and part of the mainland. After breakfast we left the Tulls and started down. Unfortunately we missed the ferry by seconds and were one hour late for tiffin. There were eighteen people waiting for us, amongst them the Resident Councillor. We at once started in on the tiffin. McNeill had arranged it all and had done things well. A menu card had been printed with the following verses by Masefield on the back:

> One road leads to London,
> One road runs to Wales,
> My road leads me seawards
> To the white dipping sails.

Leads me, lures me, calls me
    To salt green tossing sea;
A road without earth's road-dust
    Is the right road for me.

A wet road heaving, shining,
    And wild with seagulls' cries,
A mad salt sea-wind blowing
    The salt spray in my eyes.

My road calls me, lures me
    West, east, south, and north;
Most roads lead men homewards,
    My road leads me forth,

To add more miles to the tally
    Of grey miles left behind,
In quest of that one beauty
    God put me here to find.

20 Dec. Ashore early over magneto. No low tension magnetos are to be had in Penang, and high tension ones are no use with the slow fly-wheel starting. When I got on board Enden resigned for some rather obscure reason. His resignation followed a remark I had made that he was using a lot of fresh water. That seems to be the modern so-called sailor all over; if a word of reproof is uttered he throws his hand in. At 5 p.m. Peal, the Harbour Master, came off. Strangely enough, he was in command of the *Rhododendron* when she was torpedoed. We were sent from Kirkwall in the *Tay and Tyne* to look for her survivors.

21 Dec. Rain all night. Sent Enden off by the 8 a.m. ferry to Prye and thence to Singapore. I was very glad to see the last of him. A Lascar, Abdul Rahman, then appeared on the scene and I engaged him at 25 dollars a month and food, his return fare to be paid. I then called on Peal, who had another man, a cook of sorts, a Malay, Hashim. Him also I engaged at the same rate. Many people have visited the yacht, among them Mr. and Mrs. Voules, the Resident Councillor and his wife, Dr. and Mrs. Tull, Mr. and Mrs. Callan, Dr. Gossip, Mr. and Mrs. Dick, and Mr. McNeill.

CHAPTER VII

HOMEWARD BOUND

22 Dec. At 6 a.m. we weighed and left for Sabang. We have had a most delightful time in Penang, and I was very sorry to go. At the same time it is grand to be again under way. Off Muka Head we picked up a breeze, and Hashim succumbed to *mal de mer.* At noon the longitude came down from three to two figures, as we had passed 100° E. Abdul does not know the compass points.

23 Dec. The sky cleared at noon and I got a meridian altitude sight, which put us in 5° 10′ N. The wind which has been variable, has come N.W. and we are now heading in for Sumatra at a fair pace. I shall take the topsail off at dark, as this is the home of the "Sumatra" squall, and also the breeding ground of waterspouts, two very nasty things. The wind continued light all night and shifted about. At midnight it altered 4 points quite suddenly and at 1 a.m. it went 4 points back. It was very pleasant but slow sailing.

24 Dec. Stéphane has to make breakfast now, as there is still some bacon which the Mahomedans will not touch. Land was about 15 miles off at dawn and we could soon make out Diamond Point Lighthouse. The wind was light and variable; it finally came north, a nice breeze. By the evening, however, it had fallen and the ship was rolling heavily in a confused swell.

25 Dec. [*The whole entry in the Diary for this day is here inserted.*] I got very little sleep, none until after midnight, and then it was broken by calls to look at lights. At 4 a.m. I meditated calling Abdul, as I was so sleepy, but managed to turn out. It was awful sitting at the wheel trying to hold it still, with the ship rolling so badly. A bad time. There are few things worse than no wind and a swell. I shall be glad to be away from this part of the world. The weather is too uncertain. We got a squall during the morning and took the topsail off. Set it again later. In the afternoon the wind became light, and I tried to start the engine, but it refused duty. The batteries are weak. I tried all we had on board, including four new ones Tadgell bought just before we left. They had no current and I threw them away. Had to give it up in the end. Calm all night. At sunset I took the mainsail off. She rolled heavily but not quite so much as the night before. I put Hashim on from 8 to 10 p.m., as there was nothing to do except to report lights and wind, if any came. We all had eight hours' sleep.

At dinner Hashim asked for fish, sardines, for his "makan." They did not want the meat. For supper he made a curry. The meat was very tough. So passed Christmas Day. Tough meat was our portion.

26 Dec. The wind is now light and the sky overcast, with rain squalls about and a nasty confused sea. If possible we must keep the engine going until we get to Sabang. Things would, of course, have been much better with a suitably rigged ship, a ketch, for instance.

(*From a letter of earlier date.*) I shall sell the ship in Sydney if I can find a buyer, and return for another one, ketch or schooner rigged, and fitted up properly for the Tropics. I know now what is required. This ship is good and a magnificent seaboat, but the yawl rig is no use for ocean work.

(*From the diary.*) On we toiled, rolling sometimes up to the gunwales, and after passing Sabang Lighthouse stood into the Bay. After having nearly run down two canoes which tried to cross our bows without lights, we finally arrived at our anchorage. Sabang is most beautifully situated. The harbour is entirely landlocked and the hills are covered with trees and make a fine picture.

27 Dec. The Captain of the *Johan de Wit*, en route for Amsterdam, gave me the time. The chronometers seem about right and the error on the three was only two seconds.

29 Dec. I went ashore and walked along the wharf to the hill and then across to the sea on the other side. Magnificent rollers came sweeping up; they began to curl far out and then broke in masses of foam. A fascinating sight. In the harbour the water is very clear and full of gold and green fish.

30 Dec. In the afternoon we cast off and left the quay, hoisting the mainsail in the harbour. Outside we found a nice N.E. breeze but a nasty sea, especially off Pulo Rondo. I could not trust Abdul at the wheel so took his watch. Everyone here has been very kind and much interested in the trip.

31 Dec. I have been reading up the Red Sea. We are going to have a rotten time there, on account of head winds and a heavy sea in the northern part. At noon we were 5 miles off Great Nicobar, but decided not to call in there. I should have liked to go to the Nicobars; no one ever goes there. Accounts of the natives are very confused; some say that they are very savage, and others that they are inoffensive folk. After dark a light air came N.N.E. and we crawled along. The heavy rain had knocked the sea down to a great extent and she went along quietly.

1 Jan. 1923. There is now at 9 a.m. a heavy N.E. swell but a fine breeze and we are bowling along well and not bumping too much. I have just dressed Hashim's foot which is festering. Boils in places. Abdul and Hashim will not eat our food and now Stéphane has joined their mess; the only thing seems to be for Tadgell and me to do likewise.

There is now more wind and I have set the reaching stay-sail. We have been doing six knots most of the day. At dark, heavy clouds hung all round, so we got in the reaching staysail and topsail. At 9 p.m. heavy rain started. At 10 p.m. the wind dropped and we got the sheets in. At 11 p.m. a light air came from N.N.E. Trimmed the sails. . . . At 3 a.m. a squall came from the east. Gybed over and went S.W. by W. At 4 a.m. the wind dropped somewhat. At 6 a.m. it was calm and remained calm until 9 a.m. when heavy rain came out of an evil-looking cloud. We had set the spinnaker and topsail at 8 a.m. At 9 a.m. we took them in. There is nothing settled about this sailing; we are always hoisting and lowering sails. After the rain came a flat calm. This is dreadful weather; squalls and heavy rain or calms, all the time. We should be having "clear settled weather, a smooth sea and a steady breeze."

3 Jan. The wind freshened during the morning and at noon we got the topsail off to ease her. At 2 p.m. I stowed the mizzen and set the stay-sail spinnaker. This had a marked effect on the

277

speed and has steadied her somewhat. She is now rushing along at a good speed. At dark we took in the spinnaker, the wind being still fresh and the sea very heavy. In the evening the combined rope taking the boom tackle parted. It was then raining in torrents. I turned all out except Hashim, and dived into the sail locker with a candle and matches to find a new piece. Stéphane put the hatch on when I was in to keep the rain out. Got a length of new 3-inch manilla and seized the thimble in. Turned in again. Later on found that the manilla was stretching badly and looked like parting. Put on bathing costume and got out a piece of combined rope and replaced the manilla. Turned in again, time being 11 p.m.

4 Jan. Calm. Heavy swell. Lay hove to. Could not get a noon sight or even an ex-meridian. Something unusual must be happening in the Bay, as the barometer is behaving very unsteadily and all this rain is wrong for this time of year.

5 Jan. At 4 a.m. Abdul gybed accidentally. I tried to get her back, but this was hopeless. Was about to stay her when the hook of the boom tackle straightened and the boom flew across. Abdul got a blow just above the ankle from something and retired from the scene. Stéphane turned out without being called and we got the sheet in and the runner set up, and let her go off S.W. I steered most of the morning, as I feared Abdul at the wheel. We are getting to the end, 250 miles to Dondra Head, 340 to Colombo and 530 behind us.

6 Jan. The dawn was cloud-covered, as they all have been this trip. In fact we have not seen the sun, and I have not been able to get sights for days and do not know where we are. Still a stream of traffic passes by day and night, so we must be about right for latitude. We have now a nice breeze and she is going fast. Large numbers of flying fish, 50 or 60 at a time, have been getting out of our way all day. The sea must be full of them; they all come out together. One came on board. We have been one week at sea and have progressed in spurts. At night we are stopped but during the day we rush ahead.

7 Jan. The wind held all night, the first time for months. The sea was on the beam, but she is a great little ship and kept fairly dry. I shall never have such a fine sea-boat again. The day is fine so far and the sun is shining for the first time since we left Sabang. We ought to see land soon; it cannot be far off. Our bread is finished and we are on real hard tack. Just before dark a flock of very tame birds came on board and sat on the jib bolt rope, topping lifts, mizzen and anywhere. They would not go away and remained on board all night. I found one below, wrapped it in a towel and discharged it over the side. I stepped on another on deck. They sat all over the deck and showed no fear. At dark we sighted Point de Galle and Dondra Head.

8 Jan. With little wind and that ahead, and a foul tide we only did about two miles an hour over the ground, although the engine struggled gamely along. In the afternoon a squall came off the land. The way she plunged was frightful.

9 Jan. A most unpleasant morning. Fresh head wind, heavy, short steep sea and rain. Squalls too. Colombo Harbour was obscured by rain, but we hoisted "S" flag and went on. Presently the lighthouse at the end of the pier loomed up and a tug came out towing the pilot, who proved to be Hamilton of the Q-ship *Ready.* The ship at once became the target of scores of boats, and ship-chandlers, dhobi-men and engineering "runners" poured on deck.

11 Jan. Went and had a looksee aloft. All seems right. Have decided to give up Bombay, as it would take too much time, and the ship would be close-hauled in a short sea. Hashim has failed as a caterer; he went ashore and spent ten rupees for very little. His ideas of quantities are vague and he suggested 8 lbs. of rice for the trip to Aden, whereas we have used 40 lbs. since Penang. They eat a lot of it. He ordered a vast quantity of spices for curry, also 72 lbs. of dried fish. It has been a distracting day, workmen all over the place, engineers, sailmakers, shipwrights, ship-chandler. Dr. Bridger, who had seen notices about the ship in the papers, and whom I met in Barbados, came on board. Dined with him and Mrs. Bridger. Then went on to the theatre where we saw a well acted play, "Ambrose Applejohn's Adventure."

13 Jan. Tiffin with Pearcey and Logan, Captain of the Sailing

Club. Then on to the Garden Club where I met an old friend, Yates, who took me over his compound, a lovely garden, full of flowers and orchids. Dined with Dahl.

16 Jan. Another day with workmen on board all the time. Had the hull scrubbed. Chased a cockroach. Summoned Hashim to assist. He did not know what I was after and armed himself with a steel, but on catching sight of the quarry, he laughed and caught it in his hand. "This no matter," he said.

(*From a letter.*) This is not such a delightful place as Penang, though there is greater variety of climate. The island is intensely interesting, historically, but we shall not have time to go inland and visit the ancient cities. . . . I have got the moonstones for you. One could spend hundreds in these fascinating shops, full of the most beautiful things. I should like to come back here and have a real look round up country.

17 Jan. Engaged in squaring bills, drawing money and so on. Tiffin with Howard and others. All came on board afterwards. Went to the Yacht Club, where they presented me with a small burgee. At last the engineers have succeeded in making the engine go. They sold me an accumulator, as the batteries were of no use.

18 Jan. Weighed at 1 p.m. and went out under power. The sails were full of large cockroaches; they came sliding down the mainsail as it went up, and there were several in the staysail.

19 Jan. Hashim is very sick, Abdul too when below. I did not like letting the latter steer last night, but he managed quite well. There is now a smart breeze and a lot of sun and we are going along well; but the beam sea is unpleasant. Every now and then a huge wave rolls up and looks as if it were coming bodily on board, but she usually rides it somehow. Moving about is quite an exercise, and below one gets hurled about when she heaves down. If we can only hold this wind it will be great. We did 28 miles in 4 hours this afternoon without topsail or mizzen and with a double reefed mainsail. . . . A lovely, cloudless night, the stars magnificent. The wind is gradually dying away.

20 Jan. Hashim has recovered. He does not seem to understand economy of water. I tried to explain by showing him the chart and telling him it will take three weeks to make Aden; but he did not take it in. We saw the Pole Star last night for the first time since we were in the Caribbean Sea early in 1921.

21 Jan. The dawn was splendid. A bank of dark clouds on the horizon, their upper edges tipped with golden light; above them an amber strip, and higher still clouds bathed in sunshine. It was ideal sailing, a smooth sea, sun and a fair breeze. The sunset was practically cloudless and for the first time I saw the green flash insisted on by Sir G. W. Haddon-Smith of Grenada, as the sun dipped.

22 Jan. Another lovely day. This is a most pleasant change from recent trips. I had Hashim at the wheel yesterday afternoon for a few minutes. The idea is to get him to take the 4 to 6 a.m. watch. He did quite well. I am getting on with the book; this fine weather enables me to do so.

23 Jan. Rather more wind and a confused sea. The ship jumped about so much in the cross sea that I took the topsail off and set the reaching staysail. She is all the better for the change, though perhaps not quite so fast. Last night we saw the Southern Cross and the Pole Star at the same hour.

I am growing a beard to save water for shaving; and Abdul and Hashim now wash in a cupful of water.

A steamer passed us and steamed down to enquire where we were bound. The captain wished us a pleasant voyage by flags, then blew his siren in a series of blasts to cheer us up. He seemed quite pleased to meet us and waved his hat with great vim. The wind keeps up well and so does the sea. Our new log, governor and all, has gone. I rigged up a dummy governor of wood and used some small line.

24 Jan. It is a lovely day and the old ship is snoring away very comfortably. I make the total distance from Colombo to Aden 2,102 miles, of which we have done about 630.

25 Jan. There is now rather more wind and we are carrying reaching jib and staysail. . . . At sunset I changed to working jib but left the reaching staysail. This was quite as much as she wanted, if anything, more.

26 Jan. The breeze kept up all day. At noon I took the topsail off; she seems to go quite as fast without it and is much easier. To-morrow I shall load the fire-arms, as we may have trouble with dhows, which it seems are in the habit of stopping steamers for water and stores. We are however rather far north for them.

27 Jan. Thirteen flying fish came on board last night. Abdul is now making a curry powder, grinding up his own ingredients, and is going to curry them for tiffin.

We have been doing between 7 and 8 knots all day. Last night we passed the line of "no variation," and have now changed from west to east variation for a space. I have stopped issuing water rations; we should be all right now, bar accidents. The dews are very heavy, almost like rain. For a time last night the sea was white with phosphorescence, and the spurts of spray that came on board looked like liquid fire. It was a cloudless night with a full moon and brilliant stars.

29 Jan. We are now nearing Socotra, and should pass 45 miles north of it this afternoon. It seems that the N.E. monsoon is often strong in the Gulf of Aden; we are finding it so at any rate. At 4 p.m. we hove to and double reefed the mainsail, and then let her go along without the staysail. She is well within herself and is not pressed, but the sea is very trying. Abdul's stout heart seems to have failed him at the prospect of steering in such a heavy sea, and when he was due at the wheel after supper he decided to be sick. We have not seen Socotra, which was hidden in mist.

31 Jan. The sea has gone down to a great extent. We have been sailing through swarms of jelly-fish all the morning. It has been a perfect day, barring a total absence of wind. I have been running the engine all day.

1 Feb. We are now entering the Gulf of Aden, which is about 160 miles wide just here, Arabia to the north, Africa to the south. The wind has been very light and variable.

3 Feb. A good breeze. A biggish sea, a following sea, rolled along, and every now and then broke alongside. It was quite like a switchback.

(*From a letter.*) You are quite right about the run across

the Arabian Sea; it is a long way for a little ship. However we
are getting along fairly well. . . . You ask if I have a white
man with me. Yes, I am giving a young Australian a passage
home. The crew now consists of him, a Lascar, a Malay cook,
and of course Stéphane and myself. The Lascar is a fairly useless person, very apt to tear off superfluous clothes and dance
about the deck in emergencies. The Malay has the face of an
angel, but is a very wily young man really.

4 Feb. Our port is in sight and we have all day to get to it.
This swell is quite absurd, considering how little wind there is.
It comes rolling along and breaks alongside in the most im-
pudent way. Yesterday we hooked two fish, the first broke the
hook, the second broke the line. To-day Abdul has been fishing
for some gaudy blue and yellow fish, about $2\frac{1}{2}$ ft. long. The sea
seems full of them. He threw a line out and caught one, but
Hashim in his excitement seized the line and pulled it in too
fast, and the fish broke away.

We gradually closed the land and lowered sail off Elephant
Point. We hoisted our number and ensign, which were repeated
by the signal station. As we came round Steamer Point a
launch came off with a pilot, who guided us to an anchorage
off Prince of Wales's pier. A number of boats collected round
us, but we did not allow anyone on board.

Aden from the harbour is a fascinating place. It is very
parched looking, but its Moorish buildings give it an Oriental
look which is charming. The peninsula is a mass of high peaks
of fantastic shape. Not a blade of grass anywhere. Did not go
ashore, turned in and had a great sleep.

(*From a letter.*) At Aden we received the usual kind welcome.
The Port Captain had reports from ships in the Red Sea sent
in for our benefit. A whole gale was reported off Perim and a
heavy sea in the Abu Ail Channel. The Red Sea, I may
mention, is never used by sailing ships going home, as very
strong northerly winds prevail in the northern half.

5–10 Feb. Drove to the Tanks, of unknown origin, re-
discovered in 1854. The way lay through endless "lines,"
camel, transport, etc., past the Crater, the native quarter, a
mass of varied colour. We also drove right across the Penin-

sula into Arabia, past the salt pans and the heaps of white salt. Dined on shore one night with the 41st Dogras, but had to refuse an invitation to dine in H.M.S. *Northbrook* another night, as I was not well.

11 Feb. As I was feeling better and there was less wind, we weighed at 9 a.m. and left the harbour under power and sail. Saluted *Northbrook*, who replied with greetings. We are now fairly committed to the critical trip of the whole voyage, and have at any rate made a good start. The distance to Suez is roughly 1,300 miles.

12 Feb. At 6 a.m. Perim was close; it is a low, flat island, quite parched and desolate looking, without the fascinating peaks of Aden.

13 Feb. At 1 a.m. Stéphane called me for a squall. A couple of hours later the wind was so strong and the sea so heavy that I had the mainsail double-reefed. This is really very bad luck. It is usual to have a fair wind to Jidda, but we have found a strong head wind down here at Mohka. It is an awkward place to be beating about in, as there are so many rocks, and there is nowhere where we can anchor for a rest anywhere along. The only thing is to plug along. Anyway the sun is shining and we know where we are more or less. If the gear and hull, etc., stand we shall be all right. Hashim is laid up, and Stéphane is doing all the work. Abdul has been asleep nearly all day, but as he is no use when awake there is little harm in that.

14 Feb. At dawn we were a few miles off the Arabian coast, which is low, so it is impossible, or very difficult, to fix the ship from it. The wind remained light all the morning, and at noon we had only made good 21 miles. Of course we sailed more, but with the wind dead ahead it did not all count. I started the engine at noon. Stores—water and food—will run out if we do not get along faster.

15 Feb. In the morning a fairly steady breeze came S.W., and we set all the sail we could. The wind has been right round the compass to-day. A great game this, one never knows what to expect. Still just now we are romping along on the course. . . . The wind fell at dark and it became calm. At

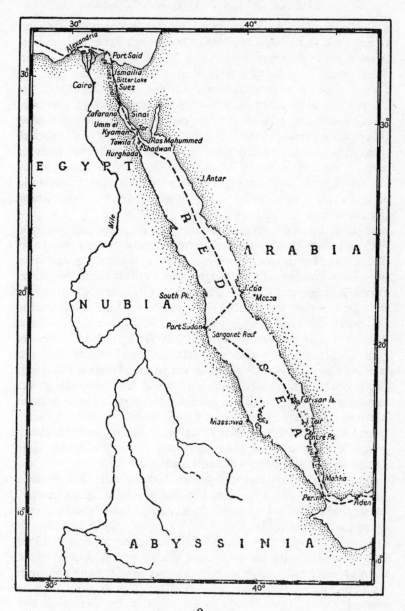

285

4 a.m. the sky looked bad and I took that watch in addition to my own, as I feared Hashim at the wheel. An extraordinary swell rolled up; there must be a lot of wind farther south. The morning was very misty, almost foggy, and the light on Centre Peak with a range of 30 miles was invisible at 15. Provisions are going to be a trouble; we have enough for three weeks with care, but we may be much longer. We took stock this morning; the potatoes are all going bad, and we have not been able to get any biscuits. There are no ports to speak of along these coasts, so we must make good 50 miles a day, to get through on our stock. Jebel Teir did not appear until we were within 5 or 6 miles. It is utterly barren, a lava heap; the *Northbrook* has to water it and give it stores. At noon we had made good 92 miles, probably more, as the horizon was bad and the refraction is great hereabouts. We passed Jebel Teir on the north side and ran on N. by E. until 1 p.m. when we were 15 miles off the reef on the Farisan Bank. We then gybed and went off N.W. This part is full of reefs and low islands; the channel itself is 60 miles wide. The breeze tailed off in the afternoon and left us rolling in a quite shocking big swell. We had to gybe and put her N.W. by N., a dangerous course, as it means heading for reefs, not far off, either. Still she is quieter so. On the other course she was shaking the ship with the boom. I am now running on hoping that something will turn up. The wind is shifting for one thing; this may improve matters. We are not well placed and should have done better to gybe past Jebel Teir, but I ran on with the idea of coming round at dark and having a long stretch of clear water. The wind has however frustrated this and left us in a hole.

17 Feb. A steamer came up astern last night. I did not want her wash and altered away, but she followed and came by close. She called us up on a signal lamp, but I shouted that I had no lamp, and she passed on. I ran the engine for a couple of hours, although I am not sure that it is wise to run it, as we may want it badly later on, and the supply of fuel is small. To-day there has been constant change, calms, light airs from anywhere, entailing continual shifting of sails, and now a slight breeze. I took a sight at 2 p.m., but the chief difficulty about the Red Sea is the refraction, on account of which one cannot rely on sights. In fact the sun is seldom used, but so far we have not had the chance of star sights.

18 Feb. Head winds and heavy seas right down in 16° N.! However shall we get to Suez? We have now been out one week and have done 400 miles, just about one-third of the distance. We should have been halfway had the wind been usual. At noon, after a morning's thought, I decided to get in somewhere and replenish and not to risk going on. At first I fixed on Jidda, but it has many disadvantages. The approach is encumbered with dangerous reefs, and we have no charts. It is the shipping port for Mecca, but there are no whites living there. The approach to Port Sudan on the Egyptian coast is however fairly clear. That seems the place. There are many whites, about 1,000, and facilities of all sorts. I now feel much easier in my mind; I felt responsible for the shortness of stores by having accepted the statement that there would surely be a fair wind to Jidda. A stream of steamers passes all day as we labour from side to side of the channel, beating up to windward. They are very useful, as they indicate our longitude more or less. We have no other means of getting it.

19 Feb. Lovely day. Progress very slow. We have lifted the embargo on the water and are having more food. I had put the ship on rations as a precaution, but this should not be necessary now, so we had sardines for breakfast. At noon we were on the 18th parallel; it is curious how we drift along. I could not get any twilight sights, except Sirius, owing to clouds. In future I must turn out regularly at twilight; it is the only way of fixing the ship.

20 Feb. At 5.30 a.m. Hashim called me, and I got sights of Jupiter and Venus, and later of the sun, all of which agreed very well. Taking star sights is very difficult in a small ship on account of the trouble of "bringing the star down." Moreover it is difficult to read the sextant by an oil lamp. The breeze still keeps dead ahead, and we are toiling along plunging in a heavy swell. Just now we are giving her plenty of sheet, which she seems to like. She sails within 7 points, i.e. $3\frac{1}{2}$ points each way, but does not get along like that. When we give her more sheet she travels faster and within 8 points. Gradually we work along, but it is a tedious business.

22 Feb. I am running the engine a good deal, as this swell kills the pace. We seem to have been set a long way to the west by a current, and are not far off a number of low 4 feet high islands. We cannot see them, but they are there all right. So the situation is, no wind, uncertain position, strong current setting us ashore, and engine running very badly, in addition a nasty swell quite 10 feet high. Could things be worse?

23 Feb. There is a fair wind up the Sea, but we must get to Port Sudan and re-stock. It is sad to waste the fair wind, but there is no help for it. We are now standing in at about 7 knots, but we cannot go on long after dark, as we do not know where we are. It would never do to run in on a reef-fringed shore in the dark. Perhaps we shall see Sanganeb Light at dark, though it is almost too much to hope for. According to the noon sight, for what that may be worth, we are north of Port Sudan, but if there is refraction which would raise the horizon, reduce the altitude, increase the zenith distance, and so increase the latitude, we may be right. It all depends now on what sights we get at twilight. Sirius and Capella would give a fix if we could get them. . . . The strong wind continued, and at dark, lo and behold, there was Sanganeb Light in exactly the right position, a piece of marvellous luck. We stood on in a heavy sea until the light bore north and then hove to. I did not care to run on with the Wingate Reef in the way.

24 Feb. The morning was misty, almost foggy, and we could not see the Wingate Beacon. On and on we went and no beacon. At length when I was getting rather anxious, a beacon loomed up in the mist, but not the S.W. one. The wind was then very high, and we hove to and double reefed the mainsail, and then went on. The beacon we saw was the E. one, and after a time we could see the sea breaking on the reef, and then we sighted the S.W. beacon and could stand on with an easy mind. As there is no chart of Port Sudan in the ship I hoisted "S" flag and hove to off the entrance. After we had anchored we were rowed across the harbour and at last were on African soil. Not a tree, not a shrub, not a blade of grass; just sand, level sand, some big, ugly, flat-roofed houses, wide open spaces, wide streets, two high beacons, telegraph posts, natives as black as coal, and light-coloured Egyptians.

(*From a letter.*) Here we are in a spot we did not mean to touch and all well. . . . Yesterday we went to the local races, which were very good, and were introduced to the Governor and his wife. The scene from the race-course was a real African desert scene, a level expanse of sand extending for miles, a stunted tree in the distance, two or three men on camels, a crowd of natives, and in the middle of the crowd a man making obeisances towards the east, touching the ground with his forehead. A fascinating scene. In the morning the *Madura* had come in, and Dr. Wilson, a member of the Royal Cruising Club, and his wife, seeing the burgee, had themselves rowed over. After them came Turner, the Secretary of the local Club, and Curry, whom we met in Tulagi. To-day another man, Monkhouse, came over from the *Madura*. He also is R.C.C. It is most unlikely that three R.C.C. men will ever meet in Port Sudan again, a place which fifteen years ago was pure Nubian desert. It is going to be a big place in the future. They are damming the Blue Nile and will then be able to produce all the cotton the Empire needs, and of the best quality. The harbour is capable of considerable development.

27 Feb. I bought some curios from a squint-eyed native, a real ruffian. I first saw him on the beach, but the bargaining took place in his shop, where we sat on chairs and had the things spread out for us. An ornamented pumpkin gourd I simply had to buy; it formed part of every bargain. The dealer wanted badly to sell it, and in the end I took it with a Sudanese shield.

28 Feb. Weighed at 8.30 and left the pleasant little spot of Port Sudan, where we have been very kindly received and generously treated. And now we have stores and water for the trip and have learnt much as to anchorages, etc. We found a heavy sea and a good deal of wind outside and double reefed the mainsail under the lee of Wingate Reef.

1 Mar. At 4 a.m. I called Hashim, who said he could steer, although he was still bad. In a few minutes he had her aback and I had to turn all out, but managed to get her back without tacking, as a heavy sea hit her on the bow and drove her back. All the morning we were standing in to the Nubian coast, which was sighted at ten o'clock through mist. The Sailing Directions recommend the Arabian coast if working northwards, as there is at times a fair current, and land and sea breezes. We therefore decided to get across. The Harbour Master at Port Sudan, however, strongly recommended the Egyptian coast, but solely on account of the hostile natives, I gathered.

3 Mar. I got sights of Jupiter and Venus, which worked out very well considering the difficulty I had in keeping upright to take them, in fact I once thought I should fall overboard. In the afternoon the mizzen had to come off, and at 4 p.m. we hove to and put in the third reef. We also reefed the staysail, as the wind had the force of a moderate gale.

4 Mar. Still blowing hard. The conditions on board are frightfully uncomfortable. A sea came over and squirted into my cabin, wetting charts, books, everything, including my bunk. A series of star sights fixed us at dark, and we also saw South Peak in Nubia at sunset. We could therefore stand in towards the shore fairly safely.

5 Mar. Up to now we have always had wind; but at 11 a.m. it fell calm. Extraordinary place, this Red Sea! It has been a beautiful day, in fact most days are beautiful, and the nights are glorious, stars simply blazing. We crawl on and on, and must be about two-thirds up the Red Sea. I am very pleased with the way the old ship gets on. Of course the worst is still to come. It is a pity there are so many reefs off the Arabian coast, 20 and 30 miles off, as I should like to get nearer in. In the evening there was a lot of wind and sea and we had to double reef her in the dark. She plunged heavily all night in a nasty short sea.

6 Mar. We are now out of the Tropics, in lat. 23° 42′ N. The day's run was again very bad, only 38 miles. There must be a foul current, as the star sights put us 10 miles farther back. At dusk as the clouds had spread all over the sky, I expected a fair wind, such as we had last night. I therefore decided to be cunning and double reef the mainsail. The wind, however, tricked me again and instead of a smart breeze we had a flat calm. It was very absurd to be lying stopped for want of wind with two reefs in the mainsail, but there we were. At 11 p.m. I got tired of steering a ship without way and started the engine.

7 Mar. The dew last night was very heavy, quite like rain. The decks were quite wet and so was the cabin floor. We have now been a week at sea and have made good roughly 289 miles. The sunset last night was magnificent, and the green flash visible. Just after the sun set the sky in the west was a glow of yellow-salmon colour, and the bases of the clouds were tipped with gold. The salmon colour gradually faded to green and this to blue. It has been a flat calm all day and very hot, the sea is like burnished metal. A number of flying ants appeared at breakfast time; they must have been blown out to sea.

Commander Draper urged me to fit brails to the gaff to control it when reefing. Yesterday I used the topsail sheet with good results, but it is hardly heavy enough.

8 Mar. Sky overcast, strong wind, heavy sea.

9 Mar. At noon the wind eased and I meditated taking out reefs, but soon after tiffin it hardened up and three of us could hardly get the mainsheet in, notwithstanding the two reefs. We are now lurching along in a horrible sea. The mainsail is getting ripe, but I do not want to get a new sail now that the trip is ending. Abdul reported himself sick and unable to do any work. I found him in his bunk, weeping with a pain in his tummy, and gave him a dose of castor-oil. Natives are bad patients, real cases of auto-suggestion. I am feeding him on Allenbury's food. I hope to be able to send him home from Port Said and get an Italian seaman or a white of some sort.

10 Mar. There is now a heavy sea and not much wind. We are just on the point of getting on to the last chart. This is great. The day's run was 46 miles.

11 Mar. Another calm. Amazing! I took four stars at dawn, Jupiter, Venus, Vega and Arcturus, which worked out well and agreed with a bearing of Jebel Antar, a mountain with a marked cleft in its summit.

12 Mar. The dawn was delightfully fresh; dawns and sunsets at sea are fine. This Red Sea is a strange part. Down south we expected fair winds and had foul. In the middle we expected light and had some heavy winds, while here we expected heavy and have light winds. Just now we are ambling along quietly. Very pleasant.

13 Mar. Lovely day. Rather more wind in the afternoon, but still light. The Sinai Peninsula is in sight ahead. It looks as if we should not be able to call in at Hurghada, as the wind is west.

14 Mar. At 6 a.m. Shadwan was in sight ahead with Ras Mahummed on the beam. Both Shadwan and the Sinai Peninsula are quite barren and arid, not a green thing to be seen, mere sandheaps. I am delighted with the progress we have made and the present weather conditions. With luck we should be through the Straits by dark. . . . But we were not. At 2 p.m. as the wind was getting heavier and heavier we decided to make for the anchorage off Towila Island. Tadgell went aloft and was able to indicate the reefs and shoal patches. We brought up in 5 fathoms. After tea we housed the topmast, as we shall probably have heavy weather from now on. . . . Well, here we are comfortably at anchor, instead of plunging about in a heavy sea. I should have been up all night if we had gone on. I shall try to work up in day trips, until we are clear of reefs, say north of Tor. We have averaged 36 miles daily from Port Sudan.

15 Mar. At 3 a.m. I heard the cable dragging and turned out. Tadgell also turned out. We roused Stéphane and got the cable ready to veer. The strain on it was very great. At first we tried heaving it out, but it took charge and threw Stéphane down. Abdul remained turned in until I called him out. These Indians are curiously apathetic. Fancy stopping in one's bunk with all the noise of cable-veering going on! The rope break parted and the cable ran out until it stuck in the pipe. We fixed new rope and then we found that we had veered all the cable, nearly 60 fathoms, and that in a depth of 5 fathoms. That ought to hold her. We left the cable in the compressor and also round the capstan, and then got the second anchor ready.

17 Mar. The wind remained high all day yesterday, but at dawn this morning we decided to have a shot at the Straits. After a time we got the cable in and the anchor on deck, and hoisted sail. Tadgell went aloft to look for reefs and we got out with difficulty. There was rather a nasty little jump in the Straits, and I decided to take the Kawarat Channel through the reefs to get smooth water. We therefore bore away for the entrance and soon sighted the low sandy island at the south end of Kawarat Reef. We passed between South Gaysum and this island in deep water. The wind went north which enabled us to lay right through the channel with one board. There is a reef at the north end, but it was visible from the deck and we passed out without trouble. It was a much better way of making Umm El Kyaman than plunging along up the Straits. At 4 p.m. we let go in 5 fathoms. There are some deserted buildings on the beach. After we had anchored two men appeared on the shore, one of them a black official clad in a khaki overcoat and shako. He blew whistles and as we did not pay any attention he got a rifle and fired a shot. I had the boat put over and went ashore, leaped into the water and cursed him up hill and down dale. He was probably speaking Arabic and I did not understand a word, but he could see that I was annoyed and was apparently full of apologies. Another Nubian, a man with a most delightful smile, tried to act as peacemaker. The first man was probably quite in order; he was a policeman of sorts set to watch the coast and prevent smuggling, and as he has no boat and we disregarded his whistles all he could do was to fire.

The Gulf is fairly narrow and the coasts are low, but inland are ranges of barren hills with high peaks, like the teeth of a saw. To-day they looked fine; the sun shone, a mist hung about and they took on all shades, blue, purple and yellow. The barometer is low, which may mean a south wind or at least light breezes. If it is high it means strong northerlies. It has been a most interesting day and most enjoyable.

18 Mar. To our surprise the wind at dawn was S.E., very rare in the gulf. We are booming along at about 6 knots. As it was a rough night we double-banked the watches, and worked three hours each watch, Tadgell and Stéphane, Abdul and I. A frightful, confused sea got up, and then the wind flew about, now on one side, and now on the other. At one moment we were sailing and at the next all aback, and then full again before anything could be done. We were sailing about in so many directions that before long I did not know where the ship was, and as the Gulf is very narrow just there, about nine miles, the chances of running ashore were great. I decided to run back and sight the Zafarana Light again. On we ran with the ship crashing about in the confused sea caused by the sudden change of wind, and at last the Light appeared. We made sure of its bearing and then hove to. It was a very anxious night. The Gulf is the worst lighted thoroughfare in the world, I should think. Several important points have no lights, and such as there are, are small. To-day is fine, but the wind is paltry and shifting. . . . Still we crawled on and passed Newport Lighthouse just before 6 p.m. A fresh breeze came along, which was lucky, as the engine was running badly and almost stopped. So at last we had reached Suez, after a great struggle. We have been five weeks doing 1,300 miles. . . . Had a mighty sleep.

20 Mar. Called on the consul, Monk Mason, who put us up for the Club. He arranged a tiffin in the Government steamer *Aida*. Then to the Club, where we met Bolitho, of the R.C.C. Then to tiffin in the *Aida* with Commander Morewood.

21 Mar. Met the correspondent of one of the London papers who wanted copy and was prepared to pay for it. Nothing doing. Later on went to the Golf Club, and met Bolitho and Mudie, a friend of a college friend of mine. Thence to dinner at Surgeon-Major Davy's, where we met Mrs. Monk Mason, Mr. and Mrs. Wyllie.

23 Mar. A large number of visitors called, among them two of the most skilful engineers in Egypt, who spent a whole day tuning up my engine, free. Englishmen abroad will do anything for another Briton.

24 Mar. Went by train to Port Tewfik to see the Consul about returning Abdul. Dined with the Turners.

26 Mar. Following the example of the Government vessels, we dressed ship in honour of the birthday of the local king, Fuadard.

27 Mar. Went up to the Atakah Hills with Bolitho and Tadgell.

(*From a letter.*) Car for part of the way and then camels, my first ride on one of those ungainly, sneering brutes. They fold themselves up, when kneeling, in an extraordinary way, usually uttering loud protests. At the foot of the hills we got off and had lunch, and then climbed up and had a fine view. The first part was on hands and knees and then we could walk more or less upright. The day was clear and the colour of the water in Suez Bay was a wonderful blue; the shoals shaded off to light blue and then green. Behind lay the bare, parched hills, cut up into wadis and in front lay the flat, sandy plain. Nothing green in sight in the way of vegetation. Sand everywhere. The hills are not volcanic, but are arranged in unbroken lines of sedimentary deposit, and, most curiously, the wadis must have at one time carried off a very heavy rainfall. On the way back we took the wrong spur and had a difficult climb down.

28 Mar. I have decided to start to-morrow, so I went to the Canal Company about dues. They sent off a measurer. The system worked out at 25 tons in my case.

29 Mar. Weighed at 6.30 a.m. and left Suez where we had been received most kindly. We started up the Canal with a pilot. Although the tide was fair and the engine ran well, our progress was slow, as the wind was too strong. At noon the tide would be against us, and, as it is not safe to leave such a ship as *Amaryllis* tied up to a bank for hours while traffic passes, I decided to return and get a tow.

30 Mar. The tug *Lynx* came at 5 a.m. and we secured alongside and proceeded up the Canal, which is roughly 65 yards wide. There is nothing to be seen in the Canal except the banks, but owing to the clear atmosphere the colouring is great, yellow sand and blue sky. On the way we saw two wolves swimming across. At noon we were off Ismailia and cast off, making the anchorage under our own power. We had at first towed alongside the tug, but in the Bitter Lake there was a slight swell, and as the *Amaryllis* was "suffering" according to the captain, we dropped astern and finished the trip so. Ismailia is a pleasant little spot, nestling amidst palms, an oasis among the sands.

31 Mar. We packed our bags and prepared to leave by train for Cairo. Stéphane was very pleased at being left in charge. After leaving Benha we saw the Pyramids in the distance, behind the flat-roofed mud houses bordering the track. We passed Tel el Kebir, the scene of the battle. At last we reached Cairo and drove to Shepheard's. After lunch we took a carriage and drove out to the Pyramids, or rather to Mena House Hotel. At intervals of a couple of hundred yards or so along the road were police armed with rifles, and mounted police were a good deal in evidence.

(*From a letter.*) Well, we found the Pyramids in their usual place. They are not beautiful, but the general effect is impressive on account of the size, also because the great labour of building them appeals to the imagination. The Sphinx is wonderful; it is greatly mutilated, but yet remains very fascinating and strangely impressive.

(*From the diary.*) We also visited the Museum and were shown round by the Director, Mr. Quibell. In the afternoon we drove to the Citadel with a dragoman. Inside the Citadel is the Mosque of Mohammed Ali. After putting on slippers over one's boots one enters the courtyard, on to which the Mosque opens. The Mosque is of great height, and there are two minarets shooting up from the roof. The floor is covered with a huge carpet. From the roof, which is beautifully carved and decorated, hang a great number of electric lights and big chandeliers. The walls are of alabaster over the stone. We visited the old palace adjoining the Mosque and obtained a fine view of the city, with its innumerable minarets, and the surrounding plains.

2 Apr. Drove to the Palace to see Castle Smith Pasha, the Commodore of the Alexandria Yacht Club. Lunched with him and his wife. We are to be the guests of the British Boat Club in Alexandria, and everybody here prophesies that after the round of festivities we shall be unfit to go to sea for a few days.

3 Apr. Returned to Ismailia and arranged for a *patron* for to-morrow.

4 Apr. At 5.30 a.m. the *patron* came on board and we started under power. Last night there had been a moderate northerly breeze, but at dawn it dropped. However, as the day drew on the wind increased and came right ahead, and in the end we had to lower the jib, staysail and mizzen, which we had hoisted at 8 a.m. Progress became very slow, but we advanced crawling between the banks of sand, passing "Gares" at intervals. At 1 p.m. we had only 14 miles to go but the speed had fallen from two knots to one, and to avoid being left steaming during the night, or having to tie up, risking damage to the ship against the bank, I decided to send for a tug. In due course it appeared and we gave it a line. Two steamers dipped their ensigns to us as they passed. The tug dragged us into Cherif Basin (Port Said), where we let go.

Another stage done. On leaving here we shall be in the Mediterranean. So far I have crossed the Atlantic Ocean, Pacific Ocean, Tasman Sea, Coral Sea, Arafura Sea, Java Sea, Bay of Bengal, Red Sea, nearly 28,000 miles.

5 Apr. Went ashore and called on British Coal Depots, who had had our letters sent back by mistake. The Consul, Hough, came off to tea. While he was there we changed and went with him to the Club and then on to Mr. Williams's, where we met his wife and family.

6 Apr. Yeilding came on board. I went ashore with him and drove to see Elliot, Captain of the Port, about going on a slip at Alexandria. Then to Hardy with a list of stores, to lunch at Girandolo's and back on board. Several visitors came in the afternoon.

7 Apr. Played golf with the Consul and Dr. Goss. Dined with the Hardys. Abdul went ashore to wait for his ship due on Monday.

8 Apr. More visitors came off, Captain Elliot and his wife, Hardy and his daughter. Hardy has put the items in at little over cost, and declares himself glad to have supplied such a famous ship.

9 Apr. Out at 6 a.m. bidding farewell to Port Said. We had been very well received and many people had visited the ship. In fact interest seems to be growing.

At last we are in the Mediterranean where we may get anything in the way of wind and weather. At present things are very pleasant and we are sliding along over a smooth sea at about 4 knots. Captain Elliot said that our trip up the Red Sea in thirty sailing days from Aden was good, with northerlies as far south as Perim.

10 Apr. It was a lovely night last night, gentle breeze and brilliant stars. The Southern Cross has gone; we saw it last in the Red Sea. A schooner was with us all yesterday afternoon. and at dawn there she still was, but we had caught up. The fore and mainsails were Bermuda cut, the bowsprit was of great length, with two jibs set on it. Yesterday she carried a mizzen staysail. We are just about to pass Aboukir Bay. The wind is S.E. fresh and we must be doing 6 to 7 knots. . . . We made good progress and at 4 p.m. were nearing Alexandria. As we got near the *Suzanna* appeared beating out and with her a launch. The Captain of the Port at Port Said had cabled when we started and all the lighthouses had orders to report us as we passed, so that the Alexandria yachts and dinghies might come out to meet us. Unluckily, the last lighthouse reported us when we appeared on the horizon, instead of when we passed, and the unfortunate dinghies were outside the harbour all the morning, with the result that some of their occupants were sea-sick and had to return, and finally all went in except the *Suzanna* and the launch. These closed us and Grogan Pasha told us to follow the *Suzanna*; she led us to an anchorage off the Clubhouse, which was dressed in flags in our honour. The Police and Grogan then came alongside in their launches, also Bolitho in his dinghy, and hosts of other people. I gave the Police particulars and guaranteed the crew, i.e. made myself responsible for their not running away. We all then adjourned to the Club for drinks.

11 Apr. At the Club we met Bolitho, who took me round to Colin Marshall, a sailing enthusiast. Then back to the Club for Van Zeller, Chief of Coastguards, and Peel, owner of the *Suzanna*.

12 Apr. Went ashore and met Van Zeller, who drove me up to town to his office, where he has a model of every type of ship and fishing boat working on the coast of Egypt, also every kind of net used. I mentioned to him the incident of the Gulf of Suez and recommended the black enthusiast for promotion. . . . Met Bordon, the Postmaster, Macaulay, Chief of Customs, Peel and Streatfield, the Captain of the royal yacht. Then all went to see a game of pelota, a Spanish game, on the principle of fives. It is played in a huge court, and the players use a sort of basket to catch and fling the ball. It seems very difficult. They players were professionals, and are said to be short-lived, but I doubt it.

13 Apr. A launch came to ask us to go into the Arsenal Basin, to enable a diver to measure the hull for the slip. All the chiefs were waiting for us, and let loose a crowd of workmen to make us fast. After the turmoil had subsided we went ashore. Back on board to meet a party of Italian Boy Scouts, who arrived in a fine six-oared galley. Flowery speeches were the order of the day. I was assured that the trip, or "raid on the world," was unique and rivalled the performances of one Christopher Columbus, that the honour of being near me was overpowering, etc. An invitation was given me to review the Scouts on Sunday. Van Zeller arrived in the middle of the fray. In the end they left, but only to return with their female relatives.

14 Apr. The Arsenal people wanted us to go on the slip at once instead of on Tuesday, and we went. They had prepared a cradle.

15 Apr. Had an amazing morning. I was fetched to inspect the Scouts. I found a crowd of Arabs at the gate, and many heavily plated officers, the Italian Consul, and several notables on the pavement. A guard of honour lined the entrance. Many people were presented, scout-masters and others, then, accompanied by my glittering retinue, I advanced into the square.

The Band played "God save the King," and every one stood at attention. I then inspected the Boy Scouts, the Girl Guides, and the Aspirantes. A boy read an Address of Welcome, and then I was led off to take a glass of wine and sign a beautiful book. I then went round the school, into classrooms and through workshops, engineering, book-binding, etc., and finally I took my leave. (*From a letter.*) I did not really recover until the next day.

16 Apr. Scraped the hull. She was not very dirty, but the copper was bad in places, and it has been replaced by Muntz metal.

17 Apr. Back on board to receive Mr. and Mrs. Van Zeller, Mr. and Mrs. Manson, Mrs. Stevens and others. In the evening they gave me a dinner at the Savoy. There were thirty-one present. The menu card had a signal, L.I.V. - - - W.G.K.F., i.e. "Well done, *Amaryllis*." The items were fitted with appropriate terms, such as: Vol au Vent, Sauve qui peut; Asperges Belaying Pins; Sauce Pacifique; Fruits au Tour du Monde. A vase of Amaryllis lilies was on the table. The dinner was excellent. Grogan presented me with a burgee, which they had had made. The Italian paper publishes an account of my visit to the Don Bosco Institution, and describes me as a lord. I protested strongly.

19 Apr. Lunched with Captain Streatfield and his wife. Their house is in front of the palace; they have made a garden on very unpromising soil. Captain Streatfield informed me that I have been made an Honorary Life Member of the Royal Yacht Club of Egypt. Dined with Colin Marshall. He has a collection of valuable prints of old sailing ships. He is very keen on sailing, and a tower of strength to the Boat Club. I have engaged Israel Horowitz as seaman, though I doubt if he is one.

20 Apr. Came away at 8 a.m. and anchored once more off the Clubhouse. Had tiffin on board, the first, I think, since we came in. Dressed ship for the New Constitution. Many visitors came off. Dined with Bolitho; had a great evening. The British Boat Club presented me with a bottle of Mumm to be drunk when I cross my outward bound track.

22 Apr. The day of departure. The wind was light from the

N.E., working round to N.N.W. Young had asked us not to weigh before 11 a.m. All the morning we lay surrounded by boats of many kinds, and several people came on board. At last the time came; the *Suzanna* was lying alongside, but she cast off when we started weighing; we hoisted the mainsail and then hove in. Our escort sailed, steamed or rowed alongside. There must have been well over thirty boats of all kinds, outriggers, dinghies, yachts and launches. Madaro and his Scouts gave us a cheer and hoisted oars. Signals flew from the Club. It was a great send-off. Indeed we have had a great time and feel we are going to sea for a rest. Everyone has been extremely kind and invitations for lunches and dinners have flowed in. . . . To-day has been magnificent, sun and a nice N.N.W. breeze, but cold. We are now sailing a trifle to wind-ward of our course, close hauled. The wind drew round at dark to E.; it was light, but we kept moving. The night was clear and quiet, the stars giving plenty of light. I called Horowitz at 2 a.m. next morning; the wind was then well aft, but he could not keep the ship on her course, so I had to send him away. . . . The wind shifts slowly about from S.E. to N.E. This fair wind is a piece of luck. . . . At Alexandria the slip still exists where Mahommed Ali built his ships, and there are three granite bollards set horizontally in one of the walls, which were used to take the tackles.

24 Apr. It seems to me that I must get rid of Horowitz, as he is useless, though a hard worker. He cannot steer, row, or even coil down a rope. We are not getting along fast, it is true, but conditions could hardly be better otherwise. At noon we had made good 95 miles and 641 to go.

25 Apr. At 2 a.m. it fell calm for an hour or two, then an air came from the east. We gybed and continued W.N.W. Another calm was followed by a nice breeze from E.S.E. I am trying sailing a bit to windward to get all the sails drawing. This is what three and four-masted schooners always do, but in our case there is the difficulty of the sea.

26 Apr. The wind fell away at dawn, and I started the engine. We have had an easterly swell for some reason, but very little wind. The swell made us roll considerably. . . .

Scraping the woodwork has been going on all day, Hashim lending a hand.

27 Apr. The ship was going well at 4 a.m.; we had gybed at midnight as the wind was working aft. A cloudy dawn, but I got a sight. Fresh wind all day, shifting about in a most peculiar way, from E.N.E. to E.S.E. There was a row forward this morning, and Stéphane kicked Hashim. Hashim nearly wept from emotion. Just a quarrel. The two accused each other of various misdeeds. . . . At noon we were well over half-way, 390 miles to do, 428 made good I shall be glad to be in, as we are short-handed, Horowitz being a passenger. To-day has been the biggest run so far, 94 miles. The wind here is most peculiar, and at times we get what are really whirlwinds. At 5 p.m. we had a fresh E.S.E. breeze, at 5.30 it fell light, and a minute later it came N.W., taking us all aback. A few minutes later it came N., N.E., E. and back to E.S.E. What can one make of it? The same thing has happened several times in the last few days. It kept on happening too, until in disgust I lowered the mainsail, and steamed. I have never experienced anything like it before; possibly the east wind is fighting the west wind.

29 Apr. At midnight it was more calm, but in an hour's time a fresh N.N.W. breeze came and I meditated reefing, but held on as we were. . . . Horowitz tells me that his late ship has been in harbour 1½ years, consequently he has never been to sea in sail before. I told him it was a dishonest thing to represent himself as a sailor when he knew nothing about a sailing ship. He said that Italian ships were not like English ships, and implied that he would be all right in the former. Hardly a compliment to them. In himself he is all right, but quite unused to sails. We have been bowling along well this morning, but the weather is very squally. At 10 a.m. the wind dropped. A few land-birds came off, also some butterflies, Greek butterflies probably.

30 Apr. A year ago we sailed from Auckland. We are celebrating by a pudding, all we can do. The wind kept very light from the N.N.W. all the morning and we barely moved. I had to start the engine. Tadgell has put another eyebolt into the stern of the dinghy to enable us to use the rudder. Horowitz, of course, cannot row, nor can Hashim, who, by the way, proposes to buy a motor-car on his return to Penang. . . . I doubt if we shall make Malta to-morrow, we may arrive in the night but not in daylight. Still this is very pleasant, though slow. A most extraordinary swell from N.W. rolled up in the afternoon, and the ship plunged heavily into it. It went on more or less all night. Just before dark a steamer passing a long way south hoisted: "I wish you a pleasant voyage." We replied "Thank you," and she blew her syren. We had to hoist on the mizzen halliards, as the main were occupied. I do not know what ship she was but she seemed to know us. Very decent of them whoever they were. In the ordinary way, however, steamers ignore us.

1 May. The swell was very heavy this morning, and I had to get the topsail off. The mizzen is rotten, I must get a new one. The sunrise was lovely, the most beautiful gold-tipped clouds, with a light green background. In the afternoon I started the engine as the wind was ahead; we are not doing much on account of the big sea. I cannot set the topsail, as it makes her plunge heavily. She wants a bit of nursing. The day is lovely and sunny; it has been like that all this part of the trip more or less. Getting in to-day is now out of the question, with the wind ahead.

2 May. Lovely morning. W.N.W. breeze. At 9 a.m. Malta appeared. Met the *Ceres* coming out: dipped to her. No sooner had we anchored in the Imsida Creek than Lieutenant Commander Mack, C.O. of H.M.S. *Tuscan*, came on board; the Signal Station had sent him the message that *Amaryllis* was entering harbour. The Customs came off and later the doctor. Alexandria has plague, and though we were not put into quarantine, we are under observation, and the doctor comes to look at us daily. Dinner at the Club with Mack. It was a great night.

5-7 May. Arranged about caulking the decks. The Royal Navy has taken us under its wing, and we are having a hectic time. We have lunched with Admiral Luce, who is coming to tea to-day with his wife and two sons, lunched in the *Iron Duke*, and dine to-night in the *Marlborough*, while of course the *Tuscan* is our headquarters.

8 May. Mack arrived on board to help us paint topsides. Dined with Denison. He is by instinct a traveller and explorer, and has a fine library of books of travel.

9 May. Strenuous morning. Stores arrived; also Galea, whom I engaged at £12 and food, and wages and passage back. Hashim wanted to leave the ship yesterday, following a quarrel with Stéphane, but reconsidered it. In the afternoon Horowitz left. Early next morning Galea came off and as soon as Stéphane heard of the other man's pay he decided to leave the ship. I agreed that that would be best and told him to change and go and see the French Consul; but it was found that the Consulate was closed, as it was a holiday. Mack came off and we painted the starboard side with a black strake and a gold line. Dined with him in the *Tuscan*. On my return found a letter of apology from Stéphane.

11 May. Painted the port side strake. Went to the famous Villa Frere on the invitation of Commander Price. The garden is simply wonderful, terrace after terrace of flowers, trees, Japanese gardens and all sorts of beautiful things.

13 May. Car to Citta Vecchia, Vadela, Musta. The Cathedral at Vecchia is wonderful, and so is the one at Musta, which has the third largest dome in the world. The decorations are magnificent. On Friday we visited the Church of St. John's, an amazingly beautiful building.

14 May. Was to have sailed to-day, but the wind is strong from the north-west. Two farewell presents of Amaryllis lilies arrived and several visitors came off.

15 May. Weighed at 8 a.m. for Sardinia. Mack had previously arrived in the launch of the *Iron Duke*. He went ashore off Marsa Musciet. I am very glad to have met him; he has given us a real good time.

And so farewell to Malta, a very interesting place. Its history goes back to about 1400 B.C., when the Phœnicians owned it. The streets are steep and some of them are in very low steps, to allow of horses and armed knights mounting. We are now at 11 a.m. off the bay where St. Paul was wrecked.

It is a delightful day; the wind is light and backing so that we can nearly lay the course. I meant to go over to the African coast and then north to the latitude of Sardinia, but with the wind this way we shall go direct, unless we meet a heavy sea off Cape Bon. It is fine to be at sea again, though we had a delightful time in Malta; but moving on is pleasant. The wind remained very light and variable and finally a nice breeze came W.N.W., and we went along well. . . . Galea is shaping very well; he says that he likes the ship. It is a great thing to have a white man forward; natives are all very well in their way, but white men are best. We now have a good ship's company. There is a curious shoal about here, Graham Shoal, which a hundred years ago was a volcano 150 ft. high. It disappeared in 1832, and seems to be sinking. There are from 2½ to 4 fathoms over it. Sicily is now well in sight; I am very anxious to get round the end of it. It is a pity that the wind keeps so much ahead; it makes progress so slow; moreover, we are having an adverse current here. At 5 p.m. it breezed up and raised a nasty short sea. A couple of hours later it fell nearly calm, and left us crashing about in the trough. We had to come round and then a terrible time began. The ship could not get along with a light wind and rotten sea; at times she would not steer, and at 9 p.m. I had the topsail hoisted. An hour later the wind had fallen and I had to turn out, couple up the shaft and start the engine.

17 May. The wind improved and at 8 a.m. we were fairly close in to the Sicilian coast. The weather was delightful, sunny and clear. At noon we were close in and soon afterwards came round; two hours later we came round again for S. Marco. My splendid old ship got along well, but I had to take her topsail off, as she was plunging rather heavily. S. Marco Light appeared in due course, Rossello Light too; we also sighted Pantellaria Island just before dark. I did not want to be sailing towards Graham Reef in the dark, so we stood in north until the Light appeared and then came round west for the rest of the night. The wind tailed off, but increased at dawn and is now at 8 a.m. blowing fresh from the N.W. Still she is getting along easily enough. Sicily was out of sight at dawn. We are nicely to the westward and with any luck should be able to clear the west side of the island. . . . We did, but could not weather the Ægadean Islands and had to come round. The sea is rough and very trying. The wind usually drops after dark, but this time it did not; it blew hard. The motion was soon so violent that I had the mizzen taken in. Soon after midnight it began to blow in earnest and I again turned everyone out and hove to. In a couple of hours we were again under way in a heavy sea. Soon after Hashim came on he got aback, the screw on the drum of the wheel parted, and the fat was in the fire. We got her round with the stump of the tiller, but they did not get the jib in properly, but left it flapping, with the result that it split in two. Put in a fresh screw and then set the second jib. No one was getting much sleep. Then a sea slapped into my cabin and went straight into my bunk, saturating it. Altogether things were not going well. However, we toiled on. At 8 a.m. the wind suddenly lulled and then shifted to the north just as we were passing Marittimo Island. We hoisted the mizzen quickly and came round. The wind then came light. We were not in a good position, as we could not get away from the island with a light wind and a heavy sea. As a way out I tried the engine and it fired at once. Engines are amazing things. Yesterday it would not do anything. To-day the water was not circulating, so I took out a valve, just looked at it and put it back, then started the motor once more. Water came at once. Another surprise. The wind then came from its old quarter and once more we advanced. We have lost the log rotator, which got round the propeller when Hashim was taken aback.

20 May. We crept slowly on and now have less than 100 miles to Sardinia. It is a lovely day so far, sun, a smooth sea and a light fair wind. We have been fanning along at about 2 knots.

21 May. At dawn it blew fresh from the N.E. We sighted Cavoli Light at 1 a.m. and at 5 a.m. were close up to it. The wind kept fresh for a time and then dropped and came all ways. I kept the engine running until we got in to Cagliari Harbour. The harbour is small and apparently all ships tie up alongside the quays. I did not want to do this, as cockroaches and insects get on board, so when the pilot came off I got him to take us to a corner where we could lie clear. Tadgell and I went ashore and called on the Consul. Cagliari looks very imposing from the sea, with the old fort crowning the hill, but the streets are ill-paved and the general aspect ashore is rather decrepit.

22 May. Sailmaker came off, repaired the mainsail (which has now eleven patches), and took away the jib for repair. In the afternoon we met Jekyll and went with him and a guide to the Cathedral, which has been woefully pulled about. The whole front ornamentation was torn down in a search for valuables mentioned in an ancient paper. We then went up to the top of one of the two Pisan towers, where we had a wonderful view. The whole of Cagliari Bay lay in front, on the right was Cagliari Lake, behind, the mountains of Sardinia and the cultivated lands; to the left salt pans and Quarto Bay. We then went to the Arena, which is in a fair state of preservation, then back on board.

24 May. Dressed ship as it was the anniversary of Italy's entering the War, also Empire Day. Dined with the Piercys.

25 May. Weighed at 8 a.m. for Minorca and at noon were off Pula Bay, where is an ancient town submerged, said to be Phœnician, though the Sailing Directions talk of a Roman town, Nora.

The crew have been eating the new bread and giving us the old lot from Malta. Stout fellows!

We have now at 4 p.m. a fine spanking breeze, dead ahead of course. It will be ahead most likely until past Gibraltar. As long as there is not too much sea we shall manage. At sunset the wind had come round to N.W., which enabled us to lay along the land. A brigantine was ahead at noon, but she is now hull down astern. The wind dropped at sunset which was a healthy one in looks, and later on we had a flat calm.

We are now at 9 a.m. getting along well with the sheets a bit off. The glass has steadied up and is even inclined to rise. I have been working out distances; there are 750 miles to

Gibraltar and 1,070 to Dartmouth from there. We shall hardly do it by the end of June, though we might. The slow part is hereabouts, as we have to beat. In the afternoon the wind increased, and, judging by the very heavy N.W. swell that more wind was coming, we double reefed the mainsail and changed the jibs. No sooner was this done than the wind shifted to the north and eased. The swell kept up, a real bad swell. I was greatly puzzled. What caused the swell? Certainly not the wind actually blowing. After dark the wind fell light and left us bumping into the sea with reduced sail. At 11 p.m. I turned out, had the sheets hauled in and started the engine, but even then the boom swung to and fro with sickening jerks. A terrible night.

27 May. Glorious morning and a fair wind. We took the reefs out and set the topsail and staysail-spinnaker. The swell was still troublesome, but died down somewhat under the east wind. We are now sliding along at 6 knots, through thousands of nautiluses. We picked one up in a bucket; it had a purple body, a gelatine sail and legs underneath. This fair wind was most unexpected and has been a great help. If all goes well we ought to reach Minorca to-morrow. After this the trips will be more along the coasts until we cross the Bay. At sunset we got the spinnaker off and later on the topsail. The wind then gradually worked ahead until in the early morning we were heading north; I turned out and brought her round. At 9.30 land appeared ahead. The wind and the sea soon became very heavy. As we ran on we were able to identify Cape Espero, and altered course for Port Mahon. The channel up to Mahon from the entrance is very narrow, but we could just lay up. This was Nelson's port of refit when he was blockading Toulon. How his captains brought their ships in is a mystery, and how they got them out again more of a mystery. After we had anchored, the Health Officer came off; he had heard of the *Amaryllis*. After him came the Customs and the Police, both armed with swords. I explained that as we were a yacht they had nothing to do with us, to which they agreed. Stood them a drink and off they went.

30 May. The weather has improved, but we shall not go

to-day, as I want to see the menhirs, and also allow the swell to subside. . . . We drove out along a road flanked with stone walls. We arrived finally at a farm and were conducted to the stones by a labourer, who led the way ruthlessly through standing crops. The central stone supports another one point-ing east and west, while a third stone, at an angle, serves as a ladder. Round the central stone, in a circle, are upright stones. Near by are a solid tower of stone and two caves, in one of which are several alcoves hollowed out of the rock. There is no record of the builders of these monuments.

31 May. Heavy overcast day. Apparently strong south wind outside; however we weighed at 8 a.m. and left for Majorca, dipping to the Arsenal as we passed, as they seemed to expect it and had a man at the halliards. At noon we were off the lighthouse on Aire Island. It rained most of the morning. The wind fell after dark and we hardly moved all night, but lay bumping into a swell.

1 June. At dusk we were able to lay through the Cabrera Channel, getting in at eight o'clock the next morning. It was a lovely morning and the low sun on Palma showed it at its best. It is an impressive place from the sea, the Cathedral and the Castle standing out well.

3 June. Galea has gone to church, and Stéphane to the theatre where he proposes to stop for nine hours. Poor Hashim is on board, rather like a monkey in a cage.

4 June. There was a thunderstorm in the night. The glass is falling and the sky looks rather bad, so I have decided to hold on for a bit, especially as I see all the fishing boats are coming in. There is nothing gained by bumping into a head sea if it can be avoided. Stéphane has come back with a trolley full of stuff from the market. Food is very dear, except apricots and cherries, which are good and cheap.

5 June. Weighed at 6 a.m. for Gibraltar. The wind outside, when we were clear of Cape Figuera, was fresh from the N.W., and as our course was S.W. by W. we got along very well, rolling and lurching along it is true, but getting ahead. If we could only carry this wind for a bit what a help it would be. The continual beating we have had to do is very trying. In the afternoon Iviza was in sight ahead. Heavy black clouds hung in the north, but it was clear to windward. However as the weather round here is peculiar, and whirlwinds and water-spouts are fairly common, I got the topsail off.

6 June. At dawn the wind was north, fresh, and we were bowling along well. Formentera was then visible through the mist. It is the last of the Balearic Isles and we are now off towards the Spanish coast, with a fine spanking breeze pushing us along. The breeze, however, soon lost its vigour and we rolled about, jerking the boom and making the ship quiver. I had to start the engine. During the night I thought I could hear the sea rumbling, a sign of east winds.

7 June. The night was clear and quiet and the swell had died down. The wind freshened and we gybed round to S.W. Soon afterwards Cape Palos loomed up on the starboard hand. We are now rushing along at about 7 knots. I do not propose to stop at Cartagena, but to take advantage of the fair wind to Gibraltar. The wind steadily increased and at noon it was blowing a strong breeze. I found that we were farther ahead than the log showed and we had to come out south to clear the Hormigas. This brought the wind abeam, and she had all she could carry, but behaved beautifully. When clear we ran off a bit and after a time brought the wind aft. But we had too much sail up with a full mainsail and at 3 p.m. we double reefed it and altered course to W. by S. The log rotator disappeared, line chafed through apparently, and we shall now have to guess distances, as we have no more rotators. This is very awkward, especially round here. No sooner were the reefs in than the wind eased. It is amazing how things happen, also very annoying. A huge great swell is running too, and we had to set the topsail to give her some way. Moreover, we are nearing Cape de Gata, where whirlwinds and waterspouts are common.

8 June. Kept the engine running all night. At 4 a.m. light airs came from all round. I could not keep her quiet any way, but she was best at W.S.W., a course I did not want to follow, as it headed us in. At 5 a.m. Stéphane called me, as he could then see the land. . . . Had great difficulty in fixing the ship

this morning, and am not very sure of where she is even now.
. . . But all panned out well and finally Cape de Gata came in
sight from behind a hill. The huge swell kept up but the wind
fell light and finally dropped to a calm. A thunderstorm
formed over Almeria. I had half a mind to go in there, but did
not do so, as I want to get on. Still, running the engine is
expensive work.

9 June. In the early morning a light air came from the N.E.
and I stopped the engine, which had run for thirty-seven
hours. The breeze gradually improved but never got strong.
The run was 87 miles and there are now 90 to go to Gibraltar.
In another 20 miles I shall have done 30,000 miles.

This morning we passed a range of snow-covered mountains. They looked lovely with the sun's rays slanting across
them. It is a beautiful day, not a cloud in the sky.

10 June. At dawn a very unpleasant swell came from the
S.E., so I had to go off W.N.W. and start the engine. We
shall hardly get in by daylight, as the wind is very light and
there is still a long way to go. This swell is knocking the speed
down and the current is strong around here. . . . On and on
we went. I could not get any fix off the land, for the coast is
very hard to identify. It is mountainous, with no trees, but
vineyards and cultivation on the slopes and in the valleys.
A rugged coast, very picturesque. The Directions give little or
no help, but we coasted round and eventually sighted the Rock
through the mist at 2 p.m. We started and stopped the engine
several times, as the wind increased or lessened. As we rounded
Europa Point we hoisted the Ensign and our number. Under
the lee of the Rock we got a series of squalls, none of them
heavy, in fact the *Amaryllis* hardly noticed them. In anticipation of something of the sort I had taken off the topsail, mizzen
and staysail, so she was under easy sail. The Rock looked very
impressive in the setting sun, as we passed in by the north
entrance. The Health boat came out to meet us and followed
us in, and a pinnace came off with the Officer of the Day,
wearing his sword, who shouted that buoy 20 had been allotted
to us. Thereupon we took in the mainsail and went up under
power. A boat from the Dockyard came to inquire whether

we wanted anything. Ship-chandlers also came off, but I sent them away. Apparently the Navy looks after the Blue Ensign; it is very nice of them. It is now blowing in gusts, but as we have hold of a warship's mooring we are all right.

I stood Galea and Stéphane a glass of Chianti; Hashim also brought his mug, but as he is a Mahommedan I would not give him any, and pointed out that he would not cook pork. He retired, but came back and said that he would do so in future, whereupon I gave him some wine.

11 June. Called on Rear-Admiral Ellerton; saw also Commander Longstaff, King's Harbour Master.

12 June. Got charts and time signal. Commander Longstaff and Lieutenant-Commander Nowell came on board, also Benson and Anderson. There has been a strong wind all day, a Levanter.

13 June. Blowing like steam from the N.E.; the wind is making the ship quiver. Dined at the Mount with Admiral Ellerton. They showed us a snake 5 ft. long, which was killed in one of the rooms. "Flags" stood on its head and cut its neck with a carving knife.

14 June. Lunch at the R.G.A. mess with Major Matthews. The Admiral and his wife, Colonel and Mrs. Buller, Majors Matthews and Walker and Colonel Wilder came off to tea. The latter belongs to the Royal Cruising Club and was very glad to see the burgee here.

15 June. Visited the Moorish Castle, built in 704, then went about one-third of the way up the Galleries and had a grand view. Wilder drove us out across the neutral zone to his house, a wonderful place. He and his wife speak highly of the Spaniards. Back to change and dine with the Bullers. Colonel and Mrs. Sheere were there.

16 June. Slipped at 9 a.m. Strong puffs in the harbour, but not much wind outside until we got into the Straits and then it blew harder and harder. First the topsail and then the mizzen had to come off. The splendid old ship rushed along at a great pace. At 4 p.m. we were out of the Straits, for which I was really thankful. It is a bad spot. There is now not so much wind, but we are still going well. 150 miles to Cape St.

Vincent. We saw the last of the African coast this afternoon. The wind grew less and less and finally fell calm.

17 June. The wind kept light and worked round from E.S.E. to S.W. in the afternoon. I set the spinnaker as jib and changed to reaching staysail. I hope we get a good breeze to-night and do not have to run the engine; it is always a trouble at night. It will be great to get round St. Vincent and head north; I shall feel that I am getting home. We did jolly well yesterday to get through the Straits so fast; the various races did not trouble us. . . . This afternoon the wind fell away, and came ahead and we had to start the engine.

18 June. Both wind and stream against us. At dawn the coast was in sight, very indistinct. I am running the engine a lot; without it there would be no progress at all, with it we are barely doing three miles an hour. The boom swings to and fro and shakes the ship. The engine chugged manfully along and gave her steerage way, but the rotten little jobble of sea took all speed off. However, we crawled on and on. We have passed Palos on the river Tinto, whence Columbus sailed in 1492 on his first voyage to America. At 4 p.m. Sagres Point loomed through the mist. After a time the lighthouse on St. Vincent showed up over the land. I suppose we shall have to beat all up the Portuguese coast. The Sailing Directions say, "Stand out until a favourable wind is met to avoid the current down the coast."

Hashim wants to go home, and I shall be glad to see him go.

19 June. We sailed slowly past St. Vincent and then met a horrible N.W. swell. The wind failed and the ship rolled and crashed about until it seemed impossible that the masts and gear would stand. I was much perturbed. However, the night passed in the end and at dawn we got a south wind and are now running before it in a heavy swell. This is a bad bit of coast, much fog and bad weather. . . . A long ocean swell is running, but it does not trouble us. In fact the weather to-day has been delightful, and we are now getting along at about 3 knots. I do not think I shall go in to Lisbon. I am anxious to finish the next two hundred miles and cross my outward track. As a matter of fact, the track is only 30 miles to the west, but

313

on this course it is about 180 miles ahead. For all practical purposes the ship has now completed the tour of the world, but until we actually cross the track we cannot open the bottle of champagne.

20 June. We are getting along very slowly, as there is no wind; we struggle on, but it is a fight for every inch. Every night it falls calm and we stop; every day the wind seems to go round the compass. This must be the "settled summer weather" we are to expect. We are now off the most westerly point of Europe.

21 June. Rolling and tumbling about in great discomfort, and making slow progress. We ought to be past the Burlings some time to-night. That will be a great thing, as we shall head up better. It is tempting to go inside them, and if we had been here earlier I should have done so, but not now.

22 June. At 2 a.m. I had the mizzen hoisted, but at 7 a.m. it had to be taken in and the staysail reefed, as the wind had got up again and was blowing hard. At 10 a.m. the wind eased and the mizzen was hoisted again, and the reef taken out of the staysail. Half an hour later we changed the jibs and took the reef out of the mainsail. Always doing something to the sails.

Galea wants to leave at Vigo as his stomach is wrong. What a time I have with the crew. As a matter of fact, they cannot stand the discomfort.

At noon the sea was ahead and very heavy and confused, and I thought she would be easier with it abeam, but first ran off N.W. for 4½ miles to cross my outward track (Sep. 9th 1920), which we did in 40° 18′ N., 10° 18′ W., with 30,460 miles made good. It is satisfactory to think that the voyage round the world has been completed.

23 June. Early this morning we reached the line of steamers and several came past, blazing with lights. At noon we had only made good 45 miles and had 94 miles to Vigo. We have been a week at sea for 436 miles. In the afternoon a breeze came and we were doing 5 knots, though not laying the course by 2 points. It was a lovely night. At midnight strange lights started flashing about and I came round for fear of running into nets.

24 June. No wind. We are now forging ahead under power. At 5 p.m. we were about 5 miles off Cape Silleiro, at the entrance to Vigo Bay. Galea is feverishly anxious to get in, so is Hashim. I found the latter trying to measure up the distance on the chart. The sooner he goes the better pleased I shall be, as he is very dirty.

We brought up off the mole at 10 p.m.

25 June. Vigo seems a bit offhand; no doctor responded to our "Q" flag. It is not an interesting place, but the oxen carts with wheels of the Roman pattern are remarkable.

26 June. A beautiful day. Galea has decided to fulfil his bargain and go on to England.

28 June. Another lovely day. The wind was right up and the tide foul, but we weighed and came out well. I kept the engine running, as the wind was light. We are now on the last lap, as far as we know. I can hardly realize that we shall be home next week if all goes well. There are 571 miles to go.

29 June. The run will be very small to-day and most of that power work; we cannot get on with this swell and no wind. In the afternoon the wind came from N.E. and hardened into a nice breeze. Of course it is ahead, but it is much to be preferred to a calm. It is fine to feel the old ship sailing once more and homeward bound too. A beautiful French yacht passed north this morning and hoisted her colours and burgee, to which we replied. We are now plunging along into a heavy swell, but the wind is working round towards east and may eventually become fair. Every now and then she puts her bowsprit right in. Writing is very difficult, as everything falls about and one is thrown about in one's cabin.

30 June. If this head wind and heavy swell persist it will be a slow passage home. Looking back on our passages, we have only had one good one and one fair one since Singapore, Arabian Sea, good, and Alexandria to Malta, fair. . . . We are now at 9 a.m. surging along nearly on the course, probably doing about 4 knots, which is good considering the sea. Anyway it is a great thing that, though close hauled, we are very nearly laying the course, only half a point off.

1 July. At 7 a.m. took the topsail off as she was plunging

315

and it was not filling. The wind is in the east, with a very high glass. The run was 73 miles, leaving 369 to go. Two grampuses passed close alongside, rolling heavily along and blowing.

2 July. Overcast sky and a flat calm. The sea quite smooth. Light airs from the north. How things change. It seems impossible that the sea of yesterday could have gone down so completely. The horizon has disappeared and we cannot get any sights. Not a breath of air, not a ripple on the water, absolute calm. I have been writing about Ambrym, and want to go back. Not yet on land and already I am planning new trips!

3 July. The morning was cold, cheerless and grey. The wind was light but enough to raise a nasty confused bobble, without being enough to keep the sails quiet.

Two, or at most three, days should see the end of the trip. It will be great to be once more in England; everyone will be pleased to be there. At five this afternoon things were so intolerable that we took in the spinnaker and headed into the swell N.N.W. I was afraid that we should smash something as things were before. This lengthens the trip, but I shall not keep this way long. A heavy bank of clouds lies to windward, we may get wind out of that.

4 July. At 9 a.m. there was a fair breeze, and in 25 miles Ushant should be abeam, well away, but abeam. The breeze held until noon and then died away. To our surprise at 3 p.m. a light air came from the S.E. It keeps her quiet, though I still have to run the engine. Early next morning the wind was east and we could just lay the course. We did very well during the night, considering all things, and we are doing well now, though close-hauled. England should soon be in sight, at any rate some time before dark. The wind increased all the morning and at noon was a fresh breeze. We are doing about 2 miles an hour. At 8 p.m. Eddystone lit up and we could also see the land far off. Came round and bumped into a head sea all night. The wind did not drop and at 1 a.m. the jib split. Set second jib.

6 July. At 7 a.m. land appeared out of the mist. England once more! Last night was probably the last night at sea, a pleasant thought. At noon we were past the Start and then came round north for Dartmouth and the Skerry buoy. It was very misty but in due course the buoy appeared and we went on for the Homestone buoy, appropriately named in my case. Under the land we lowered the mainsail and went on under power. We came past the Yacht Clubhouse and brought up off the pontoon, and the long trip had ended, 31,159 miles.

(*From a letter.*) Our homecoming was most delightful. We struck a fine day, and Dartmouth, as we came in from the sea, looked lovely. In we came with the Quarantine flag flying and the four signal letters fluttering from the yardarm. After a time a Customs Officer had himself paddled off. Why were we flying the "Q" flag? Not at all necessary. Bill of Health? No, since all were well on board he did not want to see it. He looked at our meagre stock of tobacco and spirits and waved them aside. He filled in a few forms and took himself off. The contrast between this method and that obtaining in Sydney is paralysing. There a doctor came to examine us, then a Police boat arrived and took copies of the signatures of the crew, or thumb prints in the case of Sam, and filled in innumerable forms. Then a Customs Officer came, and I had to give a list of every store aboard, an interminable business, and then make a copy, which I lost. Then came nine reporters. But here not a soul has taken the slightest notice. It is delightful. I smile when I think of the ruses I planned to avoid reporters. Not a reporter has shown up. I am immensely relieved. This is a real homecoming to dear old casual England.

THE END